Zachary M. Baker
Editor

Judaica in the Slavic Realm, Slavica in the Judaic Realm: Repositories, Collections, Projects, Publications

Judaica in the Slavic Realm, Slavica in the Judaic Realm: Repositories, Collections, Projects, Publications has been co-published simultaneously as *Slavic & East European Information Resources,* Volume 4, Numbers 2/3 2003.

*Pre-publication
REVIEWS,
COMMENTARIES,
EVALUATIONS . . .*

"A TREASURE TROVE of lucid, intelligent essays and annotated lists describing otherwise little-known or inaccessible information on collections long unavailable. I KNOW OF NO BETTER SOURCE IN ANY LANGUAGE. This is a first-rate volume that will prove indispensable to anyone interested in the history and culture of Jews in Russia and Eastern Europe."

Steven J. Zipperstein, PhD
*Daniel E. Koshland Professor of Jewish Culture and History;
Co-Director, Taube Center for Jewish Studies
Stanford University*

More pre-publication
REVIEWS, COMMENTARIES, EVALUATIONS...

"ABSOLUTELY ESSENTIAL for anyone doing advanced research on the Jews of the former Russian and Soviet empires. Zachary Baker, the world's leading bibliographic authority on the Jews of the region, has done the scholarly world a great service by bringing together leading experts to produce this invaluable guide. Encompassing Ukrainian, Polish, and Belarusian materials as well as Russian sources, this work is also a wonderful introduction to significant holdings in Jerusalem's Central Archives for the History of the Jewish People, the Jewish National and University Library, and New York's YIVO Institute for Jewish Research. GRADUATE STUDENTS AND SEASONED ACADEMICS WILL BENEFIT TREMENDOUSLY.... THIS IS AN EXCEPTIONALLY IMPORTANT COLLECTION, SURE TO BECOME A PRIMARY REFERENCE GUIDE."

Henry Abramson, PhD
University Library Scholar of Judaica
Associate Professor of History and
Judaic Studies
Florida Atlantic University

"SPLENDID.... Brings together the most authoritative specialists.... VITALLY IMPORTANT for bibliographers, archivists, historians of Jewish culture as well as many specialists in post-Soviet Russia and Eastern Europe."

Lazar Fleishman, PhD
Professor of Russian Literature
Stanford University

"AN INDISPENSABLE RESOURCE for research in all areas of East European Jewish history, literature, libraries, and publishing.... A DEFINITIVE HISTORICAL OVERVIEW of the dramatic bibliographic and archival developments in Jewish studies in the immediate post-Soviet period."

Brad Sabin Hill
Dean of the Library
and Senior Research Librarian
YIVO Institute for Jewish Research

Judaica in the Slavic Realm, Slavica in the Judaic Realm: Repositories, Collections, Projects, Publications

Judaica in the Slavic Realm, Slavica in the Judaic Realm: Repositories, Collections, Projects, Publications has been co-published simultaneously as *Slavic & East European Information Resources,* Volume 4, Numbers 2/3 2003.

Slavic & East European Information Resources Monographic "Separates"

Below is a list of "separates," which in serials librarianship means a special issue simultaneously published as a special journal issue or double-issue *and* as a "separate" hardbound monograph. (This is a format which we also call a "DocuSerial.")

"Separates" are published because specialized libraries or professionals may wish to purchase a specific thematic issue by itself in a format which can be separately cataloged and shelved, as opposed to purchasing the journal on an on-going basis. Faculty members may also more easily consider a "separate" for classroom adoption.

"Separates" are carefully classified separately with the major book jobbers so that the journal tie-in can be noted on new book order slips to avoid duplicate purchasing.

You may wish to visit Haworth's website at . . .

http://www.HaworthPress.com

. . . to search our online catalog for complete tables of contents of these separates and related publications.

You may also call 1-800-HAWORTH (outside US/Canada: 607-722-5857), or Fax 1-800-895-0582 (outside US/Canada: 607-771-0012), or e-mail at:

docdelivery@haworthpress.com

Judaica in the Slavic Realm, Slavica in the Judaic Realm: Repositories, Collections, Projects, Publications, edited by Zachary M. Baker, MA (Vol. 4, No. 2/3, 2003). *A collection of essays, bibliographies, and research studies illustrating the state of Jewish-related publishing ventures in Eastern Europe and the former Soviet Union, and documenting efforts by Judaic scholars, librarians, and genealogists to provide access to archival collections in those countries.*

Libraries in Open Societies: Proceedings of the Fifth International Slavic Librarians' Conference, edited by Harold M. Leich, MLS (Vol. 3, No. 2/3, 2002). *"The papers collected in this book are not only the product of this international conference, but also are concrete evidence of how far Slavic librarianship has progressed over the past 30 years. Valuable–not only to those with an interest in the Slavic field but to any librarian with an interest in area studies librarianship, international networking, and collection development."* (Robert H. Burger, PhD, MLS, former Head of the Slavic and East European Library, University of Illinois at Urbana-Champaign)

Publishing in Yugoslavia's Successor States, edited by Michael Biggins, PhD, MS, and Janet Crayne, MLIS, MA (Vol. 1, No. 2/3, 2000). *"A valuable tool, one which has been sorely lacking. All regions of the area are covered. The list of vendors, most with contact information that includes Web sites, will certainly be of service to those charged with acquiring these publications. An indispensible resource for anyone needing access to the publications of this region."* (Allan Urbanic, PhD, MLIS, Librarian for Slavic Collections, University of California, Berkeley)

Judaica in the Slavic Realm, Slavica in the Judaic Realm: Repositories, Collections, Projects, Publications

Zachary M. Baker
Editor

Judaica in the Slavic Realm, Slavica in the Judaic Realm: Repositories, Collections, Projects, Publications has been co-published simultaneously as *Slavic & East European Information Resources*, Volume 4, Numbers 2/3 2003.

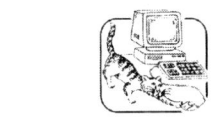

The Haworth Information Press
An Imprint of
The Haworth Press, Inc.
New York • London • Oxford

Published by

The Haworth Information Press®, 10 Alice Street, Binghamton, NY 13904-1580 USA

The Haworth Information Press® is an imprint of The Haworth Press, Inc., 10 Alice Street, Binghamton, NY 13904-1580 USA.

Judaica in the Slavic Realm, Slavica in the Judaic Realm: Repositories, Collections, Projects, Publications has been co-published simultaneously as *Slavic & East European Information Resources,* Volume 4, Numbers 2/3 2003.

© 2003 by The Haworth Press, Inc. All rights reserved. No part of this work may be reproduced or utilized in any form or by any means, electronic or mechanical, including photocopying, microfilm and recording, or by any information storage and retrieval system, without permission in writing from the publisher. Printed in the United States of America.

The development, preparation, and publication of this work has been undertaken with great care. However, the publisher, employees, editors, and agents of The Haworth Press and all imprints of The Haworth Press, Inc., including The Haworth Medical Press® and The Pharmaceutical Products Press®, are not responsible for any errors contained herein or for consequences that may ensue from use of materials or information contained in this work. Opinions expressed by the author(s) are not necessarily those of The Haworth Press, Inc. With regard to case studies, identities and circumstances of individuals discussed herein have been changed to protect confidentiality. Any resemblance to actual persons, living or dead, is entirely coincidental.

Front cover credit: Postcard of Nadrzeczna Street, Jewish Quarter of Bialystok. Courtesy of Tomasz Wisniewski.

Back cover credit: Photograph taken by Krysia Fisher.

Cover design by Lora Wiggins.

Library of Congress Cataloging-in-Publication Data

Judaica in the Slavic realm, Slavica in the Judaic realm : repositories, collections, projects, publications / Zachary M. Baker, editor.
    p. cm.
    Co-published simultaneously as Slavic & East European information resources, v. 4, nos. 2/3, 2003.
    Includes bibliographical references and index.
    ISBN 0-7890-2279-6 (alk. paper) – ISBN 0-7890-2280-X (pbk. : alk. paper)
    1. Jews–Slavic countries–Archival resources. 2. Jews–Europe, Eastern–Archival resources. 3. Jews–Slavic countries–Library resources. 4. Jews–Europe, Eastern–Library resources. 5. Jewish literature–Bibliography. I. Baker, Zachary M. II. Slavic & East European information resources.
Z6373.S55J83 2004
[DS135.R9]
016.947'0004924–dc21

    2003010479

Indexing, Abstracting & Website/Internet Coverage

This section provides you with a list of major indexing & abstracting services. That is to say, each service began covering this periodical during the year noted in the right column. Most Websites which are listed below have indicated that they will either post, disseminate, compile, archive, cite or alert their own Website users with research-based content from this work. (This list is as current as the copyright date of this publication.)

Abstracting, Website/Indexing Coverage . . . . Year When Coverage Began

- *American Bibliography of Slavic and East European Studies (ABSEES) & ABSEES Online <www.library.uiuc.edu/absees/>* . . 2000

- *CNPIEC Reference Guide: Chinese National Directory of Foreign Periodicals* 2000

- *DARE Databank (covering social science periodicals) <http://www.unesco.org/general/eng/infoserv/db/dare.html>* . . . 2001

- *IBZ International Bibliography of Periodical Literature <www.saur.de>* 2000

- *Information Science Abstracts <www.infotoday.com>* 2000

- *INSPEC <www.iee.org.uk/publish/>* 2000

- *Könyvtári Figyelő (Library Review)* 2000

- *Management & Marketing Abstracts* 2000

- *OCLC Public Affairs Information Service <www.pais.org>* 2000

(continued)

- *Referativnyi Zhurnal (Abstracts Journal of the All-Russian Institute of Scientific and Technical Information– in Russian)* 2000
- *World Publishing Monitor* 2000

Special Bibliographic Notes related to special journal issues (separates) and indexing/abstracting:

- indexing/abstracting services in this list will also cover material in any "separate" that is co-published simultaneously with Haworth's special thematic journal issue or DocuSerial. Indexing/abstracting usually covers material at the article/chapter level.
- monographic co-editions are intended for either non-subscribers or libraries which intend to purchase a second copy for their circulating collections.
- monographic co-editions are reported to all jobbers/wholesalers/approval plans. The source journal is listed as the "series" to assist the prevention of duplicate purchasing in the same manner utilized for books-in-series.
- to facilitate user/access services all indexing/abstracting services are encouraged to utilize the co-indexing entry note indicated at the bottom of the first page of each article/chapter/contribution.
- this is intended to assist a library user of any reference tool (whether print, electronic, online, or CD-ROM) to locate the monographic version if the library has purchased this version but not a subscription to the source journal.
- individual articles/chapters in any Haworth publication are also available through the Haworth Document Delivery Service (HDDS).

Judaica in the Slavic Realm, Slavica in the Judaic Realm: Repositories, Collections, Projects, Publications

CONTENTS

Introduction *Zachary M. Baker*	1
The Jewish Archival Survey: Tracing Jewish Records in the Former Soviet Archives *Marek Web*	5
The Creation of a Documentary Collection on the History of Russian Jewry at the Central Archives for the History of the Jewish People *Benyamin Lukin*	17
Hebrew Incunabula in the Asiatic Museum of St. Petersburg *S. M. Iakerson*	37
Microfilming Hebrew Manuscripts in Eastern Europe *Benjamin Richler*	59
Jewish Book Publishing Today in the Countries of the Former USSR *Alexander Frenkel*	69
Slavic Judaica in the YIVO Library: Acquisitions from 1991-2001 *Nikolai Borodulin*	89
From Odessa to Odessa: Russian-Jewish Periodicals of Ukraine, 1860-2000 *Vladimir Karasik*	119

Bibliographical Projects in Polish-Jewish Studies Since 1989   151
   Stephen D. Corrsin

Resources on the Genealogy of Eastern European Jews   169
   Zachary M. Baker

Index   185

ABOUT THE EDITOR

Zachary M. Baker, MA (Library Science), has served as Reinhard Family Curator of Judaica and Hebraica Collections at the Stanford University Libraries since 1999. He previously served as Head Librarian of the YIVO Institute for Jewish Research in New York. Mr. Baker was Contributing Editor and Style Editor of *Judaica Librarianship* (the journal of the Association of Jewish Libraries) and has published numerous articles on Judaica bibliography, Jewish history, and genealogy. The latest version of his "Bibliography of Eastern European Memorial Books" was published in *From a Ruined Garden: The Memorial Books of Polish Jewry*, translated and edited by Jack Kugelmass and Jonathan Boyarin in association with the United States Holocaust Memorial Museum.

∞ ALL HAWORTH INFORMATION PRESS BOOKS AND JOURNALS ARE PRINTED ON CERTIFIED ACID-FREE PAPER

Introduction

Judaica in the Slavic Realm, Slavica in the Judaic Realm presents a selection of articles on topics that, while certainly of relevance to Slavic studies, may be unfamiliar to many specialists in that field. This volume does not supply a comprehensive overview of developments in either of these two "realms." The contributions appearing in these pages do, however, reveal the impressive scope and scale of publications relating to Jews and Judaism that are currently being published in Eastern Europe (especially the former Soviet Union). They also describe some of the important Judaica collections in that region, along with projects directed at identifying these resources and making them accessible. We hope that these discussions will contribute to the ongoing exchange of information between archivists, librarians, and academic specialists in both Slavic and Judaic studies, and that they will stimulate new and expanded initiatives in a broad area of scholarly inquiry and documentation that was blocked for decades.

Throughout the Cold War–i.e., during the aftermath of the Nazis' attempt to exterminate all Jews who fell under their rule during World War II–public discussion of Jews and Judaism was virtually taboo within the Soviet Union proper, and permitted only under stringent controls in the rest of Eastern Europe. Local, regional, and geopolitics all played their parts in turning the "Jewish question" into one of the most conspicuous "blank spots" of an entire era. Until the second half of the 1980s, specialists in the Soviet Union and Eastern Europe were deprived of the most fundamental research tools–access to Judaica library and archival collections, and the opportunity to study the languages of Jewish scholarship: Hebrew, Aramaic, and Yiddish. Since then, they and their Western and Israeli counterparts have made an impressive start on

---

[Haworth co-indexing entry note]: "Introduction." Baker, Zachary, M. Co-published simultaneously in *Slavic & East European Information Resources* (The Haworth Information Press, an imprint of The Haworth Press, Inc.) Vol. 4, No. 2/3, 2003, pp. 1-4; and: *Judaica in the Slavic Realm, Slavica in the Judaic Realm: Repositories, Collections, Projects, Publications* (ed: Zachary M. Baker) The Haworth Information Press, an imprint of The Haworth Press, Inc., 2003, pp. 1-4. Single or multiple copies of this article are available for a fee from The Haworth Document Delivery Service [1-800-HAWORTH, 9:00 a.m. - 5:00 p.m. (EST). E-mail address: docdelivery@haworthpress.com].

http://www.haworthpress.com/store/product.asp?sku=J167
© 2003 by The Haworth Press, Inc. All rights reserved.

filling in the blank spots, as a perusal of the articles contained in this volume reveals, but much work remains yet to be done.

We begin with Marek Web's description of a remarkable cooperative venture, Project Judaica's Jewish Archival Survey, which operates under the aegis of one Russian institution and two American research organizations. Since 1991, in addition to surveying Jewish collections in former Soviet repositories, Project Judaica has trained a new generation of young Russian researchers in the languages and methodologies of Judaic scholarship. Benyamin Lukin outlines the complementary efforts of the Central Archives for the History of the Jewish People (Jerusalem) to locate and copy archival sources on Russian Jewry.

It should come as no surprise that the great libraries of Russia–like those in Western Europe and the United States–possess extensive holdings of priceless Hebrew manuscripts and early Hebrew imprints. The noted bibliographer Shimon M. Iakerson draws his readers' attention to the outstanding collection of Hebrew incunabula held by the Asiatic Museum of St. Petersburg. This is followed by Benjamin Richler's discussion of the Institute of Microfilmed Hebrew Manuscripts' ongoing efforts to acquire microfilms of Hebrew manuscripts in Eastern European and former Soviet repositories.

From "repositories, collections, [and] projects," we move to "publications." Alexander Frenkel, the editor of the aptly titled Russian Jewish bibliographical journal *Narod Knigi v mire knig* (People of the Book in the World of Books), presents an overview of Jewish book publishing in the Commonwealth of Independent States and the Baltic republics after 1990. Nikolai Borodulin's article on a decade of collecting activities by one particularly well-situated American repository, the library of the YIVO Institute for Jewish Research (New York), is a fitting companion piece to Frenkel's article. The proliferation of Jewish periodicals in Ukraine–the heartland of the Pale of Settlement (to which Jews in the Tsarist Empire were largely restricted until 1917)–is the subject of Vladimir Karasik's survey. Stephen D. Corrsin casts a westward glance, with his overview of bibliographical projects in Polish-Jewish studies. The volume concludes with Zachary M. Baker's discussion of attempts to document a specific aspect of the Eastern European Jewish heritage: its genealogical records.

Three extensive bibliographies grace this special issue, each one reflecting the rich and varied facets of the Slavic-Jewish encounter. These are:

1. Shimon M. Iakerson's listing of 38 Hebrew incunabula in the Asiatic Museum of St. Petersburg. These books' presence today in a St. Petersburg repository testifies to the legacy of two notable nineteenth-century Russian Jewish scholars and collectors.

2. Vladimir Karasik's checklist of 311 Jewish periodicals published in Ukraine from 1860 to the present. Their schematic breakdown into five different periods represents the bibliographer's reflections on the lives and fates of Jews in the Russian Empire, the Soviet Union, and post-Soviet Ukraine.
3. Nikolai Borodulin's classified bibliography of several hundred Jewish books and periodicals (in a variety of languages) from the post-Soviet republics. One hopes that these publications are a harbinger of the gradual normalization of Jewish pursuits in the post-Soviet context.

Editing this volume has been a particularly gratifying experience. It is a great privilege to work together with distinguished colleagues in Russia, Israel, and the United States, whose impressive accomplishments speak for themselves.* In addition, reading through their manuscripts brings back memories of travels to formerly dormant repositories seeking to reconstitute themselves.

One such institution is the V. I. Vernadsky National Library of Ukraine, in Kiev, which I visited in January 1992, just a few weeks after Ukraine formally achieved its independence. The insignia of Soviet power were still being removed from public buildings and the shadows of the interregnum were also perceptible in our tour of the Vernadsky Library's Jewish collections, which had only lately been moved out of remote storage for the first time since the 1940s. Meeting with the staff of the library's fledgling Judaica Section was one of the most moving experiences of my professional career.

Another story that remains to be told is the important role that commercial publishers such as IDC and Norman Ross have played in ferreting out, publishing, and disseminating previously unexplored bodies of Judaica in Eastern European libraries and archives. Appropriately, the final volume in Ross's series of reference works on Russian and Soviet bibliography is I. I. Gintsburg's *Jewish Manuscripts of the Institute of Oriental Studies, St. Petersburg* (2003). In his eloquent preface to the volume, Ross writes that the catalog "was compiled in the 1930s and 1940s by the famous bibliographer Iona Gintsburg, who starved to death during the siege of Leningrad." Ross takes note of the frequent business trips that he has made to the country that his great-grandparents left in 1897, and concludes: "I think, with these Russian-Jewish origins, that nothing

---

*I also wish to take this opportunity to thank Karen A. Rondestvedt, Editor of *Slavic & East European Information Resources*, for the critical role that she has played toward seeing this volume through.

could be more fitting than to publish this historic work as the final title in the series, compiled, as it was, by a Russian Jew about Russian Judaica. I hope the reader finds it useful."

It is in the same spirit that we offer these essays and bibliographies, which bring to light the rich documentary legacy and the continuing contributions of a people who for centuries populated the villages, cities, and towns of Central and Eastern Europe, and called these places home.

Zachary M. Baker
February 2003

The Jewish Archival Survey: Tracing Jewish Records in the Former Soviet Archives

Marek Web

SUMMARY. As the rigors of the Soviet-era prohibitions in the post-Soviet archives were eased in the early 1990s, students of Russian-Jewish history in the former Soviet Union, as well as from abroad, have been using this opportunity to search for records of the Russian-Jewish past. The Jewish Archival Survey, a joint program of the Jewish Theological Seminary of America, the YIVO Institute for Jewish Research, and the Russian State University for the Humanities has been among the earliest initiatives in this field. *[Article copies available for a fee from The Haworth Document Delivery Service: 1-800-HAWORTH. E-mail address: <docdelivery@haworthpress.com> Website: <http://www.HaworthPress.com> © 2003 by The Haworth Press, Inc. All rights reserved.]*

Marek Web, former Head Archivist at YIVO, has been coordinating the work of the Jewish Archival Survey since its inception in 1992. Mr. Web has published books on Jewish archives, and articles on the history of Polish Jewry. His most recent works are *Jewish Documentary Sources in the Moscow Archives,* co-edited with M. Kupovetskii and E. Starostin (1997), and *Poyln: Jewish Life in the Old Country*, an album of photographs by Alter Kacyzne (1999).

Address correspondence: Marek Web, YIVO Institute for Jewish Research, 15 West 16th Street, New York, NY 10011 USA (E-mail: mweb@yivo.cjh.org).

[Haworth co-indexing entry note]: "The Jewish Archival Survey: Tracing Jewish Records in the Former Soviet Archives." Web, Marek. Co-published simultaneously in *Slavic & East European Information Resources* (The Haworth Information Press, an imprint of The Haworth Press, Inc.) Vol. 4, No. 2/3, 2003, pp. 5-15; and: *Judaica in the Slavic Realm, Slavica in the Judaic Realm: Repositories, Collections, Projects, Publications* (ed: Zachary M. Baker) The Haworth Information Press, an imprint of The Haworth Press, Inc., 2003, pp. 5-15. Single or multiple copies of this article are available for a fee from The Haworth Document Delivery Service [1-800-HAWORTH, 9:00 a.m. - 5:00 p.m. (EST). E-mail address: docdelivery@haworthpress.com].

http://www.haworthpress.com/store/product.asp?sku=J167
© 2003 by The Haworth Press, Inc. All rights reserved.

KEYWORDS. Archival surveys, Jewish archives–Belarus, Jewish archives–Moscow, Jewish Theological Seminary of America (New York), Russian State University for the Humanities (Moscow), YIVO Institute for Jewish Research (New York), Russia

In the late 1980s Jews in the Soviet republics regained the right to promote Jewish learning. The subsequent opening of the former Soviet archives in the 1990s made possible once again the study of Jewish primary sources.

As the restrictions on previously classified archival materials were abandoned, interest in identifying, describing, and publishing archival records in Jewish history and culture grew stronger. In fact, some Jewish initiatives preceded by several years the "grand opening" of the post-Soviet archives. In the 1980s newly founded Jewish historical societies were planning a variety of programs in Jewish studies; projects to survey and catalog Jewish records occupied a prominent place among them. It is interesting to note here that in the specific conditions of the 1980s this work acquired a strong ideological flavor, being an expression of the drive to reclaim Jewish national past in Russia. Students of Russian-Jewish history turned their attention to the accomplishments of the pre-1917 Jewish cultural organizations such as the Society for the Promotion of Enlightenment Among Jews in Russia (known by its Hebrew name as the Hevrah Mefitse Haskalah and by its Russian name as Obshchestvo rasprostraneniia prosveshcheniia sredi evreev–OPE), the OPE Historical Commission, the St. Petersburg Jewish Historical and Ethnographic Society, and the Ansky expedition, and they embraced this period as the golden age of Russian-Jewish scholarship and as a point of departure for new endeavors.

In the absence of an established Jewish academic community, grass-root groups of young researchers, professionals and amateurs, sprang up in various places throughout the former Soviet Union and began breaking the barriers of Soviet-era prohibitions that had prevented access to archives. In many places where no such groups existed, individual enthusiasts took it upon themselves to explore local archives and libraries for Jewish records. Accessing Jewish archival collections became a high priority on every local Jewish association's agenda. To be sure, many of these early initiatives soon waned due to a variety of factors. For instance, the Jewish Historical Society in Moscow, which had pioneered the movement to collect historical materials and had conducted first surveys in the Moscow archives, ceased to exist when its most active members emigrated to Israel.[1] On the other hand, the archival program of the St. Petersburg Jewish University, which started out in the 1980s, had a much longer life although its work was not always carried out with the same intensity.

A defining event for the burgeoning Jewish scholarship in Russia and other former Soviet republics was the research conference *Jews in Russia*, organized by the St. Petersburg Jewish University in July 1992. The conference was held in remembrance of the 100th anniversary of the publication of Simon Dubnow's historic manifesto "On the Study of the History of Russian Jews and the Establishment of a Russian-Jewish Historical Society,"[2] and, on a larger plane, in honor of the school of Russian-Jewish history which Dubnow represented. The conference emphasized the continuity of Russian-Jewish scholarship, despite the gap of 70 years during the Soviet era. In substance, the conference featured papers devoted to Russian-Jewish archives and historiography. Characteristically, the authors of these papers had utilized, on a truly large scale, new archival sources that not so long ago had been kept under lock and key.[3]

Perhaps most significant among the results of this early period in the revival of Jewish historical and archival studies in Russia were the efforts to track down and report on the whereabouts of major Russian-Jewish archives and libraries. The fate of the heretofore unavailable Jewish collections at the Vernadsky Library and the Central State Historical Archives in Kiev, the Lenin Library in Moscow, the Saltykov-Shchedrin Library in St. Petersburg, the Soviet-era October Revolution Archives[4] and the Central Party Archives in Moscow,[5] to name but a few repositories, were revealed in a variety of published papers and research conferences. In the course of these early discoveries, a grim picture of destruction and fragmentation of collections unfolded.

The repositories that are today the designated custodians of Jewish historical records acquired these materials in several ways. In some cases the materials were deposited in the Russian imperial archives that were transformed into Soviet institutions following the October Revolution. Other collections belonged to Jewish learned societies until the Soviet authorities appropriated and dispersed them among state archives and libraries. Still other collections were formed in the 1920s and 1930s by the Soviet-Jewish scholarly institutions, and were transferred to a state archives when these institutions had been liquidated in recurring political purges. Many Jewish collections originated in the territories that were annexed by the Soviet Union after World War II.

The records of the Russian imperial government and those of the Soviet regime constitute an even larger source of historical documentation about Russian Jewry. As the rulers of the empire continued to impose restrictive measures on Jews throughout much of the Russian-Jewish history, so too, vast quantities of administrative records continued to accumulate that reflected the relations between the Tsarist government and the Jews. Similarly, during the Soviet period (especially during the early decades), special departments of the government as well as sections of the Communist Party were established to oversee economic, cultural and ideological activities within the Jewish community. This in turn resulted in yet another large accumulation of records that illuminate the situation of the Jews in the Soviet state.

During the Soviet period there was a constant migration of Jewish manuscripts, archival records, and collections from one archive to another. The never-ending turmoil wrought by the revolution and the two world wars, the shifting of the capital from St. Petersburg to Moscow, the appropriation of archives belonging to banned organizations and political parties, the confiscation of personal papers, the influx of archives seized by military forces in the Second World War–all of these events subjected archives to constant structural changes, breakups, relocations, and evacuations.

Furthermore, the Communist Party influenced the work of the archives by imposing political decisions on the way archival records were to be handled, and this again led to the moving around of documents and collections. Materials perceived as "superfluous" or "dangerous" were separated. In the best case, they were made inaccessible, in the worst–destroyed. The records transferred to the Communist Party archives were rearranged there, and artificial collections were carved out without much regard for their provenance.

During the final years of Stalinist rule, when the last vestiges of Jewish communal life in the Soviet Union were being obliterated, some Jewish collections were destroyed, while others were locked away or hidden. Mostly, they fell into disuse and were totally neglected. For decades, researchers had to rely on secondary sources since Jewish documents were virtually closed to them.

From 1989, articles began to appear in Jewish periodicals in Russia and in the West, reporting on the historical fate of Jewish collections and on their current condition. One notable result of these efforts was the book *Dokumental'nye materialy po istorii evreev v arkhivakh SNG i stran Baltii* (Documentary Sources on Jewish History in the Archives of the CIS and the Baltic States), compiled by Dmitrii A. Eliashevich (St. Petersburg, 1994). This modest publication contains a listing of 938 Jewish collections, which are located in 92 government and state repositories in 61 cities of the former USSR. And while the entries in this listing disclose only the most basic information (collection location, repository name, collection title, local number, collection size and inclusive dates), its importance lies in the fact that the publication was the first effort at compiling a guide to archival and documentary sources relating to Jewish history in the FSU. In the introduction, Eliashevich divides the Jewish-related collections into three categories: collections of Jewish provenance, records of state institutions and organizations appointed to work in the Jewish sector, and general records which among other things contain materials of Jewish interest. The book listed collections belonging mainly to the first two groups.

Almost from the beginning of this renewed search for Jewish records in the post-Soviet archives, the entire field became internationalized. Interest in Russian and Soviet Jewish history, combined with the desire to gain access to the mass of documents which are critical for its study, made institutions of Jewish learning in the West eager to join in the exploration of the former Soviet archives. This group included a consortium of Israeli institutions headed by the Central Archives for the History of the Jewish People, Yad Vashem Archives, the Central Zionist Archives, and the Jewish National and University Library. In the United States, the U.S. Holocaust Memorial Museum, the YIVO Institute for Jewish Research, and the Jewish Theological Seminary of America were among the earliest participants in this quest.

In 1991 the New-York based JTSA[6] and YIVO[7] joined forces with the Moscow State Historical Archival Institute–reconstituted in 1991 as the Russian State University for the Humanities (Rossiiskii gosudarstvennyi gumanitarnyi universitet–RGGU)[8]–to establish an academic program in Russia aimed at the preservation of the historical and documentary legacy of Eastern European Jewry. This two-pronged program, named Project Judaica, concentrated on the one hand on the archival search for Jewish documents in the post-Soviet archives, and on the other–on teaching students subjects in Jewish history and culture within the framework of the RGGU.

The Jewish Archival Survey of Project Judaica, or JAS, is a systematic search for Jewish documentary sources dispersed in the archives of Russia, Belarus, and Ukraine. The aim of the survey is to locate collections pertinent to Jewish history and culture, create standard descriptions at the collection (*fond*) or series (*opis'*) level, compile a database of the search results, and publish guides to important Jewish records in the archives of the former Soviet Union. The survey encompasses both collections of Jewish provenance and general collections that include records relevant to Jewish matters.

The ability of the JAS to extend its reach in these three countries, to those archival and manuscript repositories that possess Jewish records, has been of crucial importance for the survey. I should mention at this point that the fortunes of the JAS have depended very much on the political situation prevailing in each host country. As it happened, the start-up of the Project Judaica in Moscow coincided with the breakup of the Soviet Union, the August 1991 putsch, and the political turmoil during the following months. After August 1991, the archival environment in which the JAS project was carried out changed radically in comparison with the rigid pre-1991 centralized system under the Soviet-style Glavarkhiv.[9] The mammoth Soviet archival state service has been broken up along the new national borders. For the project it meant negotiating separately with each new national archival authority, and sometimes with individual repositories, about carrying out the survey in the respective territory or institution.

Still, during this period contacts were made and agreements signed with archival consortia that have under their control large networks of important archives. In Moscow, collaborative agreements were signed with the federal archives which remain under the aegis of the Rosarkhiv[10], the former Communist Party archives, several important institutional archives, manuscript divisions in libraries and museums, and with the group of the Moscow municipal archives, which is largely independent of the Russian federal network. A special agreement was reached with the Center For the Preservation of Historical Documentary Collections, the famed "Osobyi" Archive,[11] to produce folder-level finding aids to the Jewish collections that it holds. An agreement was also signed with the Committee for Archives of the Republic of Belarus, and as a result a task group headed by Evgenii Savitskii, Deputy Chairman of the Committee, was established to work on the survey in the Belarus repositories. Another task group was organized in St. Petersburg to survey the crucially important archives and libraries of the Russian imperial era. Efforts continue to expand JAS's presence in Ukraine, where hundreds of collections have been described to date. Finally, in the last three years JAS has been working on identifying Jewish records in the provincial archives of the Russian Federation.

The surveying of records is carried out with the participation of the archival institutions around the country, each of which surveys its own holdings and prepares a description of relevant materials. The survey instrument is a formatted description sheet, which comprises 35 data fields modeled on the MARC/AMC format (see Figure 1). In accordance with the agreement between the partners, the RGGU Historical-Archival Institute established the Center for Archival Research for the purpose of planning and carrying out the survey. Completed descriptions are forwarded to the Center, in Moscow, where the JAS database is maintained at present. The Center keeps in touch with participating repositories, enlists new participants, negotiates and prepares agreements, disburses funds, and arranges for traveling and inspection of work in progress. The Center also maintains ties with Jewish societies and learning centers, and with individuals in Russia and in other FSU countries who are involved in projects relating to Jewish historical records.

The other function of the Center is to process the survey data. Specially trained staff members edit drafts of descriptions received from the participating archives and enter the results in the JAS database.

Parallel to the database, the JAS staff produces finding aids to Jewish records in the FSU archives, which are published by Project Judaica. The first

FIGURE 1. Excerpt from Formatted Description Sheet, Using MARC Fields

035	*указывается только номер фонда* [collection number]
	1788
045	*хронологические рамки фонда (годы – арабские цифры, века – римские, «гг.» и «вв.» не ставится* [chronological coverage of collection]
	1917-1919
100	* *фамилия фондообразователя (для личных фондов)* [surname of collection's creator (for personal collections)]
110	* *название фондообразователя (для фондов учреждений)* [name of collection's creator (for collections of corporate bodies)]
	Совет Киевской еврейской общины; Совет объединенных общественных организаций г. Киева
	[Council of the Kiev Jewish Community; Council of the United Community Organizations of the City of Kiev]
245	*название фонда по путеводителю* [name of collection as listed in archival guide]
	Коллекция документальных материалов еврейских общественных организаций
	[Collection of documents from Jewish community organizations]

published finding aids were preliminary lists of archives and collections, such as the previously mentioned volume by Dmitrii Eliashevich which was published jointly by St. Petersburg Jewish University and Project Judaica. In 1997, the guide *Jewish Documentary Sources in the Moscow Archives* was published, the first in a series of territorial guides. The second volume, which has just been published, covers the archives in Belarus.[12] The series will include additional volumes on St. Petersburg, the rest of the Russian Federation, and Ukraine.

As explained in the introduction to the Moscow guide, the criteria used to determine which collections should be included in the database and, subsequently, in a guide,

> ... were set in the early stages of the work of locating and describing the largest possible number of pertinent collections. The presumptive existence of documents on Jewish history and culture in a collection was based upon the analysis of possible links of the collection's origi-

nator–institution or individual–to Jewish-related subjects. Thus, the preliminary list of collections to be surveyed and described included practically all collections of Jewish provenance, and collections of non-Jewish origin whose creators were in any way involved in Jewish matters. All these collections were then reviewed and those which included a significant volume of Jewish-related documents were annotated and included in the guide.[13]

The text of these guides has been excerpted from the JAS database, and the format of the entries is based on the database format. Thus, each entry contains data on collection title, local collection number, inclusive dates, quantity (number of "document units"[14]), a historical or biographical statement about the collection's creator, principles of physical arrangement, existing finding aids, and description of contents. A characteristic element that is worth noting is the extent of the historical information. In order to guide the reader through the maze of unfamiliar government and public institutions and organizations, the field containing historical information brings more data than is usually required in this type of archival guide. In the words of one reviewer of the Moscow guide, " . . . In many cases, the historical sketch of the organization is so informative that the book can be actually used as an encyclopedic source as well."[15]

The task of the guides is to concentrate on repositories in a specific geographic area and to provide an annotated list of relevant collections in each repository. A guide also cites facts about historical fates of Jewish collections in this area, and provides general information about the archival network in the region.

The Moscow guide covers for the most part the records of central state organs of the Soviet-era, and of all-Union Jewish institutions and associations of the same time period. These are augmented by a large number of personal papers of Jewish political and cultural figures. Additionally, there are archival documents going farther back, such as the records in the Russian State Archive of Early Records (Rossiiskii gosudarstvennyi arkhiv drevnikh aktov–RGADA), relating to Jewish communities in Poland and Lithuania in the sixteenth century, or records in the State Archive of the Russian Federation (Gosudarstvennyi arkhiv Rossiiskoi Federatsii–GARF) on Jews in the Russian Empire in the nineteenth century.

The Belarus volume takes the reader to the country where frequent political changes, revolutionary upheavals, devastating wars and occupations, and decades of Soviet mismanagement have left indelibly negative marks on the national archival holdings. Historically, the archives of Belarus were an integral part first of the Russian imperial, and then of the Soviet, centralized systems of records maintenance. After the Polish-Soviet War of 1920 the disputed western territories were given to Poland. They remained part of the Polish republic until 1939 before falling into the Soviet hands in result of the Molotov-Ribbentrop Pact. This brought into the Belorussian orbit many records of Polish and Polish-Jewish provenance, which to this day are dispersed through the Belarus archives. The Second World War caused wholesale annihilation of the historical collections in Belarus. As the authors of the guide remind in the introduction, less than 40% of pre-World War II archives in Belarus survived the wartime destruction. At the same time, the retreating German occupation forces left behind many records of the Nazi administration that ruled the country from 1941 until 1944.

The researchers for the Jewish Archival Survey faced the daunting task of searching for Jewish and Jewish-related records in 54 repositories of all levels, from national to local, which constitute the state archival network of the Republic of Belarus, and additionally, in institutional archives that are independent of the state network. Considering that the territory of Belarus was, until the Second World War, one of the major regions of Jewish concentration in Eastern Europe, and that the Jews until that time represented a large proportion among the peoples of Belarus, the expectations were that significant quantities of documents relevant to Jewish topics would be found among many archival collections. This was indeed the case, and it is perhaps best evidenced by the large number of records of state and local governments and of municipalities listed in the guide as containing Jewish-related documents.

As the work of the Jewish Archival Survey intensifies in Ukraine, experience gained in the Belarus archives will prove invaluable, considering both countries' common historical destinies, and many similarities in the fate of their archival holdings. The one major difference is in the quantity of the Jewish materials in the Ukrainian archives, which is considerably larger than in Belarus. That translates into the need to devote more than one volume to the Ukrainian archives.

When Project Judaica and the Jewish Archival Survey were initiated in 1991, the purpose of the JAS was defined as seeking

> to reclaim the documentary legacy of past generations of Russian and Soviet Jews, and to enable an international constituency of scholars and researchers to utilize primary sources in the study of the history of the Jewish communities in the lands of the Russian empire and the Soviet Union.[16]

More than a decade later this focus becomes, if anything, much sharper, and the need to continue the search even more pronounced. The classification system used in the Belarus archives during the Soviet period assigned collections of Jewish origin a "Third Category" status, which encompassed records possessing little if any scholarly value. Essentially, that prevented them from being properly cared for in terms of preservation and cataloging. A similar approach was prevalent in other parts of the Soviet archival colossus. Hence, the continuous need for programs such as the Jewish Archival Survey.

ENDNOTES

1. Partial results of their research were published in a collection of essays, A. Veisberg, G. Kazovskii and A. Zeltser, eds., *Istoricheskie sudby evreev v Rossii i SSSR: nachalo dialoga* (Historical Destinies of the Jews of Russia and the Soviet Union: Beginning of a Dialogue) (Moscow: 1992), and in the early volumes of the journal *Vestnik Evreiskogo Universiteta v Moskve* (Herald of the Jewish University of Moscow), which has appeared in print since 1994.

2. S. M. Dubnov (Dubnow), "Ob izuchenii istorii russkikh evreev i uchrezhdenii russko-evreiskogo istoricheskogo obshchestva," in *Voskhod*, 4:9 (April-September 1891).

3. A selection of the papers given at this conference has been published in English translation in *Eastern European Jewish Affairs* 22, no.2 (Winter 1993), and in Russian in the volume *Istoriia evreev v Rossii: problemy istochnikovedeniia i istoriografii* (History of the Jews in Russia: Topics in Documentation and Historiography) (St. Petersburg, 1993). The editor of this volume, Dmitrii Eliashevich, also contributed a paper, "Istochnikovedenie istorii evreev v Rossii: k postanovke problema" (Documentation of the History of Jews in Russia: Toward a Formulation of the Problem). Of special interest in this volume is the essay by Benyamin Lukin, "K stoletiiu obrazovaniia petersburgskoi nauchnoi shkoly evreiskoi istorii" (Centenary of the Establishment of the Petersburg Scholarly School of Jewish History), in which the author analyzes the work and accomplishments of the St. Petersburg Jewish intellectuals at the turn of the twentieth century.

4. *Tsentral'nyi gosudarstvennyi arkhiv Oktiabr'skoi revolutsii* (TsGAOR), now *Gosudarstvennyi arkhiv Rossiiskoi Federatsii* (GARF).

5. *Tsentral'nyi Partiinyi Arkhiv*, now *Rossiiskii gosudarstvennyi arkhiv sotsial'no-politicheskoi istorii* (RGASPI).

6. The Jewish Theological Seminary of America (JTSA) was founded in 1886 as a spiritual and learning center for Conservative Judaism. Among its many directions as a Jewish university, the JTSA is committed to training a new Jewish intelligentsia for Russian Jewry through Project Judaica.

7. The YIVO Institute for Jewish Research specializes in history and culture of Ashkenazic Jewry with emphasis on Eastern European Jews and their descendants in the United States. YIVO was founded in 1925 in Wilno, Poland (Russian: Vilna; Lithuanian: Vilnius), and re-established in New York in 1940.

8. The Moscow State Historical Archival Institute (*Moskovskii gosudarstvennyi istoriko-arkhivnyi institut*–MGIAI) was founded in 1930 to train professionals for the Soviet state archives. In 1991 the MGIAI was reconstituted as the Russian State University for the Humanities. The university is currently comprised of seven institutes, the former MGIAI among them.

9. *Glavnoe arkhivnoe upravlenie pri Sovete Ministrov SSSR*–GAU (Main Archival Administration under the Council of Ministers of the USSR), headed the Soviet state archival network from 1960 until 1991.

10. *Arkhivnaia sluzhba Rossiiskoi Federatsii* (Archival Service of the Russian Federation), currently administers the Russian state archival network.

11. In March 1999, it merged with the Russian State Military Historical Archives (*Rossiiskii gosudarstvennyi voenno-istoricheskii arkhiv*–RGVIA).

12. Mark Kupovetskii, Evgenii Starostin and Marek Web, eds., *Dokumenty po istorii i kul'ture evreev v arkhivakh Moskvy* (Jewish Documentary Sources In Moscow Archives) (Moscow: Project Judaica, 1997), 507 p.; Mark Kupovetskii, E.M. Savitskii and Marek Web, eds., *Dokumenty po istorii i kul'ture evreev v arkhivakh Belarusi* (Jewish Documentary Sources in Belarus Archives) (Moscow: Project Judaica, 2003), 608 p.

13. *Dokumenty po istorii i kul'ture evreev v arkhivakh Moskvy*, 18.

14. In Russian, *edinitsa khraneniia*, the smallest physical unit of an arranged collection, which is generally used within the FSU archival community as a measure to quantify the collection's volume.

15. Jeffrey Veidlinger, H-NET Book Review, *H-Russia: Russian History List*, February 1999 [Online]. Available: http://www2.h-net.msu.edu/reviews/showrev.cgi?path=1894920480545 (3 Mar. 2003).

16. Dorit Sallis and Marek Web, eds., *Jewish Documentary Sources In Russia, Ukraine and Belarus: A Preliminary List* (New York: The Jewish Theological Seminary of America, 1996), 1.

The Creation of a Documentary Collection on the History of Russian Jewry at the Central Archives for the History of the Jewish People

Benyamin Lukin

SUMMARY. At the beginning of the 1990s the Central Archives for the History of the Jewish People (Jerusalem) initiated a project to survey and microfilm sources in archives throughout the former Soviet Union. The project's aim is to create at the Central Archives a collection of archival sources on the history of Russian Jewry. The article opens with a brief description of survey activities in German and Russian archives, which preceded and inspired similar activities by the Central Archives in government archives throughout the world. It continues with a detailed description of the Central Archives' activities in government archives throughout the Commonwealth of Independent States. The Central Archives have created a database of inventories from numerous archives in Russia, Belarus, Ukraine, Uzbekistan, Moldova, and the Baltic States, as well as a massive collection of micro-

---

Benyamin Lukin is Archivist, Central Archives for the History of the Jewish People, P.O. Box 1149, Jerusalem 91010, Israel (E-mail: archives@vms.huji.ac.il).

Transliterations of place names appearing in this article are based on their Russian spellings.

This article was translated by Colleen Richey and Karen Rondestvedt.

[Haworth co-indexing entry note]: "The Creation of a Documentary Collection on the History of Russian Jewry at the Central Archives for the History of the Jewish People." Lukin, Benyamin. Co-published simultaneously in *Slavic & East European Information Resources* (The Haworth Information Press, an imprint of The Haworth Press, Inc.) Vol. 4, No. 2/3, 2003, pp. 17-36; and: *Judaica in the Slavic Realm, Slavica in the Judaic Realm: Repositories, Collections, Projects, Publications* (ed: Zachary M. Baker) The Haworth Information Press, an imprint of The Haworth Press, Inc., 2003, pp. 17-36. Single or multiple copies of this article are available for a fee from The Haworth Document Delivery Service [1-800-HAWORTH, 9:00 a.m. - 5:00 p.m. (EST). E-mail address: docdelivery@haworthpress.com].

http://www.haworthpress.com/store/product.asp?sku=J167
© 2003 by The Haworth Press, Inc. All rights reserved.
10.1300/J167v04n02_03

films relating to Jews in these areas from the sixteenth to the twentieth centuries, on a wide range of subjects. The Central Archives plan to broaden the geographic range of surveys and microfilms, as well as publish selections of the sources uncovered. *[Article copies available for a fee from The Haworth Document Delivery Service: 1-800-HAWORTH. E-mail address: <docdelivery@haworthpress.com> Website: <http://www.HaworthPress.com> © 2003 by The Haworth Press, Inc. All rights reserved.]*

KEYWORDS. Tsentral'nyi arkhiv istorii evreiskogo naroda, Central Archives for the History of the Jewish People, Jerusalem, Russia, Belarus, Ukraine, Uzbekistan, Moldova, Latvia, Lithuania, Estonia, Poland, Soviet Union, USSR, archival resources, archival surveys, documentary collections, Jewish archives, Jews

INTRODUCTORY REMARKS

Since the beginning of the 1990s the Central Archives for the History of the Jewish People (CAHJP) have been leading a broad-ranging project to uncover primary source materials on the history of Jews in archives in the former Soviet Union, and copy them. The goal of this article is to acquaint the reader with the project's background, its contents, current results, and future prospects.[1]

The opportunity for Israeli archivists to conduct research using Soviet archival collections arose as a result of *perestroika* (rebuilding) in the mid-1980s. For the first time in half a century, the doors to many archives were opened somewhat to researchers of Jewish history. By the start of the 1990s, the so-called "Jewish"[2] collections, "imprisoned" for decades in "special storage," were for the most part "liberated." This took place within the context of the fall of the USSR and the formation of independent national governments with their own archival systems. With a general tendency towards liberalization, the archival politics of each government depended on political twists and turns, as well as on the archives' administrators and their particular policies.

Perestroika also stimulated a rise in the national identity of Soviet Jews. Novice researchers of the cultural and historical past turned to government archives. At last, after many years, their collective efforts drew a source of study on Russian Jewish history out of prolonged stagnation. The opening up of "new" documentary resources, descriptions of archival collections, and inventories of Jewish archival collections have been published in academic journals and put forth in individual publications over the last ten to fifteen years.[3]

The many Western researchers and research institutions participating in the development of former Soviet archives have stimulated the overall process: they attract local researchers and archival employees to their projects, and they open the pages of academic journals to archival publications.[4] Israeli archives and research institutes are also conducting searches and copying sources on Jews in Russia and the Soviet Union as they pertain to their research topics. In contrast, CAHJP does not limit its work to developing archival collections, either in terms of territory, topic, or chronology.

THE CREATION OF THE JEWISH HISTORICAL ARCHIVES IN JERUSALEM

The Jewish Historical General Archives were established over sixty years ago in Jerusalem. It was the realization of the plans of Ben-Zion Dinaburg (Dinur), the representative of the Historical and Ethnographical Society of Israel (subsequently the Israeli minister of education), and Josef Meisl, a Jewish historian, and former secretary and librarian of the Berlin Jewish community.

With the rise of Nazism in Europe, many Jewish historians realized the urgent need to save the archives of Jewish communities and to concentrate them in a national archive in Israel. Founded in the end of the 1930s at the initiative of Meisl and his associates, the Jewish Historical General Archives were taken under the auspices of the Society of History and Ethnography in 1944. A quarter of a century later (1969) it became an independent institution–the Central Archives for the History of the Jewish People.[5]

"The archive's goal," as stated by its first director, Meisl (1947), "is to collect and prepare for scholarly use sources on the history of our people in all the countries of the Diaspora. We want to build a storage place for documents found both in our country and in the Diaspora, on the history of our people, its suffering and accomplishments in all countries of the world in the course of the whole history of its existence."[6] For Meisl, a graduate of a German-Jewish archeographical school, it became obvious that searches of archival material would be concentrated for the most part in government archives of the Diaspora. Moreover, as a result of the Holocaust, the archives of many European Jewish communities were lost.

The idea of an independent document collection in government archives to ensure full-fledged research on Jewish history was first stated publicly by the German Jewish historian Eugen Täubler, the founder (1906) and first director of the General Archives of German Jewry. Determining the task of filling the gaps in documentation of Jewish communities in Germany, Täubler attached special significance to research in government, municipal, and church archives, and also the family archives of local aristocracy. These materials related to Jewish life, and were wider in chronological reach, and topically much more diverse than the community documentation.[7]

Meisl, his colleagues and successors naturally adopted this methodology. It was not by accident that Daniel Cohen, the director of the CAHJP from 1957 to 1983, reporting at the Eighth World Congress of Jewish Studies (1981) on the Archives' thirty years of work in European government archives, emphasized that it was originally Täubler's idea.[8]

Ben-Zion Dinur, chairman of the board of the CAHJP until his death (1973), also shared the archeographic ideas of Täubler, his teacher in the Berlin Hochschule of Jewish Studies (1911) and a good friend for many years. However, in his experience with Russian Jewish historiography, Dinur also became familiar with the need to use documentation from government archives for Jewish historical research.

THE DEVELOPMENT OF ARCHIVES IN GOVERNMENT INSTITUTIONS BY HISTORIANS OF RUSSIAN JEWRY

Semyon Dubnov (Simon Dubnow) first addressed the significance of materials in government archives in the program for collecting Jewish manuscripts–and their importance for Jewish historical research in Russia–in the journal *Voskhod*, in 1891. As an example, he cited the painstaking archeographic work on court books of the sixteenth to eighteenth centuries by the historian Sergei Bershadskii, who was the first to state "that in order to construct an edifice of Jewish history in Russia it is necessary to establish a broad foundation of facts."[9] Dubnov's program received a great response among young Jewish intellectuals. Numerous helpers sent him originals and copies of documents, including those from local government archives. In St. Petersburg, in 1892, a group of young Jewish lawyers organized the Jewish Historical-Ethnographical Commission. Due to the unavailability of government archives for Jewish researchers, they took to registering published documents pertaining to the history of Russian Jewry and creating a collection of registries.[10]

Iulii Gessen, a bank clerk and amateur writer, became the first Jewish researcher to receive access to the archives of the higher and central Russian administrations (1901). He familiarized himself with all of the details of documents from the various departments of the Government Council, Senate, Jewish Committee (1840-1865), and various ministries: Internal Affairs, Justice, Public Education, Finance, Agriculture, and the Military Main Headquarter Archive. Gessen used "the richest material for the history of Russian Jews" in his articles and principal work, *Istoriia evreiskogo naroda v Rossii* (The History of the Jewish People in Russia).[11]

The February Revolution of 1917 finally granted Jewish historians the right to work in the archives of the Tsarist government. The Bolshevik government, which came to power in October, at first actually encouraged archival research in Jewish studies. In Petrograd, three Jewish archival commissions were formed under the auspices of Narkompros (Narodnyi komitet prosveshcheniia [Committee on Public Education]): "for research on the history of anti-Jewish pogroms," "for the scholarly description of Jewish affairs of the former Ministry of Public Education," and "for a scholarly edition of documents pertaining to ritual-murder trials."[12] A whole galaxy of Petrograd Jewish academics participated in the work of these commissions, including Saul Ginsburg, a well-known historian and folklorist.[13] Ginsburg's relationship to the official documents was a result of his understanding that the history of Jews in Russia is an integral part of Russian history:

> Even worse a problem for a long time was the difficulty with the obtaining of the second important type of written material–with the official archive-documents that have such great significance for the historian of Russian Judaism. Here he can study more clearly than elsewhere the politics of the Russian government and the Jewish question, its entire relationship to the Jewish population, its mostly hidden or masked motives, the Jewish legal situation, etc. Already by virtue of this alone one cannot sufficiently estimate the historiographical worth of the official archive materials. But it is a mistake to assume that they touch only the external, legal side of the erstwhile Jewish life in Russia. The government administration dealt also with the internal phenomena and events in Jewish life. It sought to regulate the Jewish life-style, Jewish literature, press, theater, Jewish religious matters, Jewish education, etc. Many, very many sides of Jewish innermost living are thereby reflected in the government documents.
>
> True one must relate to them very carefully and critically, one must continuously sift and control with the aid of other, Jewish sources. But this in no way at all diminishes the really great worth that the official sources have for the researcher of our past.[14]

For thirteen years, right up to his emigration to the U.S. (1930), Ginsburg continued to research archival collections of the Tsarist government, including the archives of the Third Division of His Majesty's Chancellery, Government

Council, Senate, Synod, the Military, the Ministry of War, the Ministry of Internal Affairs, and Ministry of Public Education.[15]

At the same time that the Jewish archival commissions were organized in Petrograd, the Jewish Historical Archeographic Commission was established in Kiev under the All-Ukrainian Academy of Sciences (1919). This commission examined collections in the Kiev Central Historical Archive. Ben-Zion Dinaburg (Dinur) was among its few employees. He constructed a plan for uncovering, collecting, and describing archival documents on the history of Ukrainian Jews. Thus, on the eve of his departure for Israel the future founder of the national historical archives took part in the archival work to reconstruct the history of Russian Jewry.[16]

THE REALIZATION OF THE CAHJP PROJECT
IN FORMER SOVIET ARCHIVES

Many years of experience copying documents in the archives of various countries prepared CAHJP management to expand this practice to the government archives of the Soviet Union. As a result of his trip to the USSR in the spring of 1991, the CAHJP's director, Aryeh Segall, decided that it was necessary to conduct a complex examination of Soviet archives in order to bring to light and then copy Jewish archival collections, as well as materials pertaining to the history of Jews. The project began to materialize in 1992, having created a foundation for:

- Databases for the materials on Jewish history that had been put in Jewish and general collections of the former USSR;
- Collections comprising copies of documents on the history of Jews in the Russian Empire and USSR.[17]

In the first years of CAHJP's work in Russia, Ukraine, and Belarus, which coincided with the establishment of the countries' archival systems, agreements-in-principle were reached with the central archival administration of each country. These spoken or written agreements (later not renewed) did not remove the necessity to sign contracts with archives individually and coordinate with the "superiors" of the archival administration. Collaborative agreements with the central archives of Moscow, St. Petersburg, Kiev, and Minsk were signed in 1992-1993 for periods of three to five years, and, as a rule, they included the archives' obligation to participate in the search and registration of related materials and to produce copies of requested documents. For its part, CAHJP took on the responsibility of managing the search of archival materials and financing the work. The contracts also expressed the parties' intentions to expand the collaborative effort–organizing joint publications, exhibitions, etc. As the archives acquired more independence, including financial independence, their management agreed to process materials "by copy orders," preferring this method to international "contracts." Over time, the registration itself of archival materials ended up in the hands of local researchers and archivists working from private agreements with CAHJP.

During the planning stages of our archival search, we took into account the work on the archival collections by Bershadskii, Gessen, Ginsburg, and Russian Jewish historians, and archival commissions that were their contemporaries, along with the opening of archival sources done in recent years (many local researchers have taken part directly in the CAHJP project). Directing our efforts to the demands of academic scholarship in Israel, we are striving to establish a documentary basis for present and future research projects.

We began the project in the central historical archives of Russia, Ukraine, and Belarus, and we are gradually extending it to municipal and district archives as well as other regions and countries (Uzbekistan, Moldova, Lithuania).

In central archives–the Russian State Historical Archive (RGIA) in St. Petersburg, the Russian State Archive of Ancient Documents (RGADA) in Moscow, and the State Archive of the Russian Federation (GARF) in Moscow–materials on the history of Jews in the Russian Empire are being uncovered and copied mainly from the archives of upper and central organs of power. However, in the Central State Historical Archive of Ukraine (TsGIAU) in Kiev, and in the National Historical Archive of the Republic of Belarus (NIARB) in Minsk, the documents are mainly from the administrative institutions of the governors-general and the *gubernii* (provinces).

In addition to the official documents in central archives, we have also copied collections from general-Russian and general-Soviet Jewish organizations: the Society for the Promotion of Enlightenment Among Jews in Russia (OPE, 1863-1929), the Society for the Attainment of Equal Rights for Russian Jews (1905-1907), he-Haluts (1917-1922), the Central Management of Jewish Communities in Russia (TsEVAAD, 1918-1919), among others; and collections from the federal and republic committees of various Jewish political parties: Poalei Zion (1916-1921), SERP (1917), Bund (1918-1921), among others. We should note that in the Central Government Historical Archive in St. Petersburg (TsGIA SPb) documents on Jewish cultural organizations whose activities were not limited to the territory of the capital have been copied, among them materials from the archive of the Jewish Historical-Ethnographical Society (1908-1929).[18]

The examination of *oblast'* (district) and municipal archives (in St. Petersburg, Vyborg, Kiev, Vinnitsa, Zhitomir, Kamenets-Podolskii, Odessa, Khar'kov, and others) has allowed us to delve into documents from provincial, district, and municipal governments and judicial institutions. Many official documents at the local level have a very direct relationship to the life of the Jewish communities of their corresponding cities and regions. They are distinguished by breadth of topic, high level of detail, and local color.

In district archives, CAHJP are also copying documentation from local Jewish communities (including birth, marriage, and death certificates), charities, educational institutions, and others. Materials from the Zhitomir Rabbinical Seminary (1848-1873) and the Zhitomir Jewish Academic Institute (1873-1886) from the State Archive of the Zhitomir District (GAZhO) hold special significance for a wide range of researchers.

In the Central State Historical Archive of Ukraine (TsGIAU) in L'vov, and also in regional archives in L'vov, Ivano-Frankovsk, Ternopol, Lutsk, Rovno, and Chernovtsy, we are having various materials on the history of local Jewish communities copied that had been deposited in the archives of the corresponding Austrian, Polish, and Romanian government institutions. Also being copied is documentation on Jewish communities and organizations of Eastern Galicia, Volhynia, and West Bukovina.

Materials from military historical archives have extended the topical reach of the developing collection. In the Russian State Military Historical Archive (RGVIA) in Moscow we have copied documents from various military departments, on recruiting, Cantonists, the service of Jews in the Russian army, the position of Jews in front-line zones and occupied territories during World War I, the relation of commanders to Jewish soldiers, etc. In the Russian State Archive of the Naval Fleet (RGAVMF) in St. Petersburg, we have copied materials on the service of Jews in Russian and Soviet fleets, the involvement of Jewish merchants in the founding and support of the Russian fleet from the end of the eighteenth century through the first third of the nineteenth century, among others.

The project participants are also trying to expand the timeframe of the collection of documents being copied. The earliest information on Jews from the middle of the sixteenth century has been discovered in judicial books from municipal and *zemstvo* courts, town councils and *ratushas* (municipal administrations). Registries of court documents from the sixteenth to the eighteenth centuries, pertaining for the most part to Jewish communities of the Grand Duchy of Lithuania (on the territory of modern Belarus), have been copied in RGADA (Moscow) and NIARB (Minsk).

In the two central Ukrainian archives (TsGIAU in Kiev and L'vov) where large collections of court books from the sixteenth to the eighteenth centuries are kept, we have systematically organized the uncovering and subsequent microfilming of documents relating to Jews. At the same time we continue to develop the work begun in the middle of the nineteenth century by the historian Bershadskii. The work of uncovering the documents and compiling inventories of them is being done by specialist paleographers who are employees of the two archives above.

The TsGIAU in Kiev has preserved record books of municipal and *zemstvo* courts, mainly from Volhynia. The oldest records are written in Old Russian,[19] and seventeenth century records are mainly in Polish. Currently, we have compiled inventories (in Ukrainian) on the record books from: Kremenets municipal court (1543-1659), Kremenets *zemstvo* court (1630-1647), Lutsk municipal court (1565-1628), Lutsk *zemstvo* court (1566-1569), Vladimir-Volynskii municipal court (1566-1613), Zhitomir municipal court (1583-1652, 1734-1773), Kiev municipal court (1684-1719), and Vyzhva *ratusha* (1608-1684). Additionally, work has begun to build a thematic collection of inventories of court records on Jews during Khmel'nyts'kyi's time (1648-1657). Over 10,000 inventories have been compiled. The court records pertaining to the history of Jewish communities are being transferred to microfilm according to the lists in their inventories. It should be noted that in cases where the record books are in poor condition, microfilm is the only way to preserve record books for historical study. For those books where the writing has practically disappeared and only fragments remain,[20] the inventories are the only source of information.

The TsGIAU in L'vov contains court and town council books from the territory of the Russian *Województwo* (*Ruś Czerwona*) of the Kingdom of Poland. The records are in Latin and Polish (predominantly the latter in eighteenth-century records). To date, we have compiled inventories (in Polish) of the court records on Jews from record books from Belz municipal court (1546-1730), Busk municipal court (1559-1765), Terebovlia (Trembowla) municipal court (1632-1872), and Sambor town council (1680-1776). Over 4,000 inventories have been compiled.

The project's timeframe extends also into the modern period. Among the documents copied from the first years of Soviet rule are unique materials on the examination of Jewish towns by Jewish organizations and Soviet institutions (1920s, mainly in Belarus). The corresponding reports provide a high level of detail about the economic, demographic, and cultural situations of communities, as well as unique statistical data. Prewar materials from collections of central, government, and party institutions and their divisions that oversaw Jewish problems, as well as from collections of the federal and Belorussian OZET committees (1925-1938) have been copied in GARF in Moscow and the National Archive of the Republic of Belarus (NARB) in Minsk. Work on discovering and reproducing materials of the postwar period requires special effort and laborious searching in order to overcome obstacles (including access to card catalogs of party organizations and personal collections) because, with rare exceptions, Jewish subjects are not distinguished in the titles of archival folders. Without conducting a systematical examination of these collections, project workers have managed to copy individual postwar documents in the collections of reorganized party archives and investigative files of the KGB.

THE RUSSIAN COLLECTION OF DOCUMENT COPIES IN CAHJP

Copies of archival materials are being made in various state archives of the former Soviet Union. CAHJP does the archival processing and cataloging (with the possible clarification or changing of names). The cataloging system of CAHJP is based on the national borders of 1939, with headings for population centers (communities) and regions. The catalog divisions by country and the headings of each division are in alphabetical order by population center and regions. Within each geographical heading, the catalog cards are added in chronological order. Every such card file reflects a collection of documents on the history of the particular community, region, or country as a whole.[21]

Currently, the "Russia-USSR" portion of the catalog includes information on more than 800 communities in the European part of Russia, Siberia, the Caucasus, and the Middle East. Material copied on the history of Jewish communities in provinces of the Russian Empire (Bessarabia, Vilna, Grodno, Kovno, Livonia, Kholm, Estonia) whose territories were not part of the Soviet Union before the beginning of World War II in 1939, are filed under the corresponding catalog sections: "Romania," "Poland," "Lithuania," "Latvia," and "Estonia." Similarly, material copied on the history of Jews in Eastern Galicia, i.e., the L'vov, Tarnopol, and Stanislavov provinces (*województwa*) of Poland, are filed under the catalog section "Poland."

The "Russia-USSR" catalog section begins with a general card file of archival records pertaining to Russian Jewry as a whole, or to the communities of several regions simultaneously. The material filed here mainly reflects the law-making processes in the Russian government and its political relationship with Russian Jewry in the social, economic, cultural, and political spheres. The general card file also includes reference cards that point to series of documents that have the same general topic but are filed in the catalog under headings of different communities (for example, documents about military recruiting, the formation of state institutions of specialized instruction, pogroms). Out of approximately 1,500 cards from the general card file, more than 1,300 pertain to the pre-Soviet period of history.

As an example, we will describe a portion of the archival collection that is classified in the general "Russia-USSR" card index in the chronological period of the rule of Nicholas I (approximately 400 files).

The thirty-year reign of Nicholas I (1825-1855) fundamentally altered all areas of life for Russian Jewry, significantly accelerating its modernization. His Majesty's Chancellery attained special significance in the federal-bureaucratic apparatus through its "Third Division," a high-level police force granted wide authority. They observed Jews who were involved in illegal keeping of taverns, wine monopolies, contraband, minting of counterfeit coins, fake loans, etc. The Third Division took part in the investigation of Jews accused of using Christian blood[22] and "profaning the Christian religion,"[23] cases of public disobedience (the Mstislav and Novoalexandrov riots[24]), and incidents of mob-rule (the Slavuta and Ushitsa cases[25]).

Being an organ of "higher surveillance" or, in other words, reporting personally to the Tsar about suspicious individuals and important events, the Third Department encouraged reports, including those from Jews. Local informants provided the basis for many reports. Jews reported on the local government and Kahal (Jewish self-rule) administrations, in the hope of receiving protection by the higher authorities; they employed denunciations against competitors. They tried to enter the capital, where they were not permitted, on the pretext of reporting personally to the Tsar regarding "affairs of governmental importance." Mostly, however, they reported in the expectation of receiving a reward. Records of informants are part of the materials copied: the Upper-Dneprovsk Rabbi Katzenellenbogen (1837) informed on a "Hasidic sect that did not recognize the government in power"; M. Blank (Lenin's great-grandfather, 1845) reported "on the harmfulness of the Jewish religion"; A. Kuperbant (1846) reported on the "agreement" of Sir Moses Montefiore and the Hasidic Rabbi Israel Friedman of Ruzhin against the Russian government, and also a whole series of reports about participants in the Polish Rebellion of 1830-1831.

The CAHJP collection has also been filled with materials about the participation of the "higher police" in developing legislative measures and in creating government political policy towards Jews (the leaders of the chancellery of the Third Division were part of the Jewish committees). Among these materials are "notes" on Jews by the agent and employee of the secret police K. Fodello (1827), a "Christianized Jew"; by the well-known Jewish Enlightenment figure (*maskil*) L. Zel'tser (1848), and many others. In addition, they include notes on various projects to reconstruct Jewish life, including those of the *maskilim* M. Gofman (1838), N. Rosenthal (1840), and the Vilna Jewish censor V. Tugenhold (1840).

Of particular interest are the documents from various institutions involved in reforming legislation about Jews. They include the Fourth Jewish Committee (1823-1835), whose activity concluded with the affirmation of a new "Position regarding the Jews." In 1832 the Department of Spiritual Affairs of Foreign Faiths of the Ministry of Internal Affairs was established as part of the development and implementation of a political policy towards Jews. The first rabbinical commission to be elected by the Jewish communities themselves gathered under its auspices in 1852. Since the government's efforts for reform did not bring the results desired, another "fundamental reformation of Jews in Russia" was entrusted to the Fifth Jewish Committee (1840-1865).

Document copies have gone into the CAHJP collection not only from the aforementioned government institutions (documents from the Fourth Jewish Committee have been copied from the archives of the General Chancellery of the Ministry of Finance), but also from the Department of Spiritual Affairs of Foreign Faiths of the Ministry of Internal Affairs, the Department of Public Education, the Central Office of Censorship, Buterlin Committee on Printing Matters, St. Petersburg and Kiev Censorship Committees, Chancellery of the Kiev Division of Censorship, Chancellery of the Kiev, Volhynia, and Podolia Governor General, the Chancellery of the Novorossiia [including the Ekaterinoslav and Kherson *gubernii*] and Bessarabia Governor General, the Podolia provincial administration, the Minsk Palace of State, the Administration of the Kiev Educational Circle, the Volhynia Jewish School Commission, and also from the archives of the Military: Chancellery of the Military Minister, Chancellery and Inspection Department of the Naval Ministry, Chancellery of the Main Naval Headquarters, the Department of Military Settlements; from the Zhitomir Rabbi School Archive; and from the personal archives of the Admirals A. Men'shikov and A. Greig.

The following is a list of some of the most characteristic topics in the archival material collected:

- Military service
  The introduction of conscription for Jews; the rights of Cantonists in army and naval departments; the use of draft duty in "debt apportioning"; converting Jewish recruits to Christianity and rewarding the converts; promoting Jews who distinguished themselves in battle to non-commissioned officer rank and awarding them medals of honor; granting some rights to Jewish medics in the Navy; marriages, divorces, and burial rules for Jewish servicemen; communities' opposition to the military draft, draft evasion by Jews; aid provided by communities to Cantonists in accordance with Jewish tradition.

- Forced Exile and Oppression
  The restriction on Jews about living in St. Petersburg, Moscow, Kiev, and Tbilisi; the eviction of Jews from villages in a 50-verst area from the border, from military settlements, and from the Black Sea ports Sebastopol and Nikolaev; prohibiting Jews from renting manors, rural and roadside inns, and post offices; prohibiting Jews from hiring Christians; banning Jews from government work and mines; prohibiting traditional Jewish attire; dividing Jews into different classes.
- Attracting Jews to Agriculture
  The resettlement of Jews from western provinces to the Tobolsk province and Omsk district, into farming colonies of the Kherson and Ekaterinoslav provinces; Jewish farming colonies in the Podolia province.
- Policies on Jewish Education
  Submitting educational institutions to the supervision of the Ministry of Public Education (1844); the organization and work of rabbinical schools, and public and private Jewish schools; the transformation of Talmud Torahs into primary and secondary-level public schools; the use of income from Jewish printing houses for the education of Jewish children.
- Policies on the Publication and Censorship of Jewish books
  The censorship of Jewish books, including those imported into Russia; the activities of the Vilna Censorship Committee; the closure of Jewish printing houses in all cities except for Vilna and Kiev; the publishing of textbooks for Jewish schools; the granting of provincial governments' right to destroy banned Jewish books.
- Regulation of Religious Life in the Communities
  The election, appointment, and dismissal of rabbis; gatherings and activities of the Rabbinical Commission (1852).
- Economic Situation of the Communities
  The payment of community debts from a retail tax on Jewish vendors; payment plans for back taxes; liquidation of community debts.
- Connection Between Russian Jewry and Eretz-Israel
  The collection of aid for Jews in Palestine; dissemination of appeals for resurrecting the Jerusalem Temple.
- Karaites
  Exemption of Karaites from restrictions pertaining to Jews.

In addition to "general" documentation on the history of Jews in Russia, a significant part of the CAHJP's "Russia" collection consists of copies of records on the history of more than 800 Jewish communities in the Russian Empire (as defined by the 1939 borders of the Soviet Union) during the sixteenth and seventeenth centuries. These documents to some extent allow the historical life of each community to be reconstructed, covering various topics, and over a long time span. The overall extent of the documentation collected on a particular community depends on the community's size, activities, and significance in Jewish history, and also on the level of development of the corresponding government archives.[26]

Thus, for example, the document collection on the history of Jews in Odessa contains more than 250 files (1799-1935), St. Petersburg–approximately 250 files (1780-1930), Minsk–approximately 200 files (1683-1935), Zhitomir–more than 150 files (1583-1918), Medzhibozh–approximately 100 files (1576-1917), and Vitebsk–approximately 80 files (1555-1916).

The following description of a collection of archival materials on the history of the Jewish community in the small Ukrainian town Tul'chin serves as an example. The archival documentation collected (1648-1933) includes more than 50 files from various archives in the Ukraine and Russia: The Central State Historical Archive of Ukraine in Kiev, the Central State Archive of the Higher Organs of the Government of Ukraine in Kiev, the State Archive of the Vinnitsa *Oblast'*, the State Archive of the Khmel'nitskii *Oblast'* (in Kamenets-Podol'sk), the Manuscript Division of the Stefanek Library of the Academy of Sciences of Ukraine in L'vov, the Russian State Archive of Ancient Records (RGADA) in Moscow, and the State Archive of the Russian Federation in Moscow. In their ensemble, the archival records copied from the collections of central, *guberniia*, and *uezd* administrative, judicial, and police institutions–and also from the collections of local Soviet and Communist Party administrations–allow one to reconstruct the main events in the community's history.

The first mention of the town Tul'chin in the Bratslav *województwo* of the Kingdom of Poland comes from the beginning of the seventeenth century. By mid-century a Jewish community had formed, which became one of the first victims of the Cossack Rebellion under the control of Bohdan Khmel'nyts'kyi (1648-1649). The story of the "Tul'chin massacre" entered into most Jewish chronicles of this era, and also into Polish and Ukrainian descriptions of the events. Many of the essential details can be clarified thanks to documents copied in CAHJP: the story of the Polish officer Rościszewski, who participated in the battle in Tul'chin (June 24, 1648), and a letter from S. Kusiewicz, a representative of the municipal government of L'vov (July 8, 1648).

Life in the Jewish community in Tul'chin resumed as early as the first third of the eighteenth century. Evidence of this comes from gravestones in a Tul'chin Jewish cemetery. Photographs of the earliest gravestones are in the CAHJP photograph collection.

By the time of the second partition of Poland (1792), the Jewish community of Tul'chin had become one of the most prominent and prosperous communities in the region. The predominance of Jews among Tul'chin craftsmen and merchants is noted in the documentation from the first part of the history of the town within the Russian Empire (this tendency was reflected in later documents: in 1832, out of the twenty-eight people registered as merchants in Tul'chin, twenty-seven were Jews). The so-called "Topographical Description of Bratslav *Uezd* of Podolia Province" (compiled at the end of the eighteenth and beginning of the nineteenth centuries) presents detailed information on the development of Tul'chin, and the industrial and trade enterprises of the Jewish population, and its numbers.

The era of Nicholas I is reflected most extensively in documentation on the history of the community. Records from the *uezd* court reveal the reaction of Tul'chin Jews to the Imperial decree about conscription of Jews (1827), to helping conscripts escape, to hiding deserters, and also to felonies like theft, horse stealing, illegal border crossing, and insulting representatives of the local government. Records from the provincial courts also reflect the conflicts between local Jews and representatives of the Kahal administration, mainly over the expenditure of community funds money and the violation of conscription laws. The abolition of the Kahal (1844) accelerated the fragmentation of communities: according to documents from 1852 there were eleven prayer houses (all members of their boards were listed by name). Documents from 1852 to 1853 present information on the fulfillment of the imperial decree in Tul'chin (1851) about "dividing Jews into categories" (i.e., "useful" and "useless" categories), and about local Jews' reaction to this decree.

Documents from the archive of the governor-general report on the innovations of Alexander II during the "era of great reform," including the election of members of "spiritual boards" in Jewish prayer houses in Tul'chin. Information on the recurring fires in Tul'chin–the worst of which broke out in 1853 and 1856–is reported there. In connection with the organization of public education for Jews, starting in the mid-nineteenth century, the government increased its control over traditional Jewish education. This is reflected in the following documents among the materials copied: a record on the Tul'chin private school for Jewish girls, and information on *heders* (elementary-level religious schools) and *melamdim* (teachers in *heders*) in Tul'chin.

The documentation collected includes statistical data on the Jewish population of Tul'chin (including the years 1852, 1866, 1889, and 1896), records about Jewish charities, a Jewish hospital, as well as a local Jewish post office, which alarmed the government.

Small anti-Jewish "disturbances" in Tul'chin itself and the pogroms in surrounding towns are reported in documents from the pogrom eras (1881-1882, 1905-1906).

Documentation from the 1910s reflects the diverse activities of Tul'chin Jewish merchants, including the savings and loan association and free-loan society that they founded.

Massacres during the Civil War (1919-20) destroyed Tul'chin, leaving dozens of children orphaned. The efforts of the Jewish aid organization were directed first toward the construction of a hospital and a school in Tul'chin (1922-23). This is reported in the documents collected.

The first actions of the Soviet power are reported in documents about the Tul'chin Jewish Pedagogical Technical School (1920s), about the organization of a local Jewish council (1925), and about the closing of Jewish prayer houses (1925).

The famine during 1932-1933 in Ukraine did not exclude Jewish towns. According to information from the Vinnitsa *Obkom* (district committee) in Tul'chin, "47 deaths among impoverished Jews" were recorded through February 15, 1933.

CONCLUSION

As a result of decades of work in the archives of the former Soviet Union, a database of materials on the history of Jews has been created in the CAHJP. The materials are located in more than eighty archives and manuscript divisions of libraries and museums in Russia, Ukraine, Belarus, Moldova, Lithuania, Latvia, Estonia, and Uzbekistan. This database includes inventories of Jewish collections, as well as record lists and documents on Jewish history in governmental and private collections. It allows CAHJP employees to plan the searching and reproduction of documents in dozens of archives in various countries and also provides convenient assistance for researchers, helping them to organize their archival search in an optimal way.

A vast collection of copied material on the history of Jews in the Russian Empire and USSR (approximately 1.5 million pages of documents in microfilm, microfiche, and photocopies) has been created in CAHJP. The microfilm collection of documents on the history of Jews in Poland, Romania, Lithuania, Latvia, Estonia, Germany, and the land of Israel has also been significantly increased.

The CAHJP plans to develop the geographical scope of the project further, by examining and reproducing documents in countries of the Baltic, Middle East, and Caucasus. Preparing documentary collections for publication is part of the project's new directions. Soon to appear are *Regesty zapisei o evreiakh v aktovykh knigakh Lutskogo grodskogo suda (vtoraia polovina XVI v.)* (Registries of Records on Jews in the Record Books of the Lutsk Municipal Court: Second Half of the Sixteenth Century) and *Dokumenty po istorii evreev iz arkhiva Tret'ego otdeleniia sobstvennoi ego imperatorskogo velichestva kantseliarii* (Documents on the History of the Jews from the Archive of the Third Division of His Majesty's Chancellery).

Even today, research on various topics relating to the history of Russian Jewry and individual communities, and genealogical work, are being conducted using the "Russian" CAHJP collection that is still in formation. Thus, the dreams of the "founding fathers" of Russian Jewish historiography to build a documentary base for historical research are being fulfilled today in Jerusalem.

NOTES

1. See also the 1996 review of CAHJP material uncovered and copied from government archives of the former USSR: Benjamin Lukin, Anat Peri, "Israeli Archives with Material on Russian Jewish History: The Central Archives for the History of the Jewish People," *Jews in Eastern Europe* 1 (1996): 65-81.

2. We refer to archives or documents from Jewish communities, societies, organizations, parties, or prominent Jewish activists as "Jewish" collections; in contrast to material pertaining to Jews in "general" collections, i.e., the archives of various federal government, social, municipal, and church institutions, as well as the personal archives of government officials or family archives from large landowners.

3. For a detailed guide to archival publications during 1989-99, see E. I. Melamed, comp. and D. A. Eliashevich, ed., *Arkhivnaia iudaika Rossii, Ukrainy i Belorussii: materialy dlia ukazatelia literatury* (Archival Judaica of Russia, Ukraine, and Belarus: Reference Materials) (St. Petersburg, 2001), 104.

4. Project Judaica, a research and pedagogical program that is carried out jointly by the Jewish Theological Seminary of America (New York), the YIVO Institute for Jewish Research (New York), and the Russian State University of the Humanities (RGGU; Moscow), has an especially wide scope. The description of "Jewish" and "general" archive collections containing materials on Jewish history, and the preparation of corresponding guides to archives, museums, and libraries fall under the scope of this project. See Dorit Sallis and Marek Web, eds., *Jewish Documentary Sources in Russia, Ukraine and Belarus: A Preliminary List* (New York: Jewish Theological Seminary of America, 1996), 164; Mark S. Kupovetskii, E. V. Starostin and Marek Web, eds., *Dokumenty po istorii i kul'ture evreev v arkhivakh Moskvy: putevoditel'* (Documents in Moscow Archives on the History and Culture of the Jews: Guidebook) (Moscow: RGGU, 1997), 503.

5. For the creation of the Jewish Historical General Archives and for the beginning stages of activities of the Central Archives for the History of the Jewish People, see: *The Jewish Historical General Archives* (Jerusalem, 1961), 19 (English), 13 (Hebrew); *The Central Archives for the History of the Jewish People, Newsletter* 1-5 (Jerusalem,

1970-1976). For the participation of Dinur and Meisel in the organization of the archives, see also: Arielle Rein, "The Historian as a Nation-Builder: Ben-Zion Dinur's Evolution and Enterprise" [Ph.D. diss., Hebrew University of Jerusalem, 2000]: 189-196.

6. From the opening speech by Meisel at the ceremony to celebrate the opening of the General Archive of the History of the Jewish People on 30 January 1947 (unpublished). See: Rein, "The Historian as a Nation-Builder," 191.

7. Eugen Täubler, "Zur Einführung," *Mitteilungen des Gesamtarchivs der Deutschen Juden* 1, no. 1 (Leipzig, 1908-9): 1-8.

8. Daniel J. Cohen, "Thirty Years of Survey in European Archives by the Central Archives for the History of the Jewish People," *Ginzei Am Olam, The Central Archives for the History of the Jewish People, Newsletter* 10 (Jerusalem, 1981): ix-xiii.

9. S. M. Dubnov, "Ob izuchenii istorii russkikh evreev i ob uchrezhdenii russko-evreiskogo istoricheskogo obshchestva" (Study of the History of Russian Jews and the Institution of the Russian Jewish Historical Society), *Voskhod* 4-9 (1891), 1-91; S. M. Dubnov, "O sovokupnoi rabote po sobiraniiu materialov dlia istorii russkikh evreev" (On the Joint Work of Gathering Materials for a History of Russian Jews), *Voskhod* 11 (1891): 34-38. Bershadskii collected, translated, and edited for publication the registries of records on Jews in court books of the fourteenth to sixteenth centuries: S. A. Bershadskii, *Russko-evreiskii arkhiv: dokumenty i materialy dlia istorii evreev v Rossii* (The Russian-Jewish Archive: Documents and Materials for the History of Jews in Russia), vols. 1-2 (St. Petersburg, 1882); vol. 3 (St. Petersburg, 1903). The registries of archival documents that remain unpublished are currently located in the collection of the Jewish Historical-Ethnographical Society, in the Central State Historical Archive (TsGIA), in St. Petersburg.

10. For the work by the Jewish Historical-Ethnographical Commission, see: Benyamin Lukin, "K stoletiiu obrazovaniia Peterburgskoi nauchnoi shkoly evreiskoi istorii" (Centenary of the Founding of the St. Petersburg Academic School of Jewish History), *Istoriia evreev v Rossii: problemy istochnikovedeniia i istoriografii* (History of the Jews in Russia: Problems in the Study of Sources and Historiography) (St. Petersburg, 1993), 13-26. The committee prepared and published: *Regesty i nadpisi: svod materialov dlia istorii evreev v Rossii*: 80 g.-1800 g. (Registries and Inscriptions: A Collection of Materials on the History of Jews in Russia: 80-1800), vols. 1-3 (St. Petersburg, 1899-1913).

11. Gessen wrote about the beginning stages of his archival research in letters to Dubnov. See: "Ia smotriu na Vas, kak na svoego uchitelia... (Pis'ma Iu. I. Gessena k S. M. Dubnovu)" (I look at you like my teacher... [Letters from Iu. I. Gessen to S. M. Dubnov]), *Vestnik Evreiskogo universiteta* 7 /22 (2000): 291-310. For Gessen's publications on Russian Jewish history, see his: *Istoriia evreev v Rossii* (History of the Jews in Russia) (St. Peterburg, 1914); *Istoriia evreiskogo naroda v Rossii* (History of the Jewish People in Russia), vol. 1 (Petrograd, 1916; 1925) vol. 2 (Leningrad, 1927). The archival documents copied by Gessen were destroyed, together with his personal archive, during the blockade of Leningrad (1941-1944).

12. The results of work by the first two commissions were published in: S. M. Dubnov and G. Ia. Krasnyi-Admoni, eds., *Materialy dlia istorii antievreiskikh pogromov v Rossii: Dubossarskoe i Kishinevskoe dela 1903 g.* (Materials on the History of Anti-Jewish Pogroms in Russia: The Dubossar and Kishinev Cases of 1903), vol. 1 (Petrograd, 1919); G. Ia. Krasnyi-Admoni, ed., *Materialy dlia istorii antievreiskikh pogromov v Rossii: vos'midesiatye gody* (Materials on the History of

Anti-Jewish Pogroms in Russia: The Eighties), vol. 2 (Petrograd; Moscow, 1923); S. M. Lozinskii, ed. and Saul Ginsburg, comp., *Opisanie del byvshego arkhiva Ministerstva narodnogo prosveshcheniia: kazennye evreiskie uchilishcha: opisanie del byvshego arkhiva Ministerstva narodnogo prosveshcheniia* (Description of Records in the Former Archive of the Ministry of Public Education: Jewish Public Schools: Description of Records from the Former Archive of the Ministry of Public Education), vol. 1 (Petrograd, 1919). The commission on ritual murder trials was dissolved in 1920 by the Jewish section of the Russian Communist Party (Bolsheviks), and did not publish its drafts.

13. When Ginsburg first came to the state archives (1917), he was already a well-known historian, author of books and articles, and editor (1908-1913) of the Jewish historical almanac *Perezhitoe* (The Past). He began the collection of materials on Jewish life with records on Jewish folklore, which went into the collection: Saul Ginsburg and P. Marek, *Evreiskie narodnye pesni v Rossii* (Jewish Folk Songs in Russia) (St. Petersburg, 1901), 332. Later, he continued to collect materials from family archives, which he used in his research and publications.

14. Saul M. Ginsburg, *The Drama of Slavuta*, translated from the Yiddish by E. M. Prombaum (Lanham: University Press of America, 1991), x-xi. Ginsburg used the majority of the archival materials during the 1930s, while preparing a series of articles on the history of Jews in Russia during the nineteenth century for the largest American Yiddish newspaper, *Forverts*. Later, these articles became the only source of historical information for many western researchers, as the documents themselves were unavailable during their decades in Soviet archival storage.

15. The collection of document copies from the archives in the aforementioned government institutions is located in Ginsberg's personal archives in the Manuscript Division of the National Library of Israel.

16. For Dinaburg's participation in the work of the Jewish Archeographical Commission, see: Rein, "The Historian as a Nation-Builder," 97. The "builders of proletarian Jewish studies" in the USSR also understood the significance of documents from the Tsarist government for reconstructing Jewish history. They liquidated the Kiev Commission and the Jewish scholarly institutions of Leningrad, and then created the Jewish Section in the Central Historical Archive of Kiev (1929), which continued work on the registration of archival documents concerning Jewish history.

17. Until 1992, the "Russian" materials in the CAHJP comprised individual documents from the archives of ORT and the Jewish Colonization Association, the personal archives of S. M. Dubnov, Solomon Mikhoels, David Mowshovitch, Leo Motzkin, Aaron Steinberg, and others, as well as individual records and documents donated to the archive by various people. The "Russian" collection included microfilms from the Public Record Office (London), the Alliance Israélite Universelle (Paris), the American Jewish Archives (Cincinnati), and others.

18. See: Binjamin (Benyamin) Lukin, "Archive of the Jewish Historical and Ethnographic Society: History and Present Condition," *Jews in Eastern Europe* 1 (1993): 45-61.

19. Recently, as a rule, the language of these and similar documents has been called the "administrative language of the Grand Duchy of Lithuania."

20. In particular, some books from the Kremenets municipal and *zemstvo* courts are in such condition.

21. Research on the "Russian" collection is facilitated by reference cards in the catalog section "Russia-USSR," as well as extra card files of personal names, private collections, and Jewish organizational collections.

22. Including cases on ritual slanders in Velizh (1823-35), Grodno (second investigation 1826-1830), Tel'cha (1827), Bobovka (1829), and Starokonstaninov (1833).

23. Including the files: "Jews insulting objects of worship during the procession" (Zhizhmory, 1851), "Jews' attack on a priest and desecration of objects of worship" (Knyshin, 1847), "Profanation of Christianity" (Polonnoe, 1854).

24. Attempts by Jews to resist the police, e.g., while the latter confiscated contraband from them, as in Novoaleksandrovsk (1839) and Mstislavl (1844), were called "riots" in the official correspondence.

25. The Slavuta case accused the owners of a Jewish printing house in the town Slavuta and the Shapiro brothers, who were publishers, of the murder of the bookbinder Protagain. The Ushitsa case accused Jews in the town Novaia Ushitsa and other nearby towns of murdering two informants; among those accused was the Hasidic Rabbi Israel Friedman, of Ruzhin.

26. CAHJP's director, Hadassah Assouline, spoke at a conference of archivists in Potsdam in July 1999 about how the CAHJP creates the historical documentation of individual communities, such as Lvov, on the basis of archival collections in various countries. See: Hadassah Assouline, "The Central Archives for the History of the Jewish People," *Preserving Jewish Archives as a Part of the European Cultural Heritage* (Paris, 2001), 220-227.

Hebrew Incunabula in the Asiatic Museum of St. Petersburg

S. M. Iakerson

SUMMARY. The formation of separate collections of Hebrew incunabula–along with their scholarly description–plays an important role on the modern stage of Hebrew book scholarship. This article is devoted to the history of the largest Russian collection of Hebrew incunabula–the collection of the Asiatic Museum (modern name: St. Petersburg Branch of the Institute of Oriental Studies, Russian Academy of Sciences). This collection comprises the earliest printed books from two private collections, those of the merchant Lev Friedland and the Orientalist Daniel Chwolson, which were incorporated into the collection of the Museum at the end of nineteenth and beginning of the twentieth centuries. The article includes a brief description of the books and fragments, along with their provenance and bibliography. *[Article copies available for a fee from The Haworth Document Delivery Service: 1-800-HAWORTH. E-mail address: <docdelivery@haworthpress.com> Website: <http://www.HaworthPress.com> © 2003 by The Haworth Press, Inc. All rights reserved.]*

S. M. Iakerson, PhD, is Senior Researcher, St. Petersburg Branch of the Institute of Oriental Studies, Russian Academy of Sciences (E-mail: shiakerson@mail.lanck.net).

This article was translated by Karen Rondestvedt, with the assistance of Zachary M. Baker.

[Haworth co-indexing entry note]: "Hebrew Incunabula in the Asiatic Museum of St. Petersburg." Iakerson, S. M. Co-published simultaneously in *Slavic & East European Information Resources* (The Haworth Information Press, an imprint of The Haworth Press, Inc.) Vol. 4, No. 2/3, 2003, pp. 37-57; and: *Judaica in the Slavic Realm, Slavica in the Judaic Realm: Repositories, Collections, Projects, Publications* (ed: Zachary M. Baker) The Haworth Information Press, an imprint of The Haworth Press, Inc., 2003, pp. 37-57. Single or multiple copies of this article are available for a fee from The Haworth Document Delivery Service [1-800-HAWORTH, 9:00 a.m. - 5:00 p.m. (EST). E-mail address: docdelivery@haworthpress.com].

http://www.haworthpress.com/store/product.asp?sku=J167
© 2003 by The Haworth Press, Inc. All rights reserved.

KEYWORDS. Asiatic Museum (St. Petersburg), Chwolson collection, Friedland collection, Hebrew books, incunabula, Wiener collection, Russia

In the history of the book the so-called "incunabula period" is exceedingly short. It begins with the first attempts by the inventor of European book printing, Johannes Gutenberg (1394-99–1468), which most likely took place in the 1430s. It ends with the deliberately chosen date 1 January 1501. For the Hebrew printed book the period of infancy was even shorter, since the first attempts at *artificosa imprimendi ac caracterizandi absque calami* (printing and stamping artifacts without a pen)[1] with Hebrew letters evidently took place only in the 1460s. During this short period, Hebrew printing began in four countries: Italy, Spain, Portugal, and Turkey. Hebrew typography appeared for a more or less extended period in 18 locations, as directly indicated in the books' colophons: 11 places in Italy, three in Spain, three in Portugal, and one in Turkey. The leaves of the books themselves preserve the names of 79 individuals who took some part in the printing process. But if one takes into account the fairly large number of anonymous works[2] and the presence of a corpus of documents connected in one way or another to book publishing activity, as well as an expanding circle of familiar names,[3] then it is entirely logical to suppose that there were more places where Hebrew printing took place in the fifteenth century and a greater number of people who participated in the process.

How many Hebrew books were produced during this initial period is still somewhat an open question. It is not always possible to determine the original structure of a particular publication from the surviving fragments.[4] There is also no doubt, at least in this author's mind, that there were publications that did not survive[5] (or, more correctly, have not been discovered and entered into the literature). There are also "marginal" publications, without bibliographical information, which could be related to late incunabula or to the earliest printed books.[6] In any case, approximately 140 to 150 Hebrew books were published in the fifteenth century (a transitional period between the times when books were copied one at a time and when they were produced continuously by typographical means), with a combined total number of copies around 30,000.[7] It is this relatively small number of publications that falls within the purview of scholars of medieval books and students of incunabula in general, as well as specialists of Hebrew.

The study of the first Hebrew printed books as a separate branch of book-lore began with the work of the Italian Biblical scholar and bibliophile Giovanni Bernardo de Rossi (1742-1831),[8] who first divided these publications into a separate group and formulated the basic principles for describing them (including, among other things, publishing the text of the colophons and their translations into Latin[9]).

Since De Rossi, the inventory and description of Hebrew incunabula has taken several directions: union and regional descriptions of incunabula; descriptions of individual collections of incunabula that include Hebrew material; descriptions of individual Hebrew book collections; textological studies; and catalogs and lists of Hebrew incunabula (items found in a region or in individual collections). In spite of the limited number of the sources themselves and the 200-year history of research on them, Hebrew incunabula as a field of study is still developing (I would even say–beginning with the second half of the twentieth century–developing intensively). Our knowledge about the origin and initial period of Hebrew printing, unfortunately, cannot be called exhaustive.[10] Consequently, compilation of a scholarly union catalog and production of a monograph on the early history of Hebrew printing are among prime desiderata for the discipline.[11]

At the same time, these comprehensive projects are impossible without substantial preparatory work, one fundamental aspect of which, I believe, is a detailed study and bibliographic description of the extant collections of Hebrew incunabula. Such work, encompassing as far as possible the history of each individual copy and how it came to be included in one or another collection, is important not only for furthering the study of Hebrew incunabula, but also for the wider history of the Hebrew book in general.

As far as it can currently be determined, Hebrew incunabula can be found in three institutions in Russia: the Russian State Library (*Rossiiskaia gosudarstvennaia biblioteka*–RSL) in Moscow, the Russian National Library (*Rossiiskaia natsional'naia biblioteka*–RNL) in St. Petersburg, and the St. Petersburg Branch of the Institute of Oriental Studies of the Russian Academy of Sciences (*Sankt-Peterburgskii filial Insitituta vostokovedeniia Rossiiskoi Akademii nauk*–SPbB IOS RAS). The RSL's collection was described briefly in the general inventory of incunabula in that library (Kiselev and Cherkasina 1973; Kiselev and Cherkasina 1979). Those in SPbB IOS RAS were described by me–with omissions and mistakes, unfortunately[12]–in a fair amount of detail in the catalog of that collection (Iakerson 1985). After that, all three collections were described together in the catalog *Evreiskie inkunabuly* (Hebrew Incunabula) (Iakerson 1988). The present article will be devoted to the history of the formation of the most significant Russian collection, that of SPbB IOS RAS.[13]

On 11 November 1818 the president of the Imperial Academy of Sciences, Count S. S. Uvarov, addressed a letter to the Board of Directors of the Academy, in which he informed them of the establishment of an Oriental Cabinet at the Academy and the appointment of Christian M. S. Fraehn as its curator.

This day is thus considered the founding date of the Oriental Cabinet, which became widely known in scholarly circles as the Asiatic Museum (*Aziatskii muzei*).[14] After that, the Asiatic Museum experienced several moves and name changes. Today it is called the St. Petersburg Branch of the Institute of Oriental Studies of the Russian Academy of Sciences. It is located in the palace of Grand Prince Michael (architect A. Stakenschneider, 1857-1861) on Dvortsovaia naberezhnaia (Palace Embankment). The Hebrew collection's last move, from the building of the Library of the Russian Academy of Sciences to the Institute of Oriental Studies' building, took place in 2001.

At the time of its founding, the Asiatic Museum received the Academy of Sciences' collections of manuscripts, woodcuts, and printed books in Eastern languages. Among the materials sent to the Museum over the years were the obligatory deposit copies of Hebrew books published on the territory of the Russian Empire received by the Academy beginning in 1811. Thus one can say that Hebrew books appeared in the Museum immediately upon its founding, although of course, there were no early printed books or incunabula among them.

The first incunabula came to the Asiatic Museum at the end of the nineteenth century, as part of the famous book collection of Lev Faivelevich Friedland (1826, Dvinsk-1899, St. Petersburg). The history of Friedland's collection deserves a separate study,[15] which goes beyond the scope of this article, but one can briefly note the following facts: Lev Faivelevich[16] Friedland was born in Dvinsk (now Daugavpils, Latvia) in 1826 into a rich and high-born merchant family. His passion for bibliography arose as a result of interest in his family tree, which originated with the so-called Ruzhan Martyrs.[17] Collecting material for the family archive kindled Friedland's interest in books in general and led him to become a bibliophile. In the popular literature there is also another explanation for his interest, evidently founded on the memoirs of Simon Dubnow (Russian name: Semen Markovich Dubnov); according to this version, Friedland began his collecting in memory of his late wife.[18] Today that is not particularly important, especially since it is obvious that only a confluence of many factors, from fortunate coincidence to certain character traits, could have led him to collect, in a relatively short time, what is arguably the largest private collection of Hebrew printed books.

Friedland was a merchant of the first guild, a hereditary and esteemed citizen, who lived far from the Pale of Settlement, in the capital, at the address Vasil'ev Island, Third Line, House 48. Friedland's collection was indisputably created by the bookman and outstanding bibliographer Samuel Wiener (Samuil Eremeevich Viner, 1860-1929). He came to Friedland in St. Petersburg in 1888.[19] That moment evidently marked the beginning of the conversion of Friedland's private home book collection into the famous "Bibliotheca

Friedlandiana." Wiener did not come to the capital empty-handed; he had with him his own library, in which was at least one incunable, the Soncino edition of Maimonides's *Mishneh Torah*. That copy, along with Wiener's entry concerning its purchase in Ekaterinoslav (now Dnepropetrovsk, Ukraine) in 1887, also came to the Asiatic Museum (Appendix, item no. 25), but, strangely, not with Friedland's books, but as part of Chwolson's collection (see later).

From Wiener's preface to the first volume of the collection's printed catalog, it is evident that the initial formation of the "Friedlandiana" took place by means of bulk book purchases–whole collections or parts of them, which came to the book market after the death of their owners or as a result of the various life circumstances of heirs, beginning at the end of the 1880s. Wiener notes the collections of I. Bampi (1823-1888) and L. Rabinovich (1830-1887) from Minsk, Sh. Tsukerman from Mogilev (d. 1879), along with approximately 2,000 volumes from the library of the famous bibliophile Joseph Mazal (Iosif Mazel') from Viazin (d. 1848), which appeared in the previously mentioned collections after the death of their owner.

Samuel Wiener not only turned ordinary serendipitous book purchasing into planned collecting, but also began the detailed bibliographic description of the books–the latter starting in 1892. That fact can be ascertained from a letter by Friedland to the Permanent Secretary of the Imperial Academy of Sciences on 14 January 1892. In the letter, in addition to the conditions of donation, he notes the motives for beginning his collecting activities and the general characteristics of the collection:

> In the course of many years I endeavored to create a collection of the most important works of Hebrew literature, at first with the goal of gathering material for the history of my family, but then from a purely bibliographical interest. [. . .] My library consists of 300 volumes of manuscripts (including a few on parchment), 32 incunabula printed in the fifteenth century, 10,000 volumes printed mostly in the sixteenth and seventeenth centuries, and a collection of books in various languages specifically on Hebrew literature and bibliography.[20]

It is obvious that the number of books indicated in the letter–10,000 volumes–is not exact. The number 13,000, twice cited by Wiener, who really knew the collection, appears to be more accurate.[21] *De facto*, the transfer of the collection to the Asiatic Museum took place on 28 February 1892.[22]

All the "Friedlandiana" books show the Friedland collection stamp, and almost all are "dressed" in standard luxurious bindings: the binding cases are covered in brown leatherine, with leather spines. The spines are stamped in gold, generally with abbreviated publication information. Unfortunately, the majority of items in Friedland's collection show no trace of where they were immediately before he acquired them. It is true that the leaves of many of the books contain glosses, marginalia, and owners' marks from the sixteenth to the eighteenth centuries (depending on the age of the books themselves). With only the rarest exceptions, however, they have no stamps or ownership marks by which it would be possible to determine to which of the private libraries listed above they belonged.

The lack of nineteenth-century ownership marks and printed catalogs from the above collections likewise makes it impossible to determine the paths that the incunabula followed into Friedland's collection. Most likely, the incunabula (or at least most of them) came to Friedland not as part of other libraries, but were bought by him from book dealers. Wiener provides indirect support for this hypothesis in his preface to the second part of the catalog, where he writes that a few thousand valuable books were acquired from Raphael Nathan Nata Rabbinovicz, of Munich. Among them, he says, were "most of the books published before 1500 that were listed in the beginning of my preface to the letter *aleph* and that are now here, including the precious Pentateuch with Rashi's commentary, Aramaic Targum, vowels, and cantillation marks (*trop*; *ta'ame ha-mikra*), which was printed on parchment in Lisbon in 1491."[23]

In addition to Rabbinovicz, Friedland also bought books from the book dealer Ephraim Deinard (1846-1930), who operated in Odessa and then in the United States. His firm's stamp ("Buchhandlung. Antiquarium. Odessa. E. Dainard [*sic*]") is preserved on the copy of Judah ben Jehiel Messer Leon's work, *Nofet tsufim* (Appendix, item no. 21).[24] This complete copy (in an amazing state of preservation!) of the first Hebrew work on rhetoric also has an ownership mark testifying to its having come to Deinard from the library of Mendel Landsberg. Landsberg (1786-1866), a bibliophile and philanthropist from Kremenets, played a significant role in the spread of Jewish enlightenment (Haskalah) in Russia. Suffice it to note that his library was a resource for his famous contemporary and fellow countryman Isaac Baer Levinsohn (1788-1860).

Another incunable, Avicenna's *Canon* (Appendix, item no. 3), also has Mendel Landesberg's ownership mark. On this same copy there are also three identifying marks from the bookseller Efraim Bislisches of Brody. Those marks show that he received the book from his brother, Mordechai Leib Bislisches of Paris, in 1816. Clearly, from Bislisches the *Canon* came to Landesberg, then to Deinard, and from him to Friedland.

From the previously cited letter to the Permanent Secretary of the Imperial Academy of Sciences, it is immediately evident that Friedland understands the value of his collection of incunabula: he divides the incunabula into a separate category and gives their number as 32. Wiener's introduction to the first volume of the printed catalog of the collection (Wiener, *List*) also begins with a list of the incunabula. In fact, it was this short bibliographic description that brought Friedland's incunabula into the scholarly literature. The descriptions do not follow a strict format, but one can nevertheless see that the entries are arranged in chronological order and generally contain the following obligatory elements: name of the work, author's name (not always), place and year of publication, and name of printer. Besides those elements, Wiener also publishes additional information: he separates out the parchment copies, indicates size in number of folds–or imposition, to use rare-book terminology–for small-format books (e.g., 12°), notes that one work is also in the manuscript collection, and makes some other supplementary notes (e.g., no. 13, Moses Kimhi's *Mahalakh shevile ha-da'at* (Appendix, item no. 36) with the note "*ne izvestnoe [izdanie]*" (unknown publication). Besides the lists of incunabula, Wiener also published, within the general arrangement of material in the published parts of the catalog *Kohelet Moshe* (or *Bibliotheca Friedlandiana*), expanded bibliographic descriptions of seven publications.[25]

The quantity of publications indicated by Wiener needs to be rendered more precise. Under numbers 13 and 14 he describes the already noted grammatical treatise by Moses Kimhi, *Mahalakh,* and *Bakashat ha-memin* (Prayers of the "Mems" [in which every prayer begins with the Hebrew letter *mem*]), by Jedaiah ben Abraham Bedersi (ha-Penini). However, these are not separate publications, but different parts of a composite volume published by the printing firm Soncino in 1488. All its parts are combined in a single pagination, and it concludes with a single colophon. For that reason, according to contemporary bibliographic rules, Wiener's items 13 and 14 comprise a single bibliographic entity.[26] To my great dismay, at the beginning of my work in describing the incunabula collection at SPbB IOS RAS in 1983, the seven leaves of the composite volume containing *Bakashat ha-memin* had already been lost. All my searching for this unique fragment has so far been unsuccessful. Wiener's list also does not contain the Constantinople publication *Turim* by Jacob ben Asher from 1493. Wiener, like the great majority of bibliographers of his time, believed that the colophon data in this item were incorrect; he dated it to 1503.[27]

Wiener's introduction to the second part of the catalog *Kohelet Moshe* ends with hearty thanks to Professor Daniel Chwolson (Daniil Avraamovich Khvol'son). In Wiener's words, the professor opened wide the doors of his house and allowed him to work in his library, which Wiener characterizes in the most complimentary terms. He notes that the "wise, old man" collected his library carefully, with great expenditure of energy, knowledge, and material means. Wiener also underscores the fact that the library contained only choice and valuable books, and for that reason, despite its relatively small size, its scholarly significance was not less than the famous collections. As the saying goes, "*mal zolotnik, da dorog.*"*

Daniel Chwolson (1819, Vilna-1911, St. Petersburg) was a very famous figure in the social and scholarly life of Russia in the second half of the nineteenth and early twentieth centuries. In childhood he received a traditional Jewish education, then continued his scholarly training in German universities. He returned to Russia in the 1850s, converted to Orthodoxy, and was appointed to the chair of Semitic languages in the Oriental Department of St. Petersburg University. From the middle of the 1850s he taught Semitic languages at various educational institutions and engaged intensively and prolifically in scholarship. He also took an active part in the life of the Jewish community in St. Petersburg and, more widely, in Russian Jewry–activity rather unusual in a Jew who had been converted to Christianity.[28]

Chwolson was, of course, not a professional bibliographer (as was, for example, Wiener), but he was also not just an amateur collector. He studied Hebrew paleography and description of manuscripts, and himself compiled a catalog of his library, which was published in Vilna in 1897. The catalog contains 2,208 descriptions of printed books, arranged in alphabetical order by title; a separate supplement has a short description of 20 manuscripts.[29]

The incunabula are described in the catalog according to the same scheme used for descriptions of other publications: short bibliographic description, including title, author, printer, place and year of publication, format of book by number of folds, and short supplementary information about the condition of the copy or its significance. It is important to note that the descriptions of incunabula are set off graphically in the catalog: the title, and place and year of publication are composed in an enlarged bold typeface. Thirty books from the fifteenth century are described in the catalog: items 1, 154, 362, 423, 535, 648, 722, 733, 736, 838, 853, 872, 873, 883, 901, 1065, 1334, 1525, 1635, 1642, 1643, 1650, 1683, 1684, 1685, 1715, 1731, 1866, 2183, and 2199.

Chwolson not only collected incunabula, but also studied them. In my opinion, it is important to remember that Chwolson published the first serious work in Russian on the rise of Hebrew book printing: *Evreiskie staropechatnye knigi* (Hebrew Early Printed Books; subsequently also published in Hebrew).[30] In that small book (all of 43 pages), Chwolson compiles in condensed form the state of knowledge at the time in the field of Hebrew incunabula. From the text of the book one can see that some of his observations are based on studying copies in his own library (cf., for example, pp. 16, 25, etc.).

Chwolson acquired his collection in 1910, shortly before his death. The incunabula from his collection are not "dressed" in standard bindings, but

---

*Literally, "The *zolotnik* [a small Russian unit of measure, whose name is a derivative of *zoloto*, 'gold'] is small but precious."

many copies bear the collection's stamp: "Professor Daniel Chwolson St. Petersburg." They generally have Chwolson's own marks on their spines or on the blank pages bound before the text. Unfortunately for us, his marks do not include information on the source of the item; rather they generally contain short characteristics of the publication and bibliographic citations to the works of De Rossi and Moritz Steinschneider.[31]

Later Chwolson's collection, the "Friedlandiana," and the Hebrew books of the Museum itself (items received by obligatory deposit) were merged into a single book collection. In Chwolson's and Friedland's collections there are many "duplicate" copies (if that word is even applicable to the first printed books), but that aspect in no way diminishes the worth of the Institute's collections. On the contrary, it makes the collection even more attractive to researchers, because it opens the possibility of comparative analysis of fifteenth-century Hebrew book production.

Today, unfortunately, the Hebrew collection of the Oriental Institute is practically inaccessible to readers. The books are partly in boxed storage and partly arranged unsystematically on shelves. The incunabula, however–which were removed to a separate repository–are available. I have not yet lost hope that the lost fragment of the composite volume that contains *Bakashat ha-memin* will be found by some miracle among the Institute's boundless book collections and returned to its rightful place next to Moses Kimhi's grammar, *Mahalak shevile ha-da'at*.[32]

BIBLIOGRAPHY

Adler*–*Adler, Israel. *Les incunables hébraïques de la Bibliothèque Nationale.* Paris, 1962.

Beizer*–*Beizer, Mikhail. *Evrei v Peterburge.* Ierusalim, 1989.

Bertel's*–*Bertel's, D. Introduction to *Aziatskii muzei, Leningradskoe otdelenie Instituta vostokovedeniia AN SSSR*, 5-80. Moskva: Akademiia Nauk SSSR, Institut Vostokovedeniia, 1972.

BMC*–Catalogue of Books Printed in the XVth Century Now in the British Museum.* Part I: *Xylographica and Books Printed with Types at Mainz, Strassburg, Bamberg and Cologne.* Part IV: *Italy: Subiaco and Rome.* London, 1908, 1916.

Census*–*Offenberg, Adri K., and C. Moed-Van Walraven. *Hebrew Incunabula in Public Collections: A First International Census* . . . Bibliotheca Humanistica & Reformatorica, vol. 47. Nieuwkoop, 1990.

Cherkashina, 1977*–*Cherkashina, N. P., and K. Bilen'kaia. *Inventar' inkunabulov.* Vol. 2, edited by E. L. Nemirovskii. Moskva: Gos. Biblioteka SSSR im. V. I. Lenina, Otdel redkikh knig, 1977.

Cherkashina, 1979*–*Cherkashina, N. P., and K. Bilen'kaia, *Inventar' inkunabulov.* Vol. 3, edited by E. L. Nemirovskii. Moskva: Gos. Biblioteka SSSR im. V. I. Lenina, Otdel redkikh knig, 1979.

Chwolson, 1896*–*Khvol'son, D. A. *Evreiskie staropechatnye knigi.* Sankt-Peterburg, 1896.

Chwolson, 1897*–*Chwolson, Daniel. *Reshit ma'aseh ha-defus be-Yisrael (Catalog der hebraeischen Buecher in der Bibliothek des Professors D. Chwolson).* Translated by Moses Eleazar Eisenstadt. Warsaw, 1897. Reprint, Tel Aviv, 1984. (In Hebrew.)

DeRossi, 1776*–*De Rossi, Giovanni Bernardo. *De hebraice typographiae origine ac primitiis seu antiquis ac rarissimis hebraicorum librorum editionibus seculi XV disquisitio historico-critica . . .* Parmae, 1776.

DeRossi, 1780*–*De Rossi, Giovanni. *De typographia hebraeo-ferrariensi commentarius historicum quo ferrarienses judaerum editiones hebraicae, hispanicae, lusitanae recensentur et illustrantur.* Parmae, 1780.

DeRossi, 1795*–*De Rossi, Giovanni Bernardo. *Annales hebraeo-typographici sec. XV. Descripsit fisocue commentario illustravit . . . 1795.* Reprint, Amsterdam, 1969.

Di Segni*–*Di Segni, R. "Nuovi dati sugli incunaboli ebraici di Roma." In *Un Pontificato ed una citta Sisto IV (1471-1484): Atti del convegno, Roma, 3-7 dicembre 1984*, 291-304. Città del Vaticano : Scuola vaticana di paleografia, diplomatica e archivistica, 1986.

Dubnov*–*Dubnow, Simon. *Kniga zhizni: vospominaniia i razmyshleniia: materialy dlia istorii moego vremeni.* Sankt-Peterburg, 1998.

Eisenstadt*–*Eisenstadt, Israel Tobias, comp. *Da'at-Kedoschim: Materialen zur Geschichte der Familien, welche ihre Abstammung von den im Jahre 1659 im litthauischen Städtchen Rushani in Folge einer Blutbeschuldigung als Märtyrer Gefallenen herleiten: aus Druckwerken und Handschriften der "Bibliotheca Friedlandiandia."* Edited by Samuel Wiener. St. Petersburg, 1897-1898. (In Hebrew.)

Ginsburg*–*Ginsburg, Christian D. *Introduction to the Massoretico-Critical Edition of the Hebrew Bible.* London 1897. Reprint, New York, 1966.

Goff*–*Goff, Frederick Richmond. *Incunabula in American Libraries: A Third Census of Fifteenth-Century Books Recorded in North American Collections.* New York: Bibliographical Society of America, 1964.

Goldschmidt*–*Goldschmidt, Lazarus. *Hebrew Incunables: A Bibliographical Essay.* Oxford: B. H. Blackwell, 1948.

GW*–Gesamtkatalog der Wiegendrücke.* Vols. 1-8 (A-Flühe). Leipzig: Komission für den Gesamtkatalog der Wiegendrücke, 1925-1978. Reprint, Stuttgart, 1968- .

Iakerson, 1985a–Iakerson, Shimon. *Katalog inkunabulov na drevneevreiskom iazyke biblioteki Leningradskogo otdeleniia Instituta vostokovedeniia AN SSSR.* Leningrad, 1985.

Iakerson, 1985b–Iakerson, Shimon. "Kollektsiia inkunabulov biblioteki Leningradskogo otdeleniia Instituta vostokovedeniia AN SSSR: istoriia vozniknoveniia; sostav." In *Problemy formulovaniia i raskrytiia fondov Biblioteki Akademii nauk SSSR: sbornik nauchnykh trudov,* 76-83. Leningrad, 1985.

Iakerson, 1988–Iakerson, Shimon. *Evreiskie inkunabuly: opisanie ekzempliarov, khraniashchikhsia v bibliotekakh Moskvy i Leningrada.* Leningrad, 1988.

Iakerson, 1990–Iakerson, Shimon. "Put' po tropam znaniia." In *Knizhnye sokrovitsa: k 275-letniu Biblioteki AN SSSR,* 240-250. Leningrad, 1990.

Iakerson, 1998–Iakerson, Shimon. "An Unknown List of Hebrew Books." *Manuscripta Orientalia: International Journal for Oriental Manuscript Research* 4, no. 1 (March 1998): 17-25.

Katsh–Katsch, Abraham Katsh. "Moshe Aryeh Leib Fridland u-sifriyato ha-meforsemet" (The Friedlandiana Library in the Leningrad Institute of Asiatic Peoples). *Perakim* (organ of the Institute of Hebrew Studies) 3 (1963): 1-27.

Kiselev–Kiselev, N. *Inventar' inkunabulov Vsesoiuznoi biblioteki im V. I. Lenina: nalichie na 1.01.1939.* Moskva, 1939.

Kondrat'ev–Kondrat'ev, P. "Evreiskie rukopisi v sobranii Instituta vostokovedeniia AN SSSR." *Palestinskii sbornik* 28 (91) (1986): 74-88.

Marx, 1944–Marx, Alexander. "The Literature of Hebrew Incunabula." In his *Studies in Jewish History and Booklore,* 277-295. New York, 1944.

Marx, 1950–Marx, Moses. "On the Date of Appearance of the First Printed Hebrew Books." In *Alexander Marx: Jubilee Volume on the Occasion of his Seventieth Birthday: English Section,* 481-501. New York, 1950.

Marx, 1953–Marx, Moses. "Catalogue of the Hebrew Books Printed in the Fifteenth Century Now in the Library of the Hebrew Union College." *Studies in Bibliography and Booklore* 1 (1953): 21-47.

Offenberg, 1971, 1973–Offenberg, Adri K. "Catalogue of the Hebrew Incunabula in the Bibliotheca Rosenthaliana." *Studia Rosenthaliana* 5 (1971): 125-143, 246-267; 7 (1973): 128-150.

Offenberg, 1990–Offenberg, Adri K. *A Short-Title Catalogue of Hebrew Books Printed in the Fifteenth Century Now in the Bibliotheca Rosenthaliana.* [Amsterdam, 1990.]

Offenberg, 1992a–Offenberg, Adri K. *A Choice of Corals: Facets of Fifteenth-Century Hebrew Printing.* Bibliotheca Humanistica & Reformatorica, vol. 52. Nieuwkoop, 1992.

Offenberg, 1992b–Offenberg, Adri K. "Literature on Hebrew Incunabula Since the Second World War." In his *A Choice of Corals,* 1-41.

Offenberg, see also: *Census*.
Richler–Richler, Benjamin. *Guide to Hebrew Manuscript Collections.* Jerusalem: The Israel Academy of Sciences and Humanities, 1994.
Starkova–Starkova, K. B. "Gebraistika." In *Aziatskii muzei, Leningradskoe otdelenie Instituta vostokovedeniia AN SSSR*, 544-559. Moskva: Akademiia Nauk SSSR, Institut Vostokvedeniia, 1972.
Tishby–Tishby, Peretz. "Hebrew Incunables" (in Hebrew). *Kiryat Sefer* 58 (1983[=1985]): 808-852; 60 (1985[=1987]): 865-962; 61 (1986/7): 521-546; 64 (1992/3): 689-726; *Ohev Sefer* 1 (1987): 23-50.
Tishby, Israel–Tishby, Peretz. "Hebrew Incunabula in Israel" (in Hebrew). *Kiryat Sefer* 59 (1984[=1986]): 946-958.
Wiener, 1893–Wiener, Samuel *Catalogus librorum impressorum hebraeorum in Museo Asiatico* (in Hebrew). Fasc. 1-7. Petropoli, 1893-1918.
Wiener, List–Wiener, Samuel. Introduction (in Hebrew) to his *Catalogus librorum impressorum hebraeorum in Museo Asiatico*. Fasc. 1 (Petropoli, 1893): i-ii.
Wiener, 1920–Wiener, Samuel. "Evreiskie rukopisi i pechatnye knigi." In *Aziatskii muzei Rossiiskoi Akademii nauk, 1818-1918: kratkaia pamiatka*, 102-106. Peterburg, 1920.
Zislin–Zislin, M. N. "Evreiskii fond." In *Vostokovednye fondy krupneishikh bibliotek Sovetskogo Soiuza*, 21-22. Moskva, 1963.

NOTES

1. From the first colophon of Fust and Sheffer, *Psalterium, 14 August 1457*, leaf 143 v., cited in BMC, vol. 1, 18.

2. The anonymous category includes here not only books without publication data, but also those which cannot be connected with known typographers even by such indirect indicators as identical handwriting. An example of such a publication is the halakhic (pertaining to Jewish law) collection *Kol bo* (Omnibus), which was undoubtedly printed in Italy in the fifteenth century, but by an unknown printer in an unknown place. Concerning this work, see the detailed article by Adri K. Offenberg, "The Dating of *Kol Bo*" (Offenberg, *Kol bo*).

3. An example is a corpus of documents related to Hebrew book publishing in Rome, published by P. Di Segni in the article, "Nuovi dati sugli incunabuli ebraici di Roma" (Di Segni). It is worth mentioning that so far it has not been possible to connect the names and numbers of copies of the first printed versions of the Pentateuch named in these documents, with names of Hebrew printers and editions of Biblical books that are known from the scholarly literature.

4. I mean particularly fragments of those texts that existed in the Jewish tradition both as independent books and as parts of more complete collections, e.g., individual books of the Bible, sections of halakhic compendia, Talmud tracts, texts of the Passover Haggadah, etc. For example, the three Biblical books printed in Naples by the

typographer Joseph Gunzenhauser–Psalms, Proverbs, and Job–can be considered either as three separate publications (as do most bibliographers) or as a single book with three parts (as does, for example, Christian Ginsburg in his *Introduction to the Massoretico-Critical Edition of the Hebrew Bible* (Ginsburg, chap. 13, no. 4)).

5. In my opinion, such books include, for example, the Sephardic edition of the treatise *Gittin* (on the laws of divorce), mentioned in the book list of 1492, which I discovered and published. For details, see my "An Unknown List of Hebrew Books" (Iakerson 1998).

6. An example of this type of item is an anonymous 31-line Bible. It is included in *Gesamtkatalog der Wiegendrücke* (GW (add) 4199/10), in Peretz Tishby's list of Israeli incunabula (Tishby, *Israel*, 75), and in Frederick Richmond Goff's index of American incunabula (Goff, *Heb*, 11), but Lazarus Goldschmidt does not consider it an incunable. He writes very precisely, "There is not the slightest trace of any evidence that this edition was printed before 1500" (Goldschmidt, 68). It is also not included by Adri K. Offenberg in *Hebrew Incunabula in Public Collections (Census)*.

7. The total number of copies was determined by the author on the basis of the number of copies indicated in the colophons, which varied from 250 to 400.

8. Particularly his fundamental monograph *Annales hebraeo-typographici sec. XV* (De Rossi 1795) and his more "modest" studies, *De hebraice typographiae origine ac primitiis seu antiquis ac rarissimis hebraicorum librarum editionibus seculi XV disquisitio historico-critica* (De Rossi 1776) and *De typographia hebraeo-ferrariensi commentarius historicum quo ferrarienses judaerum editiones hebraicae, hispanicae, lusitane recensentur et illustrantur* (De Rossi 1780).

9. In contemporary descriptions, of course, translations should be made into modern languages.

10. For a clearer understanding of the development of the study of Hebrew incunabula, I would recommend reading the survey articles by Alexander Marx, "The Literature of Hebrew Incunabula" (Marx 1944), and Adri K. Offenberg, "Literature on Hebrew Incunabula Since the Second World War" (Offenberg 1992).

11. It is true that all the previously enumerated domains do have their accomplishments, but by far the majority of the published collection descriptions are basically just lists. In my view, only a few of the catalogs can properly be called scholarly descriptions of the publications. Of those, I would give first place to the unfinished description of the "Rosenthaliana" (Offenberg 1971, 1973) and also Tishby's unfinished attempt to create a union catalog (Tishby). So far there are no full monographic studies of Hebrew incunabula, and the histories of the period in more general historical/bibliographical works seem to me inadequate.

12. The mistakes were primarily due to my having compiled the catalog during a period of almost total scholarly isolation, meaning that I had no possibility to compare the copy being described with more complete copies and no access to the contemporary bibliographical literature. As far as omissions are concerned, I mean primarily that the catalog does not include a description of the Constantinople edition of Jacob ben Asher's *Turim*. Several bibliographic imprecisions were corrected in the union catalog *Evreiskie inkunabuly* (Hebrew Incunabula) (Iakerson 1988), including, in part, the description of the previously mentioned *Turim*.

13. In principle, all three collections currently located in the two Russian capitals belong to St. Petersburg–either according to their origin (the collections of SPbB IOS RAS and RSL) or their current repository (RNL). For the history of the formation of the RSL and RNL collections, see Iakerson 1988, 11-15.

14. On the founding of the Asiatic Museum and its history, see the article by D. Bertel's (Bertel's).

15. The history of the collection's creation is set out in part in the prefaces to the published sections of the printed catalog of the collection (Wiener) and in survey articles devoted to the Institute's Hebrew materials (Wiener, "Evreiskie rukopisi;" Zislin; Kondrat'ev). The article by Professor Abraham Katsh, "The Friedlandiana Library in the Leningrad Institute of Asiatic Peoples" (Katsh) is worth separate mention, although unfortunately that article, despite its title, is primarily devoted to Friedland's state position and his role in Jewish education in Russia and not to a description of the collection.

16. In the Jewish tradition, his full name was Moshe Aryeh Leib. In the Russian tradition he is sometimes also referred to as Leib Faivelevich or Lev Pavlovich.

17. In 1657, on the eve of Passover, the corpse of a Christian child was found in the Jewish quarter of Ruzhan (Belarus). The Jews were accused of ritual murder, and the community leaders were executed. The family history inspired by Friedland was published by I. T. Eisenstadt in 1897-1898 (Eisenstadt).

18. In any case, this is what Dubnow wrote in his memoirs: "I worked a great deal in the rich book collection of the merchant L. Friedland on Vasil'evskii ostrov (Vasil'ev Island). I was led there by the bibliographer Samuel Wiener, a man with a parchment face and himself a living parchment with tracings of titles of all the Hebrew books. He had convinced a rich Petersburg merchant, inconsolable after the death of his wife, to build her a monument in the form of a book repository into which all the books ever printed in the Hebrew language could be put, as well as manuscripts. Through Wiener the widower purchased entire libraries and manuscript collections. On his advice he also later bequeathed the whole book collection to the Russian Academy of Sciences, to be put into its eastern branch, the Asiatic Museum, on condition that Wiener be designated its librarian. . . ." (Dubnow, 143). That precise motive for the founding of the "Friedlandiana" is also noted by Mikhail Beizer in his well-known guidebook, *Evrei v Peterburge* (Jews in Petersburg) (Beizer, 105).

19. In words of thanks to Daniel Chwolson written in December 1895, Wiener notes that Chwolson was his benefactor for "the entire eight years of his stay here" (Wiener, Fasc. II, xi).

20. File D 65, N 658, Manuscript Division, SPbB IOS RAS. For the complete text of this document, see Iakerson 1985b, 79-80.

21. Wiener 1893, Fasc. II, viii; Wiener 1920, 104.

22. Wiener 1893, Fasc. II, viii.

23. Wiener 1893, Fasc. II, xi.

24. Brief information about him can be found in Richler (Richler, 45).

25. Wiener 1893, items 3, 142, 1102, 1103, 3912, 4501, 4502.

26. For details concerning this publication, see Iakerson 1990. As an aside, I should note that Friedland's copy is not the only one known in the world, as observed by M. Zislin (Zislin, 22). Zislin, however, evidently misunderstood the remark made by Chwolson on the occasion that our copy was discovered (Chwolson 1896, 27). A second–and also defective–copy of this publication can be found in the Bibliothèque Nationale in Paris (Adler, no. 36).

27. See Wiener 1893, item 4502. A detailed review of the opinions on this question can be found in the article by A. Offenberg, "The First Printed Book Produced at Constantinople" (Offenberg 1992, 107-118).

28. There is a rather detailed biographical sketch of Chwolson in the *Evreiskaia entsiklopediia*, vol. 15, col. 584-587.

29. Chwolson 1897, 156-157.
30. Chwolson 1896; it is better known in its modern Hebrew translation (rendered by Moses Eleazar Eisenstadt), *Reshit ma'aseh ha-defus be-Yisra'el*, published in Warsaw in 1897 and reprinted by J. Robinson in Tel Aviv in 1984.
31. The full text of Chwolson's notes has been published in both the catalog of the collection and the union catalog (Iakerson 1985a, Iakerson 1988).
32. Strictly speaking, why not? In 1985 I found the Mantuan edition of *Nofet tsufim* from the "Friedlandiana" among the Japanese books.

APPENDIX. List of Hebrew Incunabula in the Asiatic Museum, St. Petersburg: (In the Collection as of January 1, 2002)*

1. Abudraham, David ben Joseph. *Perush ha-berakhot veha-tefilot* (Commentary on the benedictions and the prayers). Lisbon: Eliezer [Toledano], November 25, 1489. 2^0. 170 l., fols. 1r, 170v blank. Collation: [1^{10} 2-10^8 11^6 12-20^8 21^{10}]. (*Census, No. 1, GW, No. 8160*). Friedland copy (*Wiener, List, No. 19, Iakerson, 1985a, No. 1, Iakerson, 1988, No. 105*); Chwolson copy (*Chwolson, No. 1, Iakerson, 1985a, No. 2, Iakerson, 1988, No. 106*).

2. Albo, Joseph. *Sefer ha-'Ikarim* (Book of [Philosophical] Principles. Soncino, [Israel Nathan Soncino by his son Joshua Solomon Soncino(?)], October 31-December 29, 1485. 2^0. 108 l., fols. 1r, 108v blank. Collation: 1-2^8 3^6 4-13^8 14^6. (*Census, No. 3*). Friedland copy (*Wiener, List, No. 10, Iakerson, 1985a, No. 11, Iakerson, 1988, No. 33*); Chwolson copy (*Chwolson, No. 1065, Iakerson, 1985a, No. 10, Iakerson, 1988, No. 32*).

3. Avicenna. *ha-Kanon ha-gadol*. Vols 1-5. Naples: Azriel ben Joseph [Ashkenazi Gunzenhauser]. November 9, 1491. 2^0. 480 leaves in total (70, 76, 194, 96, 44). Collation (per book): Book 1 (A^4) 1-8^4 ; Book 2

---

*The Supplement contains a short description of each publication, with bibliographical citations to the *Census* and *GW*, and indications of the source for each copy (e.g., "Friedland's copy," or "Chwolson's copy") with citations to descriptions of particular copies in the corresponding bibliographies (Chwolson; Wiener 1893; Wiener, *List*; Iakerson 1985a; Iakerson 1988). The collation of the publications by signatures appeared to be a subject for a special study, which I conducted on the basis of Russian collections and the collections of the Jewish Theological Seminary of America, in New York, and the Jewish National and University Library, in Jerusalem.

(A^6) 1-8^8 ; Book 3 (A^8) 1^{10} 2-23^8; Book 4 (A^6) 1-10^8 11^6 12^4; Book 5 (A^8) 1-3^8 4^{10}. (*Census, No. 6, GW, No. 3113*). Friedland copy (*Wiener, List, No. 27, Iakerson, 1985a, No. 5, Iakerson, 1988, No. 86*).

4. Bahia ben Asher Ibn Halava. *Perush ha-Torah* (Commentary on the Pentateuch). Naples: Azriel ben Joseph Ashkenazi Gunzenhauser. July 1492. 2^0. 288 leaves, fols. 76r, 287v, 288 blank. Collation: 1-9^8 10^{10} 11-35^8 36^6. (*Census, No. 8, GW, No. 3172*). Friedland copy (*Wiener, List, No. 30, Iakerson, 1985a, No. 12, Iakerson, 1988, No. 92*).

5. Bahia ben Joseph Ibn Pakuda. *Hovot ha-levavot* (Duties of the Heart). [Naples]: Joseph [ben Jacob] Ashkenazi [Gunzenhauser], November 19 1489. 4^0. 152 leaves, fols. 1r, 151v, 152 blank. Collation: 1-19^8. (*Census, No. 9, GW, No. 3173*). Friedland copy (*Wiener No. 3912, Wiener, List, No. 30, Iakerson, 1985a, No. 14, Iakerson, 1988, No. 74*); Chwolson copy (*Chwolson, No. 362, Iakerson, 1985a, No. 13, Iakerson, 1988, No. 73*).

6. [Biblia Hebraica]. *Torah* (Pentateuch) with Targum Onkelos (Aramaic translation) and with commentary by Solomon ben Isaac (Rashi). 2 vols. Lisbon: Eliezer [Toledano], July 8-August 6, 1491. 2^0. 456 leaves. Collation: [Vol. 1] 1-13^8 14^{10} 15-26^8 27^6; [Vol. 2] 1-28^8 (*Census, No. 17*). Friedland copy (*Wiener, List, No. 25, Iakerson, 1985a, No. 54, Iakerson, 1988, No. 107*).

7. [Biblia Hebraica] *Nevi'im rishonim* (Former Prophets). With commentary of David Kimhi. Soncino: [Joshua Solomon ben Israel Nathan Soncino], October 15, 1485. 2^0. 168 leaves, fols. 1r, 21v, 22, 23r, 43v, 44, 45r, 108v, 109r, 168v blank. Collation (per Biblical book): Joshua: 1-2^8 ; Judges:1-2^8; Samuel: 1-8^8; Kings: 1-6^8 7^{12}. (*Census, No. 27*). Friedland copy (*Wiener, List, No. 8, Iakerson, 1985a, No. 56, Iakerson, 1988, No. 29*); Chwolson copy (*Chwolson, No. 1683, Iakerson, 1985a, No. 55, Iakerson, 1988, No. 27*); Fragment. Parchment. Leaves 3-6. Bound into the paper copy from the Chwolson collection (*Iakerson, 1988, No. 28*).

8. [Biblia Hebraica] *Nevi'im rishonim* (Former Prophets). With Targum Jonathan (Aramaic translation), commentary by David Kimhi and commentary by Levi ben Gershom. Leiria: [Samuel Dortas] and his three sons, January 27-February 2, 1494. 2^0. 640 leaves, fols. 1r, 80v, 400 blank. Collation: 1-20^8 21^6 22-49^8 50^{10} 51-75^8 76-77^{10}. (*Census, No. 28*). Friedland copy (*Wiener, List, No. 32, Iakerson, 1985a, No. 57, Iakerson, 1988, No. 109*).

9. [Biblia Hebraica] *Nevi'im aharonim* (Latter Prophets). With commentary of David Kimhi. [Soncino: Joshua Solomon ben Israel Nathan Soncino, circa 1475-1476]. 2^0. 294 leaves, fols. 1r, 88v, 89r, 154v, 155r, 224,

225r, 294v blank. Collation (per Biblical book): Isaiah: $1-11^8$; Jeremiah: $1-7^8\ 8^{10}$; Ezekiel: $1-8^8\ 9^6$; Minor Prophets: $1-8^8\ 9^6$. (*Census, No. 29*). Friedland copy (*Wiener, List, No. 9, Iakerson, 1985a, No. 59, Iakerson, 1988, No. 41*); Chwolson copy, copy 1 (*Chwolson, No. 1684, Iakerson, 1985a, No. 58, Iakerson, 1988, No. 40*); Chwolson copy, copy 2 (*Chwolson, No. 1685, Iakerson, 1985a, No. 60, Iakerson, 1988, No. 42*).

10. [Biblia Hebraica] *Tehilim* (Psalms). With commentary by David Kimhi. [Italy (Bologna?): Meister Joseph and Nerijah Hayyim, Mordecai and Hezekiah "Mwntrw," August 29, 1477. 2^0. 153 leaves, fol. 1r blank. Collation: $[1^9\ 2\text{-}5^8\ 6^{10}\ 7\text{-}8^8]\ 9\text{-}15^8\ 16^6\ 17\text{-}19^8$. (*Census, No. 34*). Chwolson copy (*Chwolson, No. 1715, Iakerson, 1985a, No. 61, Iakerson, 1988, No. 19*).

11. [Biblia Hebraica] *Tehilim* (Psalms). With commentary by David Kimhi. Naples: Joseph ben Jacob Ashkenazi [Gunzenhauser], March 28, 1487. 2^0. 118 leaves, fols. 1r, 118 blank. Collation: $1^6\ 2\text{-}15^8$. (*Census, No. 35*). Fragment; only one leaf, leaf 2. Bound into the copy of Psalms listed above (no. 10), from the Chwolson collection. (*Iakerson, 1985a, No. 62, Iakerson, 1988, No. 64*).

12. [Biblia Hebraica] *Mishle* (Proverbs). With commentary by Immanuel of Rome. [Naples: Joseph ben Jacob Ashkenazi Gunzenhauser], [between March 28 and September 26, 1487]. 2^0. 104 leaves, fol. 104 blank. Collation: $1\text{-}10^8\ 11^{10}\ 12\text{-}13^8$. (*Census, No. 43*). Chwolson copy (*Chwolson, No. 1731, Iakerson, 1985a, No. 63, Iakerson, 1988, No. 66*).

13. [Biblia Hebraica] *Mishle* (Proverbs). With commentary by David ben Solomon Yahya. [Lisbon: Eliezer (Toledano), circa 1492]. 2^0. 62 leaves. Collation: $1\text{-}7^8\ 8^8$. (*Census, No. 44*). Friedland copy (*Wiener, List, No. 31, Iakerson, 1985a, No. 64, Iakerson, 1988, No. 108*).

14. Gersonides, Levi. *Perush ha-Torah* (Commentary on the Pentateuch). [Mantua]: Abraham ben Solomon Conat, [circa 1474-1478]. 2^0. 412 leaves, fols. 188v, 257, 338, 410-412 blank. Collation: $[1\text{-}18^{10}\ 19^8\ 20^{10}\ 21^6\ 22^{10}\ 23^8\ 24^{10}\ 25^8\ 26^{10}\ 27^{12}\ 28\text{-}32^{10}\ 33\text{-}34^8\ 35^{10}\ 36^8\ 37\text{-}42^{10}\ 43^6]$. (*Census, No. 50*). Friedland copy (*Wiener, List No. 3, Iakerson, 1985a, No. 28, Iakerson, 1988, No. 16*); Chwolson copy (*Chwolson, No. 1650, Iakerson, 1985a, No. 27, Iakerson, 1988, No. 15*).

15. Ibn Adret, Solomon ben Abraham. *Teshuvot she'elot*. (Answers, Questions [responsa]) [Rome: Obadiah, Menasseh and Benjamin of Rome, circa 1469-1472]. 4^0. 162 leaves, fols. 1 and 162 blank. Collation: $[1\text{-}15^{10}\ 16^{12}]$. (*Census, No. 55*). Friedland copy. Addition to the catalog: On leaf 2a, notation of ownership by Hayim Yosef David Azullai (1724-1806). (*Wiener, List, No. 4, Iakerson, 1985a, No. 8, Iakerson, 1988, No. 2*); Chwolson copy (*Chwolson, No. 1334, Iakerson, 1985a, No. 9, Iakerson, 1988, No. 3*).

16. Ibn Ezra, Abraham ben Meir. *Perush ha-Torah* (Commentary on the Pentateuch). Naples: Joseph [ben Jacob] Ashkenazi [Gunzenhauser], and his son [Azriel], May 2, 1488. 2^0. 99(?) leaves, fols. 1r, 99(?) blank. Collation: 1-11^8 12$^{11(10+1)}$. (*Census, No. 56*). Friedland copy (*Wiener, List, No. 12, Iakerson, 1985a, No. 7, Iakerson, 1988, No. 69*); Chwolson copy (*Chwolson, No. 1635, Iakerson, 1985a, No. 6, Iakerson, 1988, No. 68*).
17. Ibn Gabirol, Solomon ben Judah. *Mivhar ha-peninim* (Choice of Pearls). [Soncino], Joshua Solomon ben Israel Nathan Soncino. January 14, 1484. 4^0. 60 leaves, fols. 1 and 60 blank. Collation: 1-7^8 8^4. (*Census, No. 57*). Friedland copy (*Wiener, List, No. 5, Iakerson, 1985a, No. 3, Iakerson, 1988, No. 20*); Chwolson copy (*Chwolson, No. 648, Iakerson, 1985a, No. 4, Iakerson, 1988, No. 21*).
18. Jacob ben Asher. *Arba'ah turim* (Four Orders of the Code of Law). Books 1-4. [Soncino]: Solomon ben Moses Soncino, [circa 1490]. 2^0. 350 leaves in total (94, 80, 50, 126). Collation (per volume): 1-11^8 12^6; 1-10^8; 1-5^8 6^6; 1-15^8 16^6. (*Census, No. 62*). Friedland copy, books 1-2, 4 only; bound together in 2 vols.: vol. 1–Books 1-2; vol. 2–Book 4. (*Wiener No. 4501, Wiener, List, No. 20, Iakerson, 1985a, No. 21, 24, Iakerson, 1988, No. 59, 62*); Chwolson copy, books 3, 4 only (*Chwolson, No. 423, Iakerson, 1985a, No. 22, 23, Iakerson, 1988, No. 60, 61*).
19. Jacob ben Asher, *Arba'ah turim* (Four Orders of the Code of Law). Constantinople: Brothers David and Samuel Nahmias. December 13, 1493. 2^0. 409 leaves in total (109, 90, 60, 150). Collation (per volume): [1-2^8 3$^{9(8+1)}$ 4-12^8 13-14^6; 1-10^8 11^{10}; 1-5^8 6-7^{10}; 1-18^8 19^6]. (*Census, No. 63*). Friedland copy (*Wiener No. 4502, Wiener, List, No. 20, Iakerson, 1988, No. 111*).
20. Jedaiah ben Abraham Bedersi. *Behinat ha-'olam* (Examination of the world). Soncino: Joshua Solomon ben Israel Nathan soncino, December 12, 1484. 4^0. 20 leaves. Collation: 1-2^8 3^4. (*Census, No. 76*). Friedland copy (*Wiener No. 1102, Wiener, List, No. 6, Iakerson, 1985a, No. 46, Iakerson, 1988, No. 23*); Chwolson copy (*Chwolson, No. 154, Iakerson, 1985a, No. 47, Iakerson, 1988, No. 24*).
21. Judah ben Jehiel Messer Leon. *Nofet tsufim* (Honeycomb). [Mantua], Abraham ben Solomon Conat, circa 1475. 4^0. 176 leaves. Collation: 1-7^{10} 8^8 9^{10} 10^8 11^{10} 11^{11} 12^8 13^{10} 14^8 15^{10}16^8 17^{10} 18-19^8 (*Census, No. 80*). Friedland copy (*Wiener, List, No. 2, Iakerson, 1985a, No. 32, Iakerson, 1988, No. 13*).
22. *Kol bo* (Omnibus; halakhic work). [Italy, circa 1490-1492]. 2^0. 180 leaves, fols. 1r, 6 blank. Collation: [1]^6 1-21^8 22^6. (*Census, No. 81*). Friedland copy (*Wiener, List, No. 24, Iakerson, 1985a, No. 26, Iakerson,*

1988, No. 82); Chwolson copy (*Chwolson, No. 535, Iakerson, 1985a, No. 25, Iakerson, 1988, No. 81*).

23. [Liturgies]. *Mahazor ke-minhag Roma* (Festival Prayers). Vols 1-2. Soncino/Casal Maggiore: Sons of Soncino, September 1485-August 21, 1486. 2^0. 320 leaves in total (166, 154). Collation (per volume): $1-15^8$ 16^2 $17-21^8$ 22^4; $1-18^8$ 19^{10}. (*Census, No. 83*). Friedland copy; lacks vol. 1; leaves 1-31, vol. 2, leaves 73, 115, 145 (*Wiener, List, No. 11, Iakerson, 1985a, No. 30, Iakerson, 1988, No. 36*); Chwolson copy (*Chwolson, No. 736, Iakerson, 1985a, No. 31, Iakerson, 1988, No. 37*).

24. Maimonides, Moses. *Moreh nevukhim* (Guide of the Perplexed). [Italy (Rome?), circa 1469-1472].]. 4^0. 156 leaves, fols. 1, 155v and 156 blank. Collation: $[1-15^{10}$ $16^6]$. (*Census, No. 86*). Chwolson copy (*Chwolson, No. 722, Iakerson, 1985a, No. 35, Iakerson, 1988, No. 5*).

25. Maimonides, Moses. *Mishneh Torah* (codification of Talmudic laws). [Italy (Rome??)]: Solomon ben Judah and Obadiah ben Moses, [circa 1475]. 2^0. 352 leaves, fols. 1, 184, 270, 331, 332, 352v blank. Collation: $[1-18^{10}$ 19^4 $20-23^{10}$ 24^8 25^{10} 26^6 27^{10} 28^{12} $29-33^{10}$ 34^{12} 35^{10} $36^{10}]$. (*Census, No. 87*). Friedland copy (*Wiener, List, No. 1, Iakerson, 1985a, No. 37, Iakerson, 1988, No. 9*); Chwolson copy (*Chwolson, No. 872, Iakerson, 1985a, No. 36, Iakerson, 1988, No. 8*).

26. Maimonides, Moses. *Mishneh Torah*. Soncino: Gershom ben Moses Soncino, March 1490. 2^0. 380 leaves, fols. 1r, 52r, 292, 380 blank. Collation: $1-5^8$ $6:7^{12}$ $8-29^8$ $29/1-29/8^8$ 1^8 $31-40^8$ (*Census, No. 88*). Friedland copy (*Wiener, List, No. 21, Iakerson, 1985a, No. 39, Iakerson, 1988, No. 57*); Chwolson copy (*Chwolson, No. 873, Iakerson, 1985a, No. 38, Iakerson, 1988, No. 56*).

27. *Makre dardeke* (Primary Teacher). [Naples: Joseph ben Jacob Ashkenazi Gunzenhauser] August 8, 1488.]. 2^0. 78 leaves. Collation: $1-9^8$ 10^6. (*Census, No. 91*). Chwolson copy (*Chwolson, No. 853, Iakerson, 1985a, No. 20, Iakerson, 1988, No. 65*).

28. *Mishnah*. With commentary by Maimonides. Naples: Joshua Solomon ben Israel Nathan Soncino, May 8, 1492.]. 2^0. 356 leaves, fols. 1, 56v, 214v, 356v blank. Collation: $1-2^8$ 3^{10} $4-5^8$ 6^6 $7-12^8$ $13-14^6$ $15-18^8$ 19^{10} $20-24^8$ 25^6 26^8 27^{10} $28-44^8$ 45^6 (*Census, No. 92*). Friedland copy (*Wiener, List, No. 29, Iakerson, 1985a, No. 41, Iakerson, 1988, No. 95*); Chwolson copy (*Chwolson, No. 883, Iakerson, 1985a, No. 40, Iakerson, 1988, No. 94*).

29. [Mishnah]. *Masekhet Avot* ("Ethics of the Fathers").With the introduction and commentary of Maimonides. [Soncino: Joshua Solomon ben Israel Nathan Soncino, circa 1485]. 4^0. 48 leaves, fols. 1, 48 blank. Collation: $1-6^8$ (*Census, No. 93*). Friedland copy (*Wiener, List,*

No. 7, Iakerson, 1985a, No. 43, Iakerson, 1988, No. 46); Chwolson copy *(Chwolson, No. 901, Iakerson, 1985a, No. 42, Iakerson, 1988, No. 45).*
30. Moses ben Jacob of Coucy. *Sefer Mitsvot gadol* (Great Book of Precepts). Book 1-2. [Soncino]: Gershom ben Moses Soncino, December 19 1488. 2^0. 280 leaves in total (102, 178). Collation (per book): 1-12^8 13^6; 1-21^8 22^{10} *(Census, No. 95)*. Friedland copy *(Wiener, List, No. 15, Iakerson, 1985a, No. 34, Iakerson, 1988, No. 50)*; Chwolson copy *(Chwolson, No. 838, Iakerson, 1985a, No. 33, Iakerson, 1988, No. 49).*
31. Nahmanides. *Perush ha-Torah* (Commentary on the Pentateuch). [Rome]: Obadiah, Menasseh and Benjamin of Rome, [circa 1469-1472].]. 2^0. 246 leaves, fols. 1-2, 124, 244v, 245, 246 blank. Collation: [1-11^{10} 12^{12} 13^{12} 14-24^{10} 25^{12}]. *(Census, No. 96)*. Chwolson copy *(Chwolson, No. 1642, Iakerson, 1985a, No. 15, Iakerson, 1988, No. 1).*
32. Nahmanides. *Perush ha-Torah*. Lisbon: Eliezer [Toledano], July 16, 1489. 2^0. 301 leaves. Collation: [1$^{9(8+1)}$ 2-6^8 7^{12} 8-13^{10} 14^{12} 15-28^{10} 29-30^8 31^{12}] *(Census, No. 97)*. Friedland copy *(Wiener, List, No. 18, Iakerson, 1985a, No. 17, Iakerson, 1988, No. 102)*; Chwolson copy *(Chwolson, No. 1643, Iakerson, 1985a, No. 16, Iakerson, 1988, No. 101).*
33. Nahmanides. *Perush ha-Torah*. [Naples: Joseph ben Jacob Ashkenazi Gunzenhauser] July 2, 1490.]. 2^0. 244 leaves, fols. 1r, 66, 123 blank. Collation: 1-7^8 8^{10} 9-15^8 16^{10} 17-30^8. *(Census, No. 98)*. Friedland copy *(Wiener, List, No. 22, Iakerson, 1985a, No. 19, Iakerson, 1988, No. 76)*; Chwolson copy *(Chwolson, No. 2183, Iakerson, 1985a, No. 18, Iakerson, 1988, No. 77).*
34. Kimhi, David. *Sefer ha-shorashim* (Book of Roots). Naples: [Azriel ben Joseph Ashkenazi Gunzenhauser] between August 18 and September 15, 1490. 2^0. 144 leaves, fols. 1 blank. Collation: 1-18^8 *(Census, No. 105, GW, No. 8172)*. Friedland copy *(Wiener, List, No. 23, Iakerson, 1985a, No. 48, Iakerson, 1988, No. 78).*
35. Kimhi, David. *Sefer ha-shorashim*. [Naples]: Joshua Solomon ben Israel Nathan Soncino, February 10 or 11, 1491. 2^0. 168 leaves, fols. 1r, 168 blank. Collation: 1-3^8 4$^{9(8+1)}$ 5$^{9(8+1)}$ 6-18^8 19^6 20^6 21^{10}. *(Census, No. 106, GW, No. 8173)*. Chwolson copy *(Chwolson, No. 1525, Iakerson, 1985a, No. 49, Iakerson, 1988, No. 84).*
36. Kimhi, Moses. *Mahalak shevile ha-da'at.* (with: Jedaiah Hapenini's *Bakashat ha-memin*, etc.) Soncino: [Joshua Solomon ben Israel Nathan Soncino], July 21, 1489. 12^0. 30 leaves. Collation: [1-3^8 4^6]. *(Census, No. 77)*. Friedland copy *(Wiener, List, No. 13, Iakerson, 1985a, No. 50, Iakerson, 1988, No. 48).*
37. [Babylonian Talmud] *Masekhet Hulin* (Tractate of profane things). With commentary by Rashi. [Soncino: Joshua Solomon ben Israel Na-

than Soncino], June 14, 1489. 2^0. 184 leaves, fols. 1r, 184v blank. Collation: $1\text{-}23^8$. (*Census, No. 126*). Chwolson copy (*Chwolson, No. 1866, Iakerson, 1985a, No. 51, Iakerson, 1988, No. 53*).

38. [Babylonian Talmud] *Masekhet Nidah* (Tractate on menstruation). With commentary by Rashi. [Soncino: Joshua Solomon ben Israel Nathan Soncino], July 23, 1489. 2^0. 96 leaves, fols. 1r, 94v, 96 blank. Collation: $1\text{-}12^8$. (*Census, No. 131*). Friedland copy (*Wiener, List, No. 16, Iakerson, 1985a, No. 52, Iakerson, 1988, No. 55*). Chwolson copy (*Chwolson, No. 2199, Iakerson, 1985a, No. 53, Iakerson, 1988, No. 54*).

Microfilming Hebrew Manuscripts in Eastern Europe

Benjamin Richler

SUMMARY. This article surveys the efforts of the Institute of Microfilmed Hebrew Manuscripts in the Jewish National and University Library (Jerusalem) to acquire microfilms of Hebrew manuscripts in Eastern Europe, before and after the breakup of the Soviet Union. Some collections in Hungary and Poland and a few hundred manuscripts in the Soviet Union were microfilmed before diplomatic relations with most of the Eastern Bloc countries were cut off after the 1967 war. As soon as the political climate changed in the early 1990s, the Institute launched projects to microfilm close to 20,000 manuscripts in the Russian National Library and the Oriental Institute of the Russian Academy of Sciences in St. Petersburg and in the Russian State Library in Moscow. *[Article copies available for a fee from The Haworth Document Delivery Service: 1-800-HAWORTH. E-mail address: <docdelivery@haworthpress.com> Website: <http://www.HaworthPress.com> © 2003 by The Haworth Press, Inc. All rights reserved.]*

Benjamin Richler is Director, Institute of Microfilmed Hebrew Manuscripts, Jewish National and University Library, P.O. Box 34165, Jerusalem 91341, Israel (E-mail: benjaminr@savion.cc.huji.ac.il). He has published two books and numerous articles in English and Hebrew on Hebrew manuscripts, and he has edited catalogues of Hebrew manuscripts in the Palatine collection in Parma and the Valmadonna Trust Library in London.

For further information on the Institute of Microfilmed Hebrew Manuscripts and for instructions to consult its computerized catalogue, refer to its web site http://jnul.huji.ac.il/imhm/.

[Haworth co-indexing entry note]: "Microfilming Hebrew Manuscripts in Eastern Europe." Richler, Benjamin. Co-published simultaneously in *Slavic & East European Information Resources* (The Haworth Information Press, an imprint of The Haworth Press, Inc.) Vol. 4, No. 2/3, 2003, pp. 59-68; and: *Judaica in the Slavic Realm, Slavica in the Judaic Realm: Repositories, Collections, Projects, Publications* (ed: Zachary M. Baker) The Haworth Information Press, an imprint of The Haworth Press, Inc., 2003, pp. 59-68. Single or multiple copies of this article are available for a fee from The Haworth Document Delivery Service [1-800-HAWORTH, 9:00 a.m. - 5:00 p.m. (EST). E-mail address: docdelivery@haworthpress.com].

http://www.haworthpress.com/store/product.asp?sku=J167
© 2003 by The Haworth Press, Inc. All rights reserved.

KEYWORDS. Eastern Europe, Russia, Israel, Hebrew manuscripts, Institute of Microfilmed Hebrew Manuscripts (Jerusalem), microfilms

In its fifty years of existence the Institute of Microfilmed Hebrew Manuscripts (IMHM) has accomplished what is probably a unique achievement. It has succeeded in assembling a collection of microfilm copies of over 90% of all the manuscripts extant in the world representing a single culture–in this case, literature in Hebrew and other Jewish languages written in Hebrew characters. To date, over 70,000 Hebrew manuscripts from over 600 public and private collections on all the continents have been filmed. The microfilms are all stored near the reading room so that the reader can consult manuscripts from dozens of collections within moments of filing his or her request.

The manuscripts filmed by the IMHM are primarily copies of texts that can be classified as literature in the broadest sense of the term. The texts may be canonic (Bible, Talmud and Midrash), liturgical, halakhic (related to Jewish laws, ritual and customs), philosophical, mystical, grammatical, or scientific. The authors of the texts are generally Jewish, but many of the philosophical treatises, and the astronomical, medical, and other scientific works are translations from the Arabic, Latin, or European vernacular languages. The manuscripts microfilmed date from the tenth until the twentieth centuries, with the greater part of them dating from the thirteenth to the eighteenth centuries. The earliest Hebrew manuscripts dating from the first century before the Christian era until the second or third centuries CE, i.e., the Dead Sea Scrolls and the Qumran and Judean Desert documents, were not microfilmed, as they were not made public until recently and facsimiles were published by other organizations. For similar reasons, archival material was not actively collected by the IMHM, as this task was undertaken by another institution in Jerusalem, the Central Archives for the History of the Jewish People.[1] Nevertheless, a fairly large number of *pinkasim* (registry books for communal organizations, guilds, etc.) and other historical manuscripts were microfilmed if they were included in a library's collection of manuscripts and not in its archival department.

During the medieval period the Jewish people were scattered throughout much of the world. Wherever they settled, they composed works and copied other manuscripts. The great majority of Hebrew manuscripts were copied by private persons for their own use or by professional scribes commissioned to transcribe texts for private owners.[2] Scriptoria, such as those that existed in monasteries, or stationers who produced manuscripts in mass production were almost non-existent in Jewish culture. Hebrew manuscripts were produced in Western Europe, Byzantium, the near East, Persia, North Africa, and Yemen. The majority of medieval Hebrew manuscripts that survive today were produced in Spain, France, Germany and Italy. Institutional Jewish libraries with substantial holdings, such as those found in monasteries or in royal palaces were quite rare and few existed for more than half a century. Large collections of Hebrew manuscripts are found mainly in non-Jewish university, national or public libraries in Western Europe and in Jewish institutions in the United States and Israel. The origins of some of the university and national collections date back to the sixteenth century, but most of the manuscripts were acquired in the nineteenth and twentieth centuries.[3]

At its inception the IMHM directed most of its efforts towards microfilming the collections of Hebrew manuscripts in the West, particularly in Western Europe. The first director of the Institute, Nehemiah Allony, made several trips to Europe during the first decade of its existence in order to negotiate microfilming of manuscripts. He intended to visit Poland, Czechoslovakia and Hungary, but only Hungary granted him a visa after many tribulations.[4] Considering the political situation at the time, it is not surprising that he was unable to undertake more journeys across the Iron Curtain. Nevertheless, a significant number of microfilms of Hebrew manuscripts from the Soviet realm were obtained during this period.

The account of the efforts made by the IMHM to obtain microfilms from collections in Eastern Europe may be divided into three periods. From the early 1950s until 1967 Israel maintained diplomatic relations with most of the countries in the Soviet bloc. These relations steadily deteriorated toward the end of the period and were mostly terminated with the outbreak of the Six-Day War in June 1967. Communications with the libraries in Eastern Europe were carried out mainly by correspondence. During the second period, from 1967 until the end of the Soviet regime in the late 1980s, contact was made with libraries in some of the more liberal states, but there was practically no contact with the libraries in the Soviet Union. The third period, ushered in after the fall of the Soviet regimes resulted in several large projects in cooperation with libraries in Russia and other Eastern countries.

During the first period, over a thousand manuscripts from Eastern Europe were acquired in microforms. Allony's visit to Budapest in February 1954 resulted in the filming of 114 manuscripts from the David Kaufmann collection of 594 manuscripts in the library of the Hungarian Academy of Sciences. In 1959 the Academy published microfiche copies of 116 manuscripts, and in 1962 and 1963 most of the remaining manuscripts were filmed for the IMHM. Relations between the Academy and the IMHM remained close and, after the "thaw" in the late 1980s, the fragments from the Cairo Genizah (storage place for discarded Hebrew books and manuscripts) in the Kaufmann collection were filmed anew in order to facilitate the preparation of a catalogue of these fragments to be prepared by the staff of the IMHM.

In 1958, the IMHM acquired films of 200 of the 1,913 manuscripts from the Guenzburg collection[5] in the Lenin State Library–now called the Russian State Library–in Moscow. After the delivery of the first batch of microfilms the filming was abruptly ended, not to resume until three decades later.[6] An American-Israeli scholar, Professor Abraham Katsh, had established good relations with the Lenin State Library and had obtained microfilms of over 150 manuscripts.[7] Copies of some of these manuscripts were made for the IMHM in 1972, and together with a few other copies obtained from various sources, the total number of Guenzburg manuscripts available on microfilm reached 400.

The Żydowski Instytut Historyczny (Jewish Historical Institute) in Warsaw housed over 1,000 manuscripts found in cellars belonging to the Gestapo in the Polish town of Kłodzko after World War II. Many of the manuscripts had previously belonged to other Jewish institutions such as the Jüdisch-theologisches Seminar and the Kultusgemeinde in Vienna. A handwritten catalog of the collection, written in Polish, was prepared by Ephraim (Franciszka) Kupfer and Stefan Strelcyn but was never published. Kupfer immigrated to Israel in the late 1950s and worked as a researcher and cataloguer in the IMHM for close to three decades. In the first half of 1959, a large part of the collection of manuscripts in the Jewish Historical Institute was microfilmed for the IMHM. Over a decade later, in 1971, the microfilm collection from Warsaw was augmented in rather bizarre circumstances. A Canadian bookseller, Raymond Arthur Davies, approached the IMHM with an offer to obtain microfilms of thousands of manuscripts from the National Library in Leningrad (formerly and afterwards St. Petersburg). Until then, the IMHM had obtained copies of a few of the most important Biblical manuscripts from that library, but the greater part of this magnificent collection had never been filmed and was inaccessible to most Western scholars. The first batch of microfilms to arrive raised hopes. The manuscripts filmed were indeed from the library in Leningrad, but the IMHM had already obtained copies of all of them. The second shipment contained manuscripts from the Jewish Historical Institute in Warsaw. Davies did not deny that he had tried to deceive us and agreed to take back all the duplicate microfilms and allow the IMHM to purchase only those of manuscripts that it lacked.[8]

A number of small collections of Hebrew manuscripts preserved in libraries in East Germany were microfilmed before the reunification of Germany. A few manuscripts from the Universitätsbibliothek in Leipzig were filmed in 1959, fifteen manuscripts from the Landesbibliothek in Gotha were filmed in 1960 and about a dozen manuscripts from the Landesbibliothek in Dresden in 1971. The fifty-odd Hebrew manuscripts in the Universitätsbibliothek in Rostock were not filmed until 1992. The negotiations for the filming of these collections were carried out by postal communication.

Throughout the Soviet era there was an almost mystical aura surrounding the great hoards of Hebrew manuscripts known to exist in Russia. It was estimated that about 20,000 codices and/or fragments of manuscripts were to be found in the three main depositories: the Guenzburg collection in the Lenin State Library in Moscow, the vast Firkovich collections in the Public Library in St. Petersburg and the Friedland collection in the Oriental Institute in that city. No printed catalogue of any of these collections had ever been published but brief handwritten handlists of the Guenzburg collection and the first Firkovich collection were available and whetted the appetites of Judaica scholars in the West. From time to time the IMHM was approached by various academics and businessmen who claimed to have excellent contacts with officials in some of these libraries and were willing to act as intermediaries in obtaining microfilms of Hebrew manuscripts. Not one of these contacts was able to deliver a single manuscript.

As the glasnost era began, cordial contacts were made between Israeli librarians and their counterparts in the East. Shemuel Sever of the Haifa University library met the director of the Lenin State Library (soon to be renamed the Russian State Library) at a conference, and the subject of microfilming manuscripts was raised. Israel Shatzman, then director of the Jewish National and University Library (JNUL) visited Russia in the fall of 1991 and met the director of the Lenin State Library. An agreement was signed permitting the JNUL to microfilm all the manuscripts in the Guenzburg collection.

Filming the manuscripts in the Russian State Library (RSL) was more complicated than filming similar material in the West. Payment was not to be based on a fixed rate per frame, service charges, and postage as it is in most libraries in the West. The RSL was willing to cooperate with us but expected to benefit from the project. The JNUL was to provide the photographic equipment that was to remain in the RSL after the project was completed, and staff members of the Oriental section of the RSL were to be trained and sent to Israel for courses. There were, of course, other side benefits as well.

In the summer of 1992, the head of the Reprographic Department of the JNUL, Israel Weiser, and members of his staff came to Moscow to set up the equipment and to begin microfilming. They also trained members of the photographic department of the RSL to operate the equipment. Mr. Weiser was responsible for quality control. Any Westerner attempting to operate in Russia during the period immediately after the breakup of the Soviet Union faced almost insurmountable problems, both bureaucratic and logistical. Fortunately for our party, we found an institution that was to serve as our base in Moscow. The Mekor Haim Yeshiva, sponsored by Rabbi Adin Steinsaltz of Jerusalem, afforded our staff lodgings and meals. More valuable was the logistical support ranging from the use of telephones, storage facilities, assistance in dealing with customs and other government agencies, translation services, and contacts familiar with Russian bureaucracy who helped to open doors and hearts that normally would be difficult for a Westerner to penetrate.[9]

Throughout the summer of 1992 the crew worked full-time and succeeded in filming over 1,900 manuscripts (235 reels of 35mm microfilm) in four and a half months. The entire Guenzburg collection was filmed, including those manuscripts that had previously been filmed. The superior quality and legibility of the microfilms produced with advanced equipment justified the filming of all the manuscripts. The microfilm collection of the Guenzburg manuscripts, including the original negatives, was deposited in the IMHM, but copies of the entire collection were also offered for sale and were purchased by other libraries and research institutions in Israel, Europe and North America.

The Guenzburg collection is not the only repository of Hebrew manuscripts in the RSL. A few years after the microfilm project was completed, I was invited to the library to make a checklist of the *Trofiana* collection. The *Trofiana* collection consists of World War II booty, in this case manuscripts confiscated by the Red Army from the Germans who had looted them from various Jewish libraries. Among the libraries represented are the Jüdisch-theologisches Seminar and the Kultusgemeinde in Vienna, as well as community libraries in Munich, Dresden, Vilnius and some other communities throughout Europe. Most of the manuscripts in this collection date to the eighteenth, nineteenth, and early twentieth centuries, and some are only students' notebooks or term papers presented at one of the theological seminaries in Breslau or Vienna. None of the manuscripts dates to earlier than the sixteenth century. Altogether there are a few hundred items, many of them fragmentary. The collection was arranged in files according to the presumed city of origin, but many were filed incorrectly. I prepared a short handlist of the collection, which had never been listed or registered previously. The entire issue of *Trofiana* was very sensitive at the time in Russia, and the government had issued a ban on photocopying or microfilming collections of this sort. The IMHM hopes to be able to film the collection in the near future. In addition, the RSL has a collection of several dozen Torah scrolls, probably confiscated from synagogues in the former Soviet Union.

The collections of Hebrew manuscripts in the Russian National Library (RNL) in St. Petersburg, formerly known as the Saltykov-Shchedrin Public Library, preserve unique remnants of Jewish culture especially with regard to Karaite and Samaritan literatures. The library houses many of the most ancient Bible codices extant, about 2,000 Hebrew manuscripts dating from the thirteenth to the nineteenth centuries, and about 10,000 fragments and incomplete manuscripts from *genizot* in Cairo, Jerusalem and elsewhere, many of them hundreds of pages long. The vast majority of the material was gathered by the

Russian Karaite Abraham Firkovich in the middle of the nineteenth century. Firkovich traveled to Crimea, Palestine and Egypt in his search for manuscripts and antiques, and his obsession for collecting probably saved these cultural artifacts from oblivion. No study of Karaite literature, Judeo-Arabic dialects, the Geonic period (ca. 600-1040) or medieval Hebrew poetry can afford to ignore these sources. Yet, for over half a century most of these texts were unavailable to all but a few Judaica scholars.

As soon as liberalization was introduced into the USSR, the IMHM made attempts to obtain microfilms of selected manuscripts from this huge repository. From the end of 1989 until 1992, requests for copies of individual manuscripts or small numbers of selected manuscripts were made, and in general the response was positive. No attempt was made to order copies of the entire collection. However, in the spring of 1990 negotiations began between the directors of the RNL and the JNUL, and were continued during a visit of the director of the RNL to Jerusalem. Both sides were interested in signing a viable agreement, but both sides sought to achieve the most for their respective institutions. The JNUL reckoned that, in the volatile and still unsettled political atmosphere of Russia, the good will on the part of the RNL might be only short-lived and that the opportunity to microfilm its Hebrew collections must be seized at all costs. Special funding was raised from various sources and the agreement was signed.

Given the fragile nature of many of the ancient fragments in the collection, the fact that most of the fragments were unbound separate sheets stored in folders–each of which had to be untied and retied–and the large number of leaves on which the ink had faded or had turned dark, it was impossible to film at the same rapid rate that the Guenzburg collection was microfilmed. In fact, the entire project in which 832 reels of 35mm microfilm were shot took almost four years to complete. Unlike the Moscow project, the IMHM did not send a crew from Jerusalem to St. Petersburg to operate the microfilm cameras. The director of the Reprographic Department of the JNUL, Israel Weiser, went to St. Petersburg to set up the equipment and to pick and train a local crew. The Russian operators proved to be very competent and adept at adjusting, repairing and adapting the equipment whenever necessary to accommodate non-standard material. Weiser and his staff in Jerusalem controlled the quality of the microfilms, and whenever necessary, instructed the photographers in Russia on how to correct errors or unsatisfactory results. The original negative microfilms were shipped to Jerusalem, where they served to prepare direct negative and positive copies. Some images of poor legibility were digitally enhanced on microfilms of important manuscripts. The RNL insisted upon retaining the original negatives, which were later returned to St. Petersburg. A few collections of manuscripts, mainly manuscripts in Arabic characters and non-Biblical

Samaritan manuscripts, were not filmed and are subject to future negotiations. Torah scrolls were not filmed for technical reasons.

The collections of the RNL are not the only large collections of Hebrew manuscripts in St. Petersburg. The Oriental Institute of the Russian Academy of Sciences in Leningrad, founded as the Asiatic Museum in 1818, houses 1,100 Hebrew manuscripts, including 300 from the Moses Friedland collection and manuscripts from the former Karaite National Library in Eupatoria. The collection was microfilmed on 203 reels concurrently with the collection of the RNL.

In addition to the libraries listed above, a few manuscripts and fragments in other small collections in Eastern Europe were also filmed. However, there remain several collections that have not been filmed for various reasons. The largest is in the Vernadsky Library of the Academy of Sciences in Kiev in Ukraine. The Vernadsky Library incorporated parts of the libraries of the defunct Jewish Historical Ethnographical Society of Leningrad, and the Society for the Promotion of Enlightment Among Jews in Russia (Russian abbreviation: OPE) which were removed to the Institute for Yiddish Proletarian Culture in Kiev. Included among these manuscripts are some of the codices and Genizah fragments from the library of the Russian orientalist and scholar of Jewish history and literature, Albert Avraham Harkavy. The manuscripts in the library date from early medieval Genizah fragments to nineteenth century Yiddish writings, probably over a thousand items altogether.[10] Even though there was a mutual exchange of delegations between the JNUL and the Vernadsky libraries, and letters of understanding were signed, the negotiations were never completed and except for a few dozen *pinkasim* the manuscripts in the Vernadsky Library were never filmed.

There are several other small collections of Hebrew manuscripts in Eastern Europe that remain to be microfilmed. Material similar to that found in the *Trofiana* collection in the RSL is found in the Rossiiskii Gosudarstvennyi voennyi arkhiv (Russian State Military Archive), formerly known as Tsentr khraneniia istoriko-dokumental'nykh kollektsii in Moscow. A few dozen Hebrew manuscripts, including a small number that are four or five hundred years old, and many files of documents are to be found in this archive. The IMHM has negotiated with this archive, but so far only a few manuscripts have been filmed. The documentary material is being filmed by the Central Archives for the History of the Jewish People in Jerusalem.

Smaller collections of Hebrew manuscripts exist in Vilnius, L'vov and elsewhere. Most of the manuscripts in these collections are quite recent; few date back to medieval times. Only a few of these books have been filmed by the IMHM.

Microfilming Hebrew manuscripts serves a twofold purpose. It makes the texts accessible for researchers and it preserves them in case the originals are lost or damaged. The preservation aspect is pertinent for handwritten documents anywhere in the world, but especially so for those in Eastern Europe. The unhealthy mixture of manuscripts worth tens of thousand of dollars, and guardians whose annual salary is a pittance, has resulted in the gradual erosion of some of the holdings in East European libraries. Thefts or attempted thefts of rare books and manuscripts have made headlines in the past few years, but more manuscripts have disappeared from libraries surreptitiously than have been stolen through violent means. I am aware of dozens, if not hundreds, of handwritten books from some of the libraries I have described that have shown up on the market. Since the fall of the Iron Curtain, a few dozen manuscripts from prewar Jewish communal and institutional libraries have emerged; the provenance of some can be traced to East European libraries, but the trail of ownership of many others may never be known. Unfortunately, many of these manuscripts, especially those in which more than one work was copied, have been cut up, separated, and bound in several volumes in order to fetch a higher price or to conceal their former provenance. Quite often, a search in the catalog of the microfilmed manuscripts in the IMHM will reveal the true history of these divided manuscripts.[11]

NOTES

1. See Benyamin Lukin's article, "The Creation of a Documentary Collection on the History of Russian Jewry at the Central Archives for the History of the Jewish People," elsewhere in this volume. *Ed.*

2. See Malachi Beit-Arié, *The Makings of the Medieval Hebrew Book* (Jerusalem, 1993), 43-44.

3. For more information on Hebrew manuscripts, see *Encyclopaedia Judaica* (Jerusalem, 1972), 11: 899-909; Benjamin Richler, *Hebrew Manuscripts; a Treasured Legacy* (Cleveland-Jerusalem, 1990); Benjamin Richler, *Guide to Hebrew Manuscript Collections* (Jerusalem, 1994); Colette Sirat, *Hebrew Manuscripts of the Middle Ages* (Cambridge, 2002).

4. Allony's accounts of the establishment of the IMHM and of his efforts to obtain microfilms were posthumously published in his memoirs *Ketav-yad shel Mosheh Rabenu* (Jerusalem, 1992). His visit to Hungary and his efforts to negotiate the microfilming of manuscripts in Budapest are chronicled on pp. 283-326.

5. The Guenzburg collection of over 1,900 Hebrew manuscripts, most of them copied before 1600 and many predating the fifteenth century, was compiled by three generations of the family in the nineteenth century. The last private owner of the collection, Baron David Guenzburg, who lived in St. Petersburg and in Paris, augmented the collection with hundreds of manuscripts purchased from dealers and private collectors, mainly in Western Europe. Most of the MSS were copied in Italy, Spain, Germany, or the Near East, and only a few dozen were produced or composed in Russia. The proprietorship of the Guenzburg collection remains an open question. Baron David decreed in his will that his library should be kept in an institution devoted to Jewish studies. An attempt to purchase the collection for the Jewish Theological Seminary of

America in New York was thwarted by the outbreak of World War I. In 1917 the library was purchased by Russian Zionists for the Jewish National Library in Jerusalem, but before it could be shipped abroad, the October Revolution broke out and the library was confiscated and kept in the Publichnaia Biblioteka, the forerunner of the Lenin State Library. Efforts to redeem the library were made in the 1930s but were unsuccessful. See Michael Stanislawski, "An Unperformed Contract: The Sale of Baron Gunzburg's Library to the Jewish Theological Seminary of America," *Transition and Change in Modern Jewish History* (Jerusalem, 1987): lxxiii-xciii, and, on the negotiations for the purchase of the collection for the Jewish National Library, see Mordecai Nadav, "History of the Efforts to Purchase the David Gunzburg Collection for the National Library in Jerusalem" (in Hebrew), *Essays and Studies in Librarianship Presented to Curt David Wormann on his Seventy-Fifth Birthday* (Jerusalem, 1975): Hebrew section, 81-95.

6. My former colleague at the IMHM, Ephraim F. Kupfer, informed me of his opinion why the Russians aborted the microfilming. Allony insisted upon receiving only original negative copies of the manuscripts. He refused to agree to terms stipulated by some libraries that agreed to supply the Institute with positive copies or direct negatives, retaining the original negatives for themselves. For this reason some of the largest collections in England, those in the University libraries in Oxford and Cambridge, were not filmed until Allony left the Institute when it moved to the Jewish National and University Library in 1962. The microfilms of the Guenzburg manuscripts sent from Moscow were positive copies and Allony promptly wrote to Moscow demanding the original negatives. It seems that either his letter piqued the officials in the Lenin State Library, who refused to continue the filming, or that it was brought to the attention of a higher authority who canceled the transaction.

7. These manuscripts were described by Abraham Katsh, *Catalogue of Hebrew Manuscripts Preserved in the USSR*, vol. 1 (New York, 1957).

8. Davies sold the entire collection of microfilms to the National Library of Canada as well. A few years later he offered for sale another batch of microfilms of "Russian manuscripts" that turned out to be a collection of mainly nineteenth and twentieth century Yemenite manuscripts purchased in Israel by a private American collector and acquired under questionable circumstances by Davies. This time, when the IMHM discovered the ruse, Davies insisted that the source of the manuscripts was a library in Russia that was holding manuscripts purchased in Israel by Russian agents. Though the IMHM eventually purchased the microfilms, for they were of some interest to researchers, no further contacts were ever made with Davies who passed away a few years later. The whole affair serves to underline the fascination with the unattainable Russian manuscripts and the passions they aroused. Had Davies advertised his wares as late Yemenite manuscripts, many of them copies of printed books, it is doubtful if he would have found any takers.

9. See Benjamin Richler, "Microfilming the Baron Guenzburg collection of Hebrew Manuscripts in the Russian State Library in Moscow," *Judaica Librarianship* 8, nos.1-2 (1993-1994): 142-144.

10. See Zachary M. Baker, "History of the Jewish Collections at the Vernadsky Library in Kiev," *Shofar* 10, no. 4 (1992): 31-48, and the bibliography quoted.

11. See Binyamin Richler, "Ketuve-yad 'ivriim she-nitpatslu," *Asufot* 1 (1987): 105-158 for descriptions of a hundred manuscripts that were divided. Since publishing that article, I have recorded over twice that number of divided manuscripts, some of them recently separated by new owners or booksellers.

Jewish Book Publishing Today in the Countries of the Former USSR

Alexander Frenkel

SUMMARY. This article discusses Jewish book publishing in most of the Soviet Union's successor states after 1990. All publications on Jewish history, culture, traditions, and religion (Judaism) are included under this rubric. In addition to scholarly and educational publications, fiction translated from Yiddish and Hebrew, and "Russian-Jewish literature" are also included. The author provides statistics and discusses basic themes, linguistic issues, and problems encountered in the post-Soviet states. The article lists different publishers and organizations involved in Jewish book publishing. *[Article copies available for a fee from The Haworth Document Delivery Service: 1-800-HAWORTH. E-mail address: <docdelivery@haworthpress.com> Website: <http://www.HaworthPress.com> © 2003 by The Haworth Press, Inc. All rights reserved.]*

KEYWORDS. Bibliography, Holocaust, Jewish periodicals, Jewish publishing, Azerbaijan, Belarus, Estonia, Georgia, Kazakhstan, Kyrgyzstan, Latvia, Lithuania, Moldova, Russia, Ukraine, Uzbekistan, Soviet Union

---

Alexander Frenkel is Executive Director, Jewish Community Center of St. Petersburg, Rubinshteina Street, 3, St. Petersburg 191025, Russia (E-mail: frenk@lea.spb.su). He is also Editor-in-Chief of the *Narod Knigi v mire knig* bibliographical journal.

The article was translated by Beth Feinberg and the author.

[Haworth co-indexing entry note]: "Jewish Book Publishing Today in the Countries of the Former USSR." Frenkel, Alexander. Co-published simultaneously in *Slavic & East European Information Resources* (The Haworth Information Press, an imprint of The Haworth Press, Inc.) Vol. 4, No. 2/3, 2003, pp. 69-88; and: *Judaica in the Slavic Realm, Slavica in the Judaic Realm: Repositories, Collections, Projects, Publications* (ed: Zachary M. Baker) The Haworth Information Press, an imprint of The Haworth Press, Inc., 2003, pp. 69-88. Single or multiple copies of this article are available for a fee from The Haworth Document Delivery Service [1-800-HAWORTH, 9:00 a.m. - 5:00 p.m. (EST). E-mail address: docdelivery@haworthpress.com].

http://www.haworthpress.com/store/product.asp?sku=J167
© 2003 by The Haworth Press, Inc. All rights reserved.

INTRODUCTION

"Jewish book publishing" refers here not only to publications that are issued by Jewish communities and not exclusively to those whose authors are Jewish. It refers to the full range of publications devoted to Jewish history, culture, Judaism, traditions, and the specifically Jewish experience. In addition to scholarly, semi-scholarly, and educational publications, belles-lettres (translations of Yiddish and Hebrew authors, and Russian-Jewish literature) are also included. Obviously, publications of an openly anti-Jewish character (e.g., publications by neo-Nazi organizations, missionary groups, "anti-Zionist" literature) are excluded, under this definition.

The publication genres examined in this article are highly heterogeneous. They include:

- Publications from the various countries of the former Soviet Union, written in various languages;
- Publications issued by state and private publishers, academic institutions, and Jewish communal organizations;
- Publications of varying levels of content and typography.

But in all of these cases the term "Jewish book publishing" represents an integrated phenomenon–publications that in some way reflect the Jewish spiritual legacy, publications that form post-Soviet Jewry's views about itself, as well as the views of the non-Jewish populations of post-Soviet countries regarding the Jews.

JEWISH BOOK PUBLISHING IN THE USSR UNTIL 1990

Under the policy of state anti-Semitism, Jewish book publishing in the USSR in the 1960s to 1980s was almost non-existent, and strict ideological control was exercised over the few titles that did appear.

The only Soviet Jewish periodicals were two Yiddish-language publications: the literary monthly *Sovetish heymland* (Moscow) and the newspaper *Birobidzhaner shtern*, which came out five days a week in the remote, Far Eastern city of Birobidzhan. Sovetskii pisatel' (Moscow) was the sole publisher of books in Yiddish (five or six titles per year, on average), in limited press runs–works by Soviet Yiddish writers along with Yiddish classics "recognized" by the regime (Mendele Moykher-Sforim, Sholem Aleichem, I. L. Peretz). The same titles were also published in Russian translation and in translation into other "languages of the peoples of the USSR" (Ukrainian,

Belorussian, etc.).[1] It is necessary to note that under the conditions of a state system of publishing and distribution, the circulation of books of Jewish writers in translation in Russian was fairly high. Thus a six-volume Sholem Aleichem edition in Russian was published in 1961 in a print run of 225,000 copies, and was reissued twice in following years.

Scholarly and semi-scholarly literature on Jewish history and culture was practically non-existent in the USSR. The few Jewish religious groups that were legally constituted in the different cities of the USSR were not allowed to publish any religious literature. Only the Moscow Choral Synagogue issued Jewish calendars each year, in small numbers of copies, and only once in all the postwar years was it allowed to publish a prayer book–the Siddur *Mir* (1956).

In the years of Gorbachev's perestroika, policies toward Jewish book publishing gradually liberalized. In 1985 a supplement to the journal *Sovetish heymland* commenced–the annual almanac in Russian *God za godom* (Year After Year), which included not only works of Yiddish writers in Russian translation, but also historical articles, social-political literature on contemporary topics (*publitsistika*), and memoirs. (A total of six issues were published.) In December 1988, for the first time in many years, the first legal, Russian-language Jewish newspaper in the USSR came out–the newspaper of the Obshchestvo evreiskoi kul'tury Estonii (Society for Jewish Culture of Estonia), Khashakhar (Ha-Shahar [Dawn]; Tallinn). In 1989, Jewish periodicals in Russian legally began in Riga, Vilnius, and Moscow as well. In the middle of 1990, ideological control over publishing activity ended and the free development of Jewish publishing activity on the territory of the USSR began.

DEVELOPMENT OF JEWISH BOOK PUBLISHING IN RUSSIAN AFTER 1990

During the 1990s, the number of Jewish book titles published in Russian on the territory of the former USSR was constantly increasing (although their print runs were decidedly smaller than the regular ones in the Soviet period). The results of the monitoring of Jewish book publishing in Russian, starting in 1996, are shown in Table 1. Despite the incompleteness of the information and the relativity of the criteria as to what defines a particular book as "Jewish," the data in the tables give a clear impression of the dimensions of Jewish book publishing and the pace of its development.

In the beginning of the 1990s, foreign Jewish organizations played a significant role in Jewish book publishing in the USSR: the Jewish Agency ("Sochnut"), the Israeli government organization Lishkat ha-kesher ("Nativ" [The Path]), the or-

TABLE 1. Number of Book Titles on Jewish Topics in Russian by Country

		1996	1997	1998	1999	2000	2001
Russia	Moscow	43	37	54	65	103	128
	St. Petersburg	8	13	13	25	30	33
	Other cities	11	17	18	25	34	29
Ukraine	Kiev	7	9	11	10	13	22
	Other cities	11	6	13	23	24	38
Belarus	Minsk	2	9	9	8	11	7
	Other cities	2	6	1	2	4	3
Moldova	Kishinev	–	3	7	8	7	1
	Other cities	1	2	–	1	–	–
Lithuania		2	1	1	–	–	–
Estonia		1	–	–	–	1	1
Latvia		1	2	5	2	3	3
Other countries of the former USSR		–	1	3	2	4	4
TOTAL		89	106	135	168	234	269

Notes:
This table is compiled on the basis of monitoring conducted by the journal *Narod Knigi v mire knig*.
The count also includes books with texts in both Russian and other languages.
Data from 2001 are not complete.

ganization "SHAMIR" (Soiuz evreiskoi religioznoi intelligentsii iz SSSR v Izraile–Union of Jewish Religious Intelligentsia of the USSR in Israel), and others. These organizations published reprint editions of Russian-language Israeli and American books (mostly textbooks of Hebrew and religious literature). Soon, however, local Jewish organizations established a more serious presence on the Jewish publishing scene, with foreign organizations just playing the role of financial supporters of local publishing initiatives. In addition, joint Russian-Israeli publishing projects emerged: organizations such as the Gesharim publishing house and the Institut izucheniia iudaizma v SNG, with divisions in Israel and Russia. In these cases, publication and distribution of books takes place both in Israel and the post-Soviet countries, with the place of publication on the books' title pages usually given as "Jerusalem-Moscow."

At the end of the 1990s, large Russian commercial publishing houses started to play a notable role in the publication of Jewish books. They began actively to include in their publishing programs translations of foreign books on Jewish history and culture, and also literary works by the most popular Jewish authors (e.g., Isaac Bashevis Singer, Saul Bellow, Sholem Aleichem). The majority of the commercial publishing houses are based in

Moscow (Tekst, EKSMO-Press, Vagrius, Gud'ial-Press, etc.), but also in St. Petersburg (Limbus-Press, Amfora), Rostov-on-the-Don (Feniks), and several other cities. In some instances commercial publishing houses publish Jewish books, with the financial participation of Jewish organizations. For example, the Rossiiskii evreiskii kongress (Russian Jewish Congress, Moscow) sponsored the publication of a series of books, chiefly on the history of the Holocaust, through the publishing houses Limbus-Press (St. Petersburg) and Sovershenno sekretno (Top Secret, Moscow).

During the 1990s, the participation of state organizations in Jewish publishing activity markedly decreased. Nonetheless, some Jewish publications appeared under state auspices (for example, books published by the Holovna spetsializovana redaktsiia literatury movamy natsional'nykh men'shin Ukrainy [Kiev], or the Valstybinis Vilniaus Gaono Žydų muziejus [The Publishing House of the Vilna Gaon State Jewish Museum, Vilnius]). In rare circumstances, Jewish organizations were successful in obtaining state financing in their publishing projects.

SURVEY OF BOOK PUBLISHING BY COUNTRY; LINGUISTIC ISSUES[2]

Russia

Moscow, the capital of the Russian Federation, is the most important center of Jewish publishing activity in the post-Soviet arena, as Table 1 clearly shows. This publishing activity is maintained by the Moscow-based commercial publishing houses, by small private publishing houses of "intellectual literature," as well as by numerous Jewish organizations–religious, cultural, academic. Jewish publishing in St. Petersburg is markedly less active than in Moscow, but a group of local publishing houses there publishes Jewish books regularly enough. In addition, several Jewish organizations in that city maintain publishing programs. Jewish books are also published in many other Russian cities, from Kaliningrad to Vladivostok.

Jewish book publishing in Russia appears almost exclusively in Russian. The publication of Yiddish books ceased after the breakup of the USSR.

In Makhachkala (Dagestan), books have been published in the language of the Mountain Jews (the so-called Judeo-Tat language). In 1997, the Evreiskii universitet v Moskve (Jewish University in Moscow) published the Tatsko *(evreisko)-russkii slovar'* (Tat-Russian dictionary). In Nal'chik (Kabardino-Balkariia), a *Tatsko-russkii illiustrirovannyi slovar' dlia detei* (Tat-Russian Illustrated Dictionary for Children) was published (1991).

Next we will conduct a brief survey of some fairly important publishing programs in Moscow and St. Petersburg.

Izdatel'stvo "Gesharim/Mosty kul'tury" (Moscow)

This is the largest publishing house of Jewish literature in Russian. Founded in the beginning of the 1990s in Jerusalem, it soon became Russian-Israeli, with sections in Jerusalem and Moscow. It has published about 200 titles on Jewish history and culture, both translations and texts originally written in Russian. Gesharim publishes an extensive series jointly with the Hebrew University's Chais Center for Jewish Studies in Russian, Bibliotheca Judaica, which includes translations of important contemporary research in Jewish history, along with studies by Russian and Israeli historians, originally written in Russian. The Biblioteka Flaviana series includes academic editions of the works of Josephus Flavius, plus the fundamental three-volume anthology *Grecheskie i rimskie avtory o evreiakh i iudaizme* (Greek and Roman Authors on Jews and Judaism; 1997-2002). The Literatura Izrailia (Literature of Israel) and Literatura Izrailia i diaspory (Literature of Israel and the Diaspora) series include publications of contemporary literature both in translation from Hebrew and by contemporary Russian-Jewish authors.

Izdatel'stvo "DAAT/Znanie" (Moscow)

This publishing house was founded by the "Prisoner of Zion" Iosif Begun in 1999, as a Russian-Israeli enterprise, but in reality the publishing activity occurs only in Moscow. Over three years, ten titles have been published on Judaism and Jewish history, either translations or original Russian works.

Institut izucheniia iudaizma v SNG pod rukovodstvom ravvina Adina Shteinzal'tsa (Institute for the Study of Judaism in the CIS Headed by Rabbi Adin Steinzaltz; Moscow)

The Institute carries out its publishing activity equally in Moscow and Jerusalem. Its most important publishing project comprises the edition of the Babylonian Talmud with commentaries, in Russian translation. By late 2002, four volumes had been published. Additionally, it has published Russian translations of essays by Rabbi Steinzaltz and popular literature on Judaism.

Project Judaica (Moscow)[3]

The Project Judaica publishing program is under the aegis of the Tsentr bibleistiki i iudaiki Rossiskogo gosudarstvennogo gumitarnogo universiteta

(The Center for Biblical and Jewish Studies of the Russian State University for the Humanities, Moscow), the Jewish Theological Seminary (New York), and the YIVO Institute for Jewish Research (New York). It has published several important academic and educational publications, such as the Yiddish textbook by Shimen Sandler (2001), the monograph by Igor' Tantlevskii, *Vvedenie v Piatiknizhie* (Introduction to the Pentateuch; 2000), *Antologiiia ivritskoi literatury: Evreiskaia literatura XIX-XX vekov v russkikh perevodakh* (Anthology of Hebrew Literature: Jewish Literature of the Nineteenth and Twentieth Centuries in Russian Translation; 1999). In 1999 it began a series of collections of academic articles under the title Judaica Rossica.

Rossiiskaia evreiskaia entsiklopediia (Russian Jewish Encyclopedia; Moscow)

This is another Russian-Israeli publishing project, with the editorial board located in Moscow. As of late 2002, four volumes of a projected seven-volume encyclopedia dedicated to Russian Jewry had come out.

Nauchno-prosvetitel'skii tsentr "Kholokost" (Scientific and Educational Center "Holocaust"; Moscow)

The Center publishes academic and educational literature on the Holocaust, and also memoirs. The majority of publications appear within the series Rossiiskaia biblioteka Kholokosta (Russian Library of the Holocaust).

Tsentr nauchnykh rabotnikov i prepodavatelei iudaiki v vuzakh "Sefer" (Center of Academicians and Teachers of Judaica in Institutions of Higher Education "Sefer"; Moscow)

The Center regularly publishes collections of academic articles on various aspects of Jewish studies, along with the reference guides *Iudaika v stranakh SNG i Baltii* (Judaica in the Countries of the CIS and the Baltic; parallel issues in Russian and English), which include the addresses and phone numbers of research organizations and groups, and individual researchers.

Izdatel'stvo "Lekhaim" (Moscow)

The publishing house of the Chabad Lubavitch movement publishes the essays of the Lubavitcher Rebbe Menahem Mendel Schneersohn for mass distribution, along with popular Hasidic literature. It has also published a Russian translation of the *Memoirs of Glueckel of Hameln* (2001).

Ob"edinenie religioznykh obshchin sovremennogo iudaizma v Rossii–OROSIR (Union of Religious Communities of Modern Judaism in Russia; Moscow)

This organization is the publisher of the Reform Jewish prayer book in Russian, as well as popular literature on Judaism from the position of the Reform movement.

Izdatel'stvo "Evreiskii mir" (Publishing House "Jewish World"; Moscow)

This publishing house was founded in the mid-1990s by a group of activists primarily involved in the worldwide movement of Humanistic Judaism. Accordingly, one of its first publications was a Russian translation of a book by the founder of Humanistic Judaism, Rabbi Sherwin T. Wine, *Novyi put' v iudaizme* (A New Path in Judaism; 1998). However, the publishing group has moved away from Humanistic Judaism and begun to publish popular literature on Judaism and Jewish history. In particular, it has published more than 30 educational brochures in the series Biblioteka lektora (Reader's Library), distributed under the auspices of the Assotsiatsiia narodnykh universitetov evreiskoi kul'tury v SNG (Association of People's Universities of Jewish Culture in the CIS).

Peterburgskii evreiskii universitet (in 1999 re-named Peterburgskii institut iudaiki) (St. Petersburg Jewish University, re-named St. Petersburg Institute of Judaica)

Beginning in 1990, the University started a large-scale publishing program, including six collections of academic works, the bibliographical index *Literatura o evreiakh na russkom iazyke, 1890-1947* (Literature on the Jews in the Russian Language, 1899-1947; 1995), and academic and popular books on Jewish history and Judaism. For organizational reasons its publishing activity greatly decreased in the end of the 1990s, but it continues to publish the annual guide *Evreiskie obrazovatel'nye uchrezhdeniia SNG i stran Baltii* (Jewish Educational Institutions of the CIS and Baltic; parallel issues in Russian and English).

Issledovatel'skii tsentr "Peterburgskaia iudaika" (Research Center "Petersburg Judaica"; St. Petersburg)

Founded in 2000, the Center started a publishing program on Jewish history, beginning with the publication of a bibliographical reference work *Voskhod–Knizhki Voskhoda: rospis' soderzhaniia 1881-1906 gg.* (*Voskhod* Magazine with Supplement: Index of Articles for 1881-1906; 2001).

Evreiskii obshchinnyi tsentr Sankt-Peterburga (Jewish Community Center of St. Petersburg)

The publishing program of the Center includes literature on Jewish culture, above all music and fine art. Publications on music include collections of scores, songbooks, and collections of scholarly articles on the history of Jewish music in Russia. Publications on art include catalogs of the works of contemporary Jewish artists. In 2000, the Center published a photo album in Russian and English, *Forgotten Stones: Jewish Tombstones in Moldova*.

Tsentr "ORT-Gintsburg" (St. Petersburg)

The St. Petersburg branch of the World ORT Union became a pioneer in the publishing of Jewish multimedia products in Russian. In 2000, the Center produced a Russian version of the CD-ROM, *Puteshestvie v mir Tory* (Travels in the World of Torah), and also an album on two CD-ROMs, *Evrei Peterburga: Tri veka istorii = St. Petersburg's Jewish Community: Three Centuries of History*, with parallel texts in Russian and English.

Ukraine

Kiev is the most important center of Jewish book publishing in Ukraine. Jewish works are published regularly in Odessa, L'viv, Khar'kiv, Dnipropetrovs'k, and Zaporizhzhia. From time to time Jewish books are published in other cities.

A peculiarity of Jewish book publishing in Ukraine is its bilingualism. A substantial proportion of Jewish books are published in Ukrainian, and collections including articles in either Russian or Ukrainian (depending on the language in which the author wrote the article) are widespread. It is important to note that among the books in Ukrainian there are not only translations from Yiddish, Hebrew, or English, but also original works on Jewish history written in Ukrainian. The results of our monitoring of Jewish book publishing in Ukraine from 1996-2001 appear in Table 2.

Since 1990, more than ten books have been published in Yiddish, in Ukraine. Most were published in 1994-1997 by the publisher Maiak (Lighthouse; Odessa), but after the emigration of its editor, Yiddish publishing in Odessa ceased. Several Yiddish books have also been published in Kiev with government support (see summaries following). Separate Yiddish books have also been issued in L'viv and Chernivtsi.

Here is a brief summary of the more notable publishing projects in Kiev:

Institut iudaiki (Institute of Judaica)

Founded in 1994, the Institute has a large-scale publishing program, Biblioteka Instituta iudaiki (Library of the Institute of Judaica), which includes scholarly, semi-scholarly, and literary works. Publications of the Institute include proceedings of its annual academic conferences, the monograph by the musicologist Moisei Beregovskii, *Purimshpili* (Purim Plays; 2001), the reference work *Dokumenty po evreiskoi istorii XVI-XX vekov v kievskikh arkhivakh* (Documents on Jewish History of the Sixteenth through Twentieth Centuries in Kiev Archives; 2001), collections of poetry by Peretz Markish in Ukrainian translation, and much more. The Institute is preparing for publication a popular encyclopedia, *Ukrains'ke evreistvo* (Ukrainian Jewry).

Instytut natsional'nykh vidnosyn i politolohii Natsional'noi akademii nauk Ukrainy (Institute of National Relations and Political Science of the National Academy of Sciences of Ukraine)

Its Department on Jewish History and Culture is an example of a governmental organization concerned with Jewish research and publishing. Publications of the Institute include proceedings of its academic conferences, monographs on various aspects of Jewish history, and the *Korotkyi idysh-ukrains'kyi slovnyk* (Brief Yiddish-Ukrainian Dictionary; 1996), published jointly with the Holovna spetsializovana redaktsiia literatury movamy natsional'nykh menshin Ukrainy (described in the next paragraph).

Holovna spetsializovana redaktsiia literatury movamy natsional'nykh menshin Ukrainy (Chief Specialized Editorial Board of Literature in Languages of National Minorities of Ukraine)

The Board is another government organization concerned with Jewish book publishing. In addition to the dictionary mentioned above, it has issued a collection of stories by the Kiev author Hershl Polianker, *Der oytser* (The Treasure; 1996; in Yiddish), a collection of stories by Isaac Bashevis Singer, with parallel texts in Yiddish and in Ukrainian translation (2000), and other publications. The Editorial Board has also published several issues of an anthology, *Na nashii, na svoii zemli* (Our Land, Native Land; 1995-1996), which include works by poets who live in Ukraine and write in different languages, including Yiddish (poems are printed in Yiddish with parallel Ukrainian translation).

The Ministry of Culture and Arts of Ukraine

By issuing the richly illustrated and beautifully printed album *Treasures of Jewish Culture in Ukraine*, the Ministry opened a publishing series devoted to Jewish heritage in Ukraine. The first album deals with Jewish ritual objects from museum collections in Ukraine. The second album is planned to be dedicated to synagogue architecture. It is significant that this publishing project is maintained parallel in three languages–Ukrainian, English, and Hebrew.

Evreiskii sovet Ukrainy (Jewish Council of Ukraine)

The Council publishes collections of popular essays on the history of the Holocaust in Ukraine and on the participation of Jews in the Second World War; memorial books dedicated to the events at Babi Yar; and collections of remembrances of Jewish veterans.

Belarus

The majority of Jewish books in Belarus are published in Minsk. Unlike Moscow, St. Petersburg, and Kiev, no Jewish organizations publish on a systematic basis in Minsk. As a rule, various private publishers issue Jewish books with support from the American Jewish Joint Distribution Committee (commonly referred to simply as the "Joint") and other Jewish organizations. It is worth mentioning the collection of academic articles *Evrei v Belarusi: istoriia i kul'tura* (Jews in Belarus: History and Culture) that has been published regularly since 1997; so far, six issues have been published. Various publishing houses (including the academic publisher Belaruska navuka) publish collections of documents and materials on the history of the Holocaust in Belarus. The Belorusskii nauchno-issledovatel'skii institut dokumentovedeniia i arkhivnogo dela (Belaruski navukova-dasledchy instytut dakumentaznaustva i arkhiunai spravy–Belorussian Scientific Institute of Document and Archive Research) has published some valuable collections of documents on Jewish

TABLE 2. Number of Book Titles on Jewish Topics Published in Ukraine

	1996	1997	1998	1999	2000	2001
In Russian only	15	10	14	27	28	47
In Ukrainian only	2	5	10	1	9	7
With texts in both Russian and Ukrainian	3	5	7	6	9	13
TOTAL	20	30	31	34	46	67

Notes:
This table is compiled on the basis of monitoring conducted by the journal *Narod Knigi v mire knig*.
Data from 2001 are not complete.

history including the thick tome *Bund v Belarusi, 1897-1921* (Bund in Belarus, 1897-1921; 1997).

There is an interesting publishing program in Vitebsk, devoted mainly to the history of the Jewish community of the city. An outstanding publication from Vitebsk is a detailed guide to the local Jewish cemetery (2001).

Jewish books are also published occasionally in Brest, Grodno, Gorki, and other cities.

As in Ukraine, bilingualism exists in Belarus also, but not to so noticeable a degree as in Ukraine; Russian dominates overwhelmingly. We know of only four books on Jewish history published in Belorussian after 1990 (one is a translation from English, the other three were written in Belorussian). Some collections include materials in two languages, but the majority of materials are in Russian. Yiddish books have not been published there in the past decades.

Moldova

Jewish book publishing is concentrated almost exclusively in Kishinev and is almost always in Russian. Books are issued by various publishers, mainly with support from the "Joint." The Institut mezhetnicheskikh issledovanii AN Respubliki Moldova (The Institute of Inter-ethnic Research of the Academy of Sciences of the Republic of Moldova) has issued some academic publications, including the basic collection of documents and materials *Kishinevskii pogrom 1903 goda* (Kishinev Pogrom of 1903; 2000). The Obshchestvo evreiskoi kultury Kishineva (Jewish Cultural Society of Kishinev) published two issues of a literary almanac on Jewish writers of Moldova, *Vetka Ierusalima* (Jerusalem Spray; 1998-2000).

We know of only four publications written in Romanian on Jewish topics published in Moldova after 1990 (all were issued separately in Russian as well). In 2000, a book of prose by the Kishinev Yiddish writer Iekhiel Shraibman, with parallel text in Yiddish and Russian translation, came out.

Lithuania

Jewish books are published mainly in Vilnius, but also in Kaunas. During the 1990s, the relative prominence of the Russian language in Jewish book publishing gradually decreased, and Lithuanian became dominant. Russian is gradually ceasing to be used even in the fairly numerous publications that have parallel texts in several languages, with English taking the place of Russian as the second language. In some instances the omission of Russian is affected and is clearly done for political reasons. For example, *The Book of Sorrow* (1997), an album with photographs of all of the memorials at the places in

Lithuania where Jews were murdered during the war, includes text in four languages–Lithuanian, English, Hebrew, and Yiddish.

At the same tim, this language shift reflects an important qualitative change in Jewish book publishing in Lithuania. Because the Jewish population in Lithuania has decreased and interest in Jewish heritage has grown in Lithuanian society as a whole, Jewish book publishing is more and more oriented to non-Jews. To a noticeable degree non-Jewish publishers conduct it with government support. It is significant that research and memoirs on the history of the Jews of Lithuania dominate, especially on the history of the Holocaust in Lithuania–both translated from other languages (English, Hebrew and Yiddish) or written originally in Lithuanian. The change in the language situation is clear from the results of our monitoring in Table 3.

We know of only one title exclusively in Yiddish, published in Lithuania since 1990. But there were some books with parallel Yiddish texts or with Yiddish résumés or prefaces.

Valstybinis Vilniaus Gaono Žydų muziejus (The Publishing House of the Vilna Gaon Jewish Museum, Vilnius)

The Museum has published catalogs of its exhibitions and collections of academic articles on the history and culture of the Jews of Lithuania. In 1994 the first issue of the almanac *Žydų muziejus = Evreiskii muzei = The Jewish Museum*, with articles written by employees of the museum (all texts are parallel in Lithuanian, English, and Russian) was published. The second issue of the almanac (2001) was alreadye in Lithuanian only. A two-volume list of names of prisoners of the Vilnius ghetto (1996-1998) was issued as a supplement to the almanac. The Museum also published a two-volume publication of materials on Lithuanians who saved Jews during the war, *Hands Bringing Life and Bread* (1997-1999; parallel texts in Lithuanian and English).

TABLE 3. Number of Book Titles on Jewish Topics Published in Lithuania

	1996	1997	1998	1999	2000	2001
In Russian only	1	1	–	–	–	–
In Lithuanian only	–	7	3	7	4	10
Parallel in Lithuanian and English	1	5	–	1	–	2
Parallel in Lithuanian, English, and Russian	1	1	1	–	1	–
TOTAL	3	14	4	8	5	12

Note:
This table is compiled on the basis of monitoring conducted by the journal *Narod Knigi v mire knig*.

Estonia

Jewish books are published mainly in Tallinn, but also in Tartu. As in Lithuania, they are oriented in the main not to the comparatively small Jewish community, but to the non-Jewish population, and therefore they are published almost exclusively in Estonian. From 1992 to 1998, a specialized publishing house, Aviv, operated in Tallinn, having as its charge the presentation of Jewish culture to the Estonian reader. This publishing house issued about ten titles in Estonian–translations of Jewish classics (Sholem Aleichem, Isaac Bashevis Singer), books on contemporary Israel–but at the end of the 1990s it closed for economic reasons. Eesti Juudi Kogukond (the Jewish Community of Estonia) published some books and brochures on the history of the Jews in Estonia–in Estonian, but some also with parallel texts in Estonian, English, and Russian.

Latvia

Jewish books are published mainly in Riga, but some also in Daugavpils, Jurmala, and Rēzekne. Unlike Lithuania and Estonia, the majority of Jewish books here are published in Russian, because the Jewish community of Latvia is bigger, and is traditionally to a greater degree oriented to the Russian language. At the same time, the number of Jewish books published in Latvian is growing. The publishing house of the Latvian Institute of History has issued several important academic monographs on Jewish history in Latvian, and has also published translations of these books in English. The Center for Judaic Studies at the Latvian University also issues publications on Jewish history. Beginning in 1996, the Center, together with Jewish community organizations of Latvia, has published collections of academic articles in Russian, *Evrei v meniaiushchemsia mire* (Jews in a Changing World). To date, three volumes have been printed.

Georgia

Jewish books are published mainly in Georgian. Unfortunately, the author of this article does not have detailed information on Jewish book publishing in Georgia.

Azerbaijan

Publishing of popular books on Judaism occurs in Baku, mainly in Russian and not on a large scale. In addition, one should note the publication of a bibliographical reference work *Gorskie evrei v Azerbaidzhane* (Mountain Jews in Azerbaijan; 2000), and a collection of reminiscences by the prominent leader of Mountain Jewish culture, Iakov Mikhailovich Agarunov, in Judeo-Tat (2001).

Kazakhstan, Kyrgyzstan, Uzbekistan

Jewish publishing in Central Asia is not extensive, and chiefly comprises books on the history of local Jewish communities, and popular works on Judaism and Jewish traditions. Books are written almost exclusively in Russian. An exception is the publication (probably with propagandistic intentions) in 2000 in Bishkek, of the illustrated work *Iz evreiskikh predanii* (From Jewish Legends), with parallel texts in Russian, Kyrgyz, and Hebrew.

Bukharskii gosudarstvennyi arkhitekturno-khudozhestvennyi muzei-zapovednik (Bukhara State Architectural and Art Museum/National Park, Bukhara, Uzbekistan)

The Museum has published several books on the history and folklore of Bukharan Jews.

JEWISH LOCAL HISTORY LITERATURE

Jewish local history (*kraevedenie*)–books on the history of local Jewish communities–is a widespread Jewish publishing genre in the former USSR, especially typical for small towns. The geographical coverage of this literature is exceptionally broad. Jewish local histories are published both in large cities possessing rich Jewish pasts and large Jewish populations even today (Kiev, Odessa, Kishinev, St. Petersburg, etc.), and in small towns whose Jewish communities today number only 200-300 people (e.g., Konotop, Sumskaia oblast' [Ukraine], or Soroki [Moldova]). These books are published in cities in the former Pale of Settlement and in places far from its borders, where a large Jewish population appeared only after the Second World War (Cheliabinsk, Orenburg, Perm', Vladivostok). There are publications on the history of the Jews in regions that cannot be described as traditionally Jewish (Bashkortostan, Zapadnoe Zabaikal'e, Yakutia, Kyrgyzstan, Kazakhstan). As a rule these books are published by the local Jewish communities, or sometimes by a government academic institution, and occasionally jointly. The scholarly level of this literature varies from highly professional to amateur. The production standards also vary. But on the whole, Jewish local history publications are a clear witness to the growth of the national self-consciousness of post-Soviet Jewry, in search of a historical continuity and authenticity for its renewing communal life.

The total number of titles on Jewish local history published in the former USSR since 1990 approaches 150. Some notable publishing ventures are mentioned in this section:

Nizhnii Novgorod (Russia)

In 1993-1999, five issues of the collection *Evrei Nizhnego Novgoroda* (The Jews of Nizhnii Novgorod) appeared, with articles on the history of its Jewish community; stories on prominent Jews, leaders in science and art; memoirs.

Krasnoiarsk (Russia)

The Institut sotsial'nykh i obshchinnykh rabotnikov (The Institute of Social and Community Workers), which works under the auspices of the local division of the "Joint," has published the series of academic books *Istoriia evreiskikh obshchin Sibiri i Dal'nego Vostoka* (The History of Jewish Communities of Siberia and the Far East) since 2000. Professional historians from various cities in the region have participated in its publication. To date, ten issues have been published.

Nal'chik (Russia)

The Evreiskii kul'turnyi tsentr "Tovushi" (The Jewish Cultural Center "Tovushi") has published some collections on the mountain Jews of Kabardino-Balkariia. The collections include articles, archival documents, and memoirs of elderly Jews.

Zaporizhzhia (Ukraine)

From the beginning of the 1990s, the Zaporizhzhia State University, together with Jewish organizations, has published academic collections on the history of the Jews in southern Ukraine. *Materialy k istorii evreiskoi obshchiny Aleksandrovska (Zaporozh'ia)* (Materials on the History of Jewish Community of Aleksandrovsk [Zaporizhzhia]), six issues; *Zaporozhskie evreiskie chteniia* (Zaporizhzhia Jewish Readings), five issues; *Evreiskoe naselenie Iuga Ukrainy* (Jewish Population of Southern Ukraine), a two-volume set of documents and memoirs. These publications include texts in both Russian and Ukrainian.

Daugavpils (Latvia)

From 1993-2001, the Daugavpils Jewish Community published a three-volume set of historical essays, *Evrei v Daugavpilse* (Jews in Daugavpils). There are also some books on various aspects of the history of Jews of the city. All publications are in Russian.

St. Petersburg (Russia)

A group of Petersburg and Jerusalem researchers have founded a series of historical guides, *100 evreiskikh mestechek Ukrainy* (100 Jewish Shtetls of Ukraine), which include detailed descriptions of the past and present of former shtetls (small towns), together with photographs and maps. Two volumes have been published to date, dedicated to the Jewish small towns of Podolia.

LITERATURE ON THE HISTORY OF THE HOLOCAUST

The conscious attempt of Soviet propaganda, from the 1950s through the 1980s, to stifle discussion of the Holocaust in the Soviet Union–in effect crossing out this page from the historiography of the Second World War–was especially painful for Soviet Jews. It is not surprising, then, that from the very beginning of the 1990s the Holocaust became the most important topic of Jewish publishing in the countries of the former USSR. Publications include general works on the history of the Holocaust, on the history of the Holocaust in individual post-Soviet countries (Ukraine, Belarus, Moldova, Latvia, Lithuania, Estonia) and of large regions (Western Ukraine, Transnistria); works on the history of individual ghettos; accounts by former prisoners of ghettos and concentration camps; and collections of archival documents.

The geographical diffusion of publications on Holocaust history is especially broad. Books have been published in many small towns, relating the tragic history of their Jewish populations in the years of occupation (Baranovichi, Simferopol', Yalta, Brest, Rovno, Gorki, Slavuta, Orsha, Dubossary, Kaliningrad, and others). An extensive literature has been published on the history of the Holocaust in large cities in occupied Soviet territory (Kiev, Odessa, Khar'kiv, Minsk, Kishinev, Vilnius, Riga, and others). The publication of martyrologies–lists of Jews murdered by the Nazis–has been undertaken in some cities (Kiev, Borisov, Gorki, Artemovsk, Vitebsk, Mogilev, and others). Memoirs by Jews who survived the ghettos and concentration camps have been published in many cities including those that were not under German occupation (Samara, Yaroslavl', Syktyvkar).[4]

An important landmark event was the publication in 1993, in Vilnius, of the complete text of the *Chernaia kniga* (Black Book), prepared at the end of the 1940s by Ilya Ehrenburg and Vassily Grossman but not published under Stalin's anti-Semitic repression.[5]

Jewish participation in the war against Nazism (which is closely connected with the history of the Holocaust) is a topic that was also ignored by Soviet propaganda. Associations of Jewish war veterans and invalids in several cities have published collections of remembrances of their members (these have been published in St. Petersburg, Kiev, Vinnitsa, Khar'kiv, Kishinev and many other cities). Since 1995, the Soiuz evreev–invalidov i veteranov voiny (Union of Jewish Invalids and War Veterans, SEIVV), based in Moscow, has published the multi-volume *Knigi pamiati voinov-evreev pavshikh v boiakh s natsizmom, 1941-1945* (The Memorial Book of Jewish Soldiers Fallen in Battles with Nazism, 1941-1945). It includes names, photographs, and short biographies of Jews killed in the years of the war. By late 2002, seven volumes had been published. Similarly, the *Kniga pamiati voinov-evreev Dnepropetrovska* (The Memorial Book of Jewish Soldiers of Dnipropetrovs'k) was published in 1999-2001, in three volumes. In 2001, the Evreiskii sovet Ukrainy (Jewish Council Ukraine; Kiev) published the *Knyha pam'iati voiniv-evreiv, zahyblykh pid chas Velykoi Vitchyznianoi viiny, 1941-1945* (The Memorial Book of Jewish Soldiers Fallen in the Years of the Great Patriotic War, 1941-1945).

JEWISH PERIODICALS IN THE FORMER USSR[6]

As mentioned earlier, the publication of Jewish periodicals resumed at the end of 1988. Since then, the number of Jewish newspapers, journals and bulletins in post-Soviet countries has been constantly increasing. Monitoring of periodicals is conducted by the Hebrew University's journal, *Jews in Eastern Europe*, which regularly publishes articles with bibliographical information, and analyses of tendencies and developments.[7] In this article, we will list only some of the more authoritative and important periodicals.

- *IEhupets* (Kiev)–literary journal, published since 1995 by the Kiev-based Institut iudaiki. To date, ten issues have been published. The journal uses the traditional format of the Russian "thick" (*tolstyi*) literary journal. It includes materials in both Russian and Ukrainian.
- *Evreiskoe obrazovanie* (Jewish Education; St. Petersburg)–pedagogical journal, published since 2000 by the Peterburgskii institut iudaiki, in cooperation with the Hebrew University. Three issues have been published.
- *Mishpokha* (Vitebsk)–Jewish local history journal, dedicated to the history of Jewish communities of the cities and shtetls (small towns) of Belarus. Published since 1995, eleven issues have been published to date.
- *Narod Knigi v mire knig* (The People of the Book in the World of Books, St. Petersburg)–critical and bibliographical journal, dedicated to ques-

tions of Jewish book publishing in the former USSR. Issued once every two months since 1995.
- *Novaia evreiskaia shkola* (New Jewish School, St. Petersburg)–pedagogical journal, dedicated to the problems of Jewish education in the former USSR. Published since 1998. Eleven issues have been published.
- *Vestnik evreiskogo universiteta* (Herald of the Jewish University, Moscow-Jerusalem)–academic publication, issued from 1999 together by the Evreiskii universitet v Moskve and the Hebrew University (the journal is a continuation of the *Vestnik evreiskogo universiteta v Moskve* (Herald of the Jewish University in Moscow), which was published from 1992-1998).

PROBLEMS OF JEWISH BOOK PUBLISHING IN THE FORMER USSR

The decline of the general publishing culture after the breakup of the USSR, resulting from the economic crisis and the radical change in political conditions in post-Soviet countries, is paralleled in the Jewish book-publishing realm. At the same time, the difficult situation with Jewish book publishing is exacerbated by the universal shortage of authors, editors, and translators qualified in Jewish subjects. As a result, many Jewish publications are issued with serious errors in typography and content. The quality of translations of Jewish books (from English, Yiddish, Hebrew, and other languages) is often very low, especially those released by large commercial houses that for economic reasons do not hire qualified editors. Thus, the Russian translations of Irene Korn's album, *Celebration of Judaism in Art*, Isaac Bashevis Singer's novel, *Meshugah*, Martin Gilbert's illustrated monograph, *The Jews in the 20th Century*, and many other books were published with the coarsest errors.

Another issue is the lack of reference books and dictionaries to normalize the use of Russian terminology for Jewish subjects and forms of Jewish personal names. There is no generally accepted system of Russian transliteration for Yiddish and Hebrew texts. Unfortunately, we do not know of any academic institution working on the elaboration of an appropriate normative base.

Another serious problem is the dissemination of Jewish publications. There are no specialized book trade organizations interested in the circulation of Jewish books in post-Soviet countries. Jewish academic publications, memoirs, and local histories of small Jewish communities appear in small print runs (as a rule, 100-500 copies), with limited distribution beyond their cities of publication.

Bibliographical registration of Jewish literature in post-Soviet countries is also problematic. The breakup of a unified USSR and the actual disappearance of a legal deposit system mean that many books (especially those from small cities) are not held even by the large libraries of Moscow, St. Petersburg, Kiev, and other capitals–and accordingly, do not turn up in official bibliographical publications. At the beginning of the 1990s, an experiment was undertaken in Moscow to arrange the publication of bibliographical indexes *Problemy iudaiki* (Problems of Judaica, 1993-1994), based on the entries of Moscow academic libraries. It was therefore fragmentary, and the publication quickly ceased for economic reasons.

The Petersburg journal *Narod Knigi v mire knig* is today in practice the only active bibliographical project to track books on Jewish topics that are published in the entire post-Soviet arena. The editorial board monitors Jewish book publishing with the active cooperation of the library of the Jewish Community Center of St. Petersburg and the libraries of Jewish organizations from other cities. Notwithstanding the breadth of scope, and the high level of completeness of the collected information, it cannot be regarded as all encompassing due to the issues described above. The results of this monitoring served as the basis of this article.

NOTES

1. For the most complete bibliography of books by Yiddish authors that were published in the USSR from 1956 to 1980, see: *Sovetish heymland* 5 (1981): 153-161.

2. Full citations for many of the titles mentioned in this and subsequent sections are found in the bibliography that accompanies Nikolai Borodulin's article, "Slavic Judaica in the YIVO Library: Acquisitions from 1991-2001," elsewhere in this volume. *Ed.*

3. For a description of Project Judaica's activities in the arena of archival documentation, see the article by Marek Web, "The Jewish Archival Survey: Tracing Jewish Records In the Former Soviet Archives," elsewhere in this volume. *Ed.*

4. For a complete bibliography of books on the history of the Holocaust, published in the former USSR from 1990-1999, see: *Narod Knigi v mire knig* 27 (2000): 7-8; 28 (2000): 8-10.

5. For the latest English translation, see Ilya Ehrenburg, Vasily Grossman, *The Complete Black Book of Russian Jewry*; translated and edited by David Patterson; with a foreword by Irving Louis Horowitz and an introduction by Helen Segall (New Brunswick, NJ: Transaction, 2002).

6. Jewish serials in Ukraine are discussed by Vladimir Karasik elsewhere in this volume, in his article "From Odessa to Odessa." *Ed.*

7. See: *Jews and Jewish Topics in the Soviet Union and Eastern Europe* 2 (12) (1990): 69-77; and 3 (19) (1992): 62-77; *Jews in Eastern Europe* 2 (24) (1994): 72-84; 2 (30) (1996): 58-83; 1-2 (38-39) (1999): 103-142; and 1 (44) (2001): 92-146.

Slavic Judaica in the YIVO Library: Acquisitions from 1991-2001

Nikolai Borodulin

SUMMARY. This article discusses the development of Jewish publications from the former Soviet Republics, which were acquired by the YIVO library during the last decade. A brief history of Slavic Judaica holdings at the YIVO library is provided, followed by an overview of new publishers and vendors of Slavic Judaica in the CIS countries, especially Russia, Ukraine, Belarus, and Moldova, and in the Baltic States. In addition, an extensive, selected bibliography on the following topics is appended: (1) Reference books, encyclopedias, dictionaries, bibliographies, sources on East European Jewry (2) History of East European Jewry; anti-Semitism, biography (3) Holocaust literature, World War II (4) East European Jewish culture (Yiddish literature in the original and translation, folklore, art, education, theater, fiction, poetry, Jewish wit and humor) and (5) Conferences, congresses, symposiums on East European Jewry. *[Article copies available for a fee from The Haworth Document Delivery Service: 1-800-HAWORTH. E-mail address: <docdelivery@haworthpress.com> Website: <http://www.HaworthPress.com> © 2003 by The Haworth Press, Inc. All rights reserved.]*

Nikolai Borodulin was Bibliographical Specialist/Cataloger in the library of the YIVO Institute for Jewish Research until November 2002. He is currently Assistant Director, Center for Cultural Jewish Life of The Workmen's Circle/Arbeter Ring, 45 East 33rd Street, New York, NY 10016 USA (E-mail: nikolaib@circle.org).

[Haworth co-indexing entry note]: "Slavic Judaica in the YIVO Library: Acquisitions from 1991-2001." Borodulin, Nikolai. Co-published simultaneously in *Slavic & East European Information Resources* (The Haworth Information Press, an imprint of The Haworth Press, Inc.) Vol. 4, No. 2/3, 2003, pp. 89-118; and: *Judaica in the Slavic Realm, Slavica in the Judaic Realm: Repositories, Collections, Projects, Publications* (ed: Zachary M. Baker) The Haworth Information Press, an imprint of The Haworth Press, Inc., 2003, pp. 89-118. Single or multiple copies of this article are available for a fee from The Haworth Document Delivery Service [1-800-HAWORTH, 9:00 a.m. - 5:00 p.m. (EST). E-mail address: docdelivery@haworthpress.com].

http://www.haworthpress.com/store/product.asp?sku=J167
© 2003 by The Haworth Press, Inc. All rights reserved.

KEYWORDS. Bibliography, conference proceedings, Holocaust, Jewish history, Jewish publications, Slavic Judaica, YIVO Institute for Jewish Research (New York), Yiddish, United States, Russia, Ukraine, Belarus, Moldova, Estonia, Latvia, Lithuania

The YIVO library, which collects printed materials on diverse aspects of East European Jewry, has always pursued a keen interest in Slavic Judaica. Among the library's books are a significant number of older Russian-language publications from its original headquarters in Vilnius. Many of these volumes were confiscated and shipped to Germany during the Nazi occupation of Vilnius (where the YIVO Institute for Jewish Research was founded in 1925) in 1941-1943, for incorporation into the Institut zur Erforschung der Judenfrage, headed by the Nazi ideologue Alfred Rosenberg. These publications deal predominantly with issues of Jewish history, Jewish community organizations, Jewish religious traditions, and anti-Semitism. Many are stamped "Sichergestellt durch Einsatzstab RR," indicating that they were selected and confiscated by the Rosenberg task force. In 1947, these important books were recovered and returned to the YIVO Institute in New York City (where its headquarters were transferred at the beginning of the war).

Another important portion of the library's Slavic Judaica originates from one of YIVO's founders, Elias Tcherikower, who until his death in 1943 was the head of the Institute's Historical Section. This collection is particularly strong in its holdings on the Jewish history of Russia and Poland, Jewish social and political movements, pogroms and anti-Semitism. It also miraculously survived the Holocaust, having been hidden during World War II in France. Portions of YIVO's Slavic Judaica collection, comprising 354 monographic titles, are available on microfilm from IDC Publishers (http://www.idc.nl).

Jewish scholarship is now experiencing a process of enormous revival and blossoming in the former Soviet Union, and there are growing concerns over preserving the centuries-long legacy of Eastern European Jewry. Consequently the YIVO library has been replenishing its Slavic Judaica collection. For the period of 1991-2001 the library acquired, through various sources, more than 800 books and periodicals from more than 40 cities of the CIS and Baltic States. The vast majority of these publications deal with multifaceted topics relating to East European Jewry. Their major centers of publication are: Moscow (257 titles), Kiev (116), St. Petersburg (100), Minsk (87), Vilnius (39), L'vov (24), Khar'kov (19), and Riga (15). The new materials reflect the growth of interest in Jewish studies in both its quantitative and–more importantly–qualitative aspects.

The books cover a wide spectrum of history and culture of Eastern European Jewry, including the history of Jews and Jewish socio-political and cultural organizations in particular places (both large cities and small towns, interestingly enough), covering not only the traditional locations of Jewish communities in the area previously known as the Pale of Settlement, but also unusual and unexpected spots, where Ashkenazi Jews left some legacy of their presence. For example, during the past two years material about the history of the Jews has come from such remote places as Ufa, Nizhnii Novgorod, the Urals, Siberia, the Far East of the Russian Federation, and Kyrgyzstan.

Another significant phenomenon–unthinkable in the Soviet era–is the emergence and success of Jewish publishing houses and publishers. These include relatively well-known publishers from Moscow (Gesharim [Moscow-Jerusalem], Nauchno-prosvetitel'skii tsentr "Kholokost" [Scientific and Educational Center "Holocaust"], Evreiskii Universitet v Moskve [Jewish University in Moscow], TSentr nauchnykh rabotnikov i prepodavatelei iudaiki v vuzakh "Sefer" [Center of Academicians and Teachers of Judaica in the Institutions of Higher Education "Sefer"]) and St. Petersburg (Peterburgskii evreiskii universitet [St. Petersburg Jewish University]). Another dynamic institution is Institut iudaiki (Institute of Judaica, Kiev <http://www.judaica.kiev.ua>), which specializes in the research, publication and coordination of scholarship in the field of Jewish history and culture in Ukraine. Founded in early 1990s, this academic institution has sponsored and coordinated a number of research projects, conferences, and lectures. Its publishing activities are impressive: the literary almanac *Yehupets [Ehupets]*, no. 1-8 (1995-2001); materials of the international academic conference "Jewish History and Culture in Central and Eastern Europe" (1994-2000); dozens of academic works and other publications on Jewish social, economic and cultural life; Jewish art albums and calendars.

Publications of the TSentr nauchnykh rabotnikov i prepodavatelei iudaiki v vuzakh "Sefer" and Peterburgskii evreiskii universitet are very instrumental in terms of reference information on Jewish scholarship in the countries of the former Soviet Union. Some important books can be mentioned in this regard: *Iudaika v vysshykh uchebnykh zavedeniiakh SNG i stran Baltii* (Judaica in Institutions of Higher Education in the CIS and Baltic Countries) (Moscow: Sefer, 1996-1999), and *Evreiskie uchebnye zavedeniia na territorii SNG i stran Baltii* (Jewish Educational Institutions on the Territory of the CIS and Baltic Countries) (Saint-Petersburg: Izd. Peterburgskogo instituta iudaiki, 2000).

Due to the significant socio-political changes in the countries of the former Soviet Union, the network of distributors has greatly expanded. In addition to the quasi-monopoly Mezhdunarodnaia kniga (Moscow), hundreds of independent book distribution organizations and dealers came into being. Among the most successful groups of this kind that deal with the West is MIPP International (http://www.mipp.msk.ru/books), a vendor of publications from the CIS and Baltic States since 1991. This dealer offers more than 32,500 titles in its database, including hard-to-find items. Books not included in the MIPP catalog may be special-ordered by customers. It has a special Slavic Judaica database, which is updated on a regular basis. In addition, YIVO receives MIPP's weekly catalogs of specific publications from particular places. Occasionally, these catalogs are solely devoted to Judaica publications.

At the same time, the collapse of the Soviet Union caused numerous problems for the compilation of proper bibliographic data. If, previously, almost all materials that were published in the Soviet Union were easily traceable, it has become very difficult to keep track of the many publications that are not registered in any centralized bibliographic work. As far as Slavic Judaica goes, the field has expanded so much in comparison with Jewish publications of the Soviet period of the late 1950s through early 1980s (when they were largely limited to translations of the Soviet Yiddish writers and anti-Zionist literature), that it became a real challenge to get hold of these important items.

In this connection, it is worth mentioning the bibliographic periodical *Narod Knigi v mire knig* = 'Am ha-sefer 'im ha-sefer = *The People of the Book in the World of Books*, the newsletter of the Jewish Library Association of the Commonwealth of Independent States. Edited by Aleksandr Frenkel[1] and published by the Evreiskii obshchinnyi tsentr (Jewish Community Center) in Saint Petersburg since August 1995,[2] these newsletters are a major bibliographical source for Slavic Judaica published in the former Soviet Union. Each issue includes bibliographic information on new Slavic Judaica books, periodicals, book reviews, articles from both Jewish and non-Jewish journals in the languages of the CIS and Baltic States. For example, issue no. 28 (August 2000) lists 85 new books, including the following subjects: Judaism and Jewish philosophy (6), Jewish history (25), anti-Semitism (5), reference books and directories (8), lives of famous Jews (11), and fiction (21). In addition, the newsletter pays special attention to Holocaust publications. Issues no. 27 and 28, for instance, list 123 publications on this subject that have come out in the CIS since 1989. Alexander Frenkel, who is also the Chairman of Saint Petersburg Jewish Community Center, also publishes supplements to *Narod Knigi v mire knig*. The first issue, *Evreiskie obshchinnye biblioteki stran SNG i Baltii* (Jewish Community Libraries in the Countries of the CIS and the Baltic States) (Sankt-Peterburg, 2000), provides information on 178 Jewish libraries in 113 cities of 13 former Soviet Republics.

The rise of national consciousness in the former Soviet Union led to the establishment of hundreds of Jewish cultural, religious, social, academic and sport organizations throughout the entire CIS and Baltic States. Many of them publish their own periodicals, and the number of newspapers and journals that have come out in the last ten years is almost impossible to register. The daily, and especially the weekly and monthly press, record the current vibrant life of numerous Jewish communities, including instances of anti-Semitism; they trace the past of East European Jews and relate it to the present and future.

Among the most significant academic and socio-cultural periodicals that the YIVO library acquires are:

- *Vestnik Evreiskogo universiteta* (Herald of the Jewish University) (Moscow-Jerusalem, no. 1-21, 1992-2000).
- *Diaspory* (Diasporas) (Moscow, 1999); the first issue deals with Jewish immigration.
- *Istoki: vestnik Narodnogo universiteta evreiskoi kultury v Vostochnoi Ukraine = Sources* (Khar'kov: "Evreiskii mir," no. 1-8, 1997-2001).
- *Korni: vestnik Narodnogo universiteta evreiskoi kultury v tsentral'noi Rossii i Povolzh'e = Roots* (Saratov: Evreiskii mir, no. 1-4, 14, 1994-1995, 2000).
- *Mishpokha = Mishpahah* (Vitebsk: Belorusskoe ob"edinenie evreiskikh obshchin i organizatsii, Vitebskii evreiskii kul'turnyi tsentr, no. 1-9, 1995-2001).
- *Yehupets = Egupets = IEhupets: khudozhno-publitsystychnyi almanakh Asotsiatsii IUdaiky Ukrainy /* [H. Aronov, editor] (Kyiv: Asotsiatsiia IUdaiky Ukrainy, no. 1-8, 1995-2001).

The remainder of the present article comprises a selected bibliography of YIVO's holdings of Slavic Judaica according to the following categories:

1. Reference books, encyclopedias, dictionaries, bibliographies, sources on East European Jewry
2. History of East-European Jewry, anti-Semitism, biography
3. Holocaust literature, World War II
4. East European Jewish culture (Yiddish literature in the original and translation, folklore, art, education, theater, fiction, poetry, Jewish wit and humor)
5. Conferences, congresses, symposiums on East European Jewry.

Additional bibliographic information on publications listed below may be obtained from the YIVO library's online catalog (http://yivo.cjh.org/yivo_search1.htm).

1. REFERENCE BOOKS, ENCYCLOPEDIAS, DICTIONARIES, BIBLIOGRAPHIES, SOURCES ON EAST EUROPEAN JEWRY

Aragunov, M., R. Guseinov, and E. Kerimov. *Gorskie evrei Azerbaidzhana: bibliograficheskii ukazatel'*. 46 p. Baku: Abilov, Zeinalov i synov'ia, 2000.

Bachyns'kyi, P. P. *Dokumenty trahichnoi istorii Ukrainy, 1917-1927 r.* 640 p. Kyiv: Okhorona pratsi, 1999.

Banchik, Nadezhda and Vasilii Shchedrin. *Dokumental'nye istochniki po istorii evreev v arkhivakh SNG: putevoditel'*. Moskva: Izd-vo "Evreiskoe nasledie," 1994-

Chlenov, Mikhail Anatolevich, Mark Kravets, and Mark Maltynskii. *Karmannaia evreiskaia entsiklopediia*. 248 p. Rostov-na-Donu: Feniks, 1999.

Dekhtiarova, Nataliia Anatoliivna. *IEvrei v Ukraini: naukovo-dopomizhnyi bibliohrafichnyi pokazhchyk, 1917-1941*. 2 vols. Kyiv: Knyzhkova palata Ukrainy, 1999-2000.

Dekhtiarova, Nataliia Anatoliivna. *Sholom-Aleikhem: bibliohrafichnyi pokazhchyk tvoriv ta literaturoznavchykh doslidzhen, vydanykh v Ukraini, 1917-1941*. 47 p. Kyiv: Kyivs'ke ievreis'ke kulturno-prosvitnie tovarystvo im. Sholom-Aleikhema, 1994.

Eliashevich, D. A. *Dokumental'nye materialy po istorii evreev v arkhivakh SNG i stran Baltii: predvaritel'nyi spisok arkhivnykh fondov*. 132 p. Sankt-Peterburg: Akropol, 1994.

Published under the auspices of Peterburgskii evreiskii universitet, Institut issledovanii evreiskoi diaspory, and its Istoriko-arkhivnyi institut, TSentr arkhivnykh issledovanii.

Fain, Tat'iana Anatol'evna. *Idish-russkii slovar: dlia shkolnikov*. 231 p. Moskva; Birobidzhan: Ministerstvo obrazovaniia Rossiiskoi Federatsii, 1993.

Feller, M. D. *Pidhotovchi materialy populiarnoi entsyklopedii "Ukrains'ke ievreistvo."* Kyiv: Instytut iudaiky, [1996?-]

Gerasimova, I. P., and S. M. Papernaia. *Istoriia kholokosta na territorii Belarusi: bibliograficheskii ukazatel'*. 104 p. Vitebsk: Vitebskaia oblastnaia tipografiia, 2001.

Guzenberg, Irina, Liudmila Sharashkina, and Svetlana Shatalova. *Žydų tema lietuvos spaudojē 1985-1989 (Bibliografijos rodykle) = The Jewish theme in Lithuanian press 1985-1989*. 150 p. Vilnius: Valstybinis Vilniaus Gaono žydų muziejus, 2000.

In Lithuanian, Russian and English.

Gurevich, V. S. and F. N. Rianskii, eds. *Evreiskaia avtonomnaia oblast': entsiklopedicheskii slovar' = Jewish Autonomous Region: Encyclopedia*. 366 p. Birobidzhan: Izd-vo "Riotip," 1999.

Kalnyts'kyi, Mykhailo. *Ievreis'ki adresy Kyieva = Jewish Addresses of Kyiv*. 1 folded map. Kyiv: Instytut iudaiky, 2001.

Kaplanov, R. M., V. V. Mochalova, and L. A. Chulkova, eds. *Iudaika v stranakh SNG i Baltii: spravochnik*. 263 p. Moskva: Tsentr nauchnykh rabotnikov i prepodavatelei iudaiki v vuzakh "Sefer," 1999.

Kel'ner, Viktor Efimovich and D. A. Eliashevich. *Literatura o evreiakh na russkom iazyke, 1890-1947: knigi, broshiury, ottiski statei, organy periodicheskoi pechati: bibliograficheskii ukazatel'*. 678 p. Sankt-Peterburg: Gumanitarnoe agentstvo "Akademicheskii proekt," 1995. Published under the auspices of the St. Petersburg Jewish University and the Russian National Library.

Khiterer, Viktoriia. *Dokumenty sobrannye Evreiskoi istoriko-arkheograficheskoi komissiei Vseukrainskoi akademii nauk*. 298 p. Moskva; Ierusalim: Gesharim, 1999.

Khiterer, Viktoriia. *Dokumenty po evreiskoi istorii XVI-XX vekov v Kievskikh arkhivakh*. 223 p. Kiev: Institut iudaiki; Moskva: Mosty kultury, 2001.

Kozak, A. F. *Vo slavu Rossii: evrei v russkoi kulture: spravochnik*. 191 p. Moskva: Fizkul'tura i sport, 1996.

Kruglov, Aleksandr Iosifovich. *Katastrofa ukrainskogo evreistva 1941-1944 gg.: entsiklopedicheskii spravochnik*. 375 p. Khar'kov: Karavella, 2001.

Kupovetskii, M. S., E. V. Starostin, and Marek Web, eds. *Dokumenty po istorii i kulture evreev v arkhivakh Moskvy: putevoditel'*. 502 p. Moskva: Rossiiskii gos. gumanitarnyi universitet, 1997. A joint project of Project Judaica, Russian State Humanities University, the Jewish Theological Seminary of America, and YIVO Institute for Jewish Research.

Lukin, V. M. and B. N. Khaimovich. *100 evreiskikh mestechek Ukrainy: istoricheskii putevoditel'*. 2d ed. Ierusalim; Sankt-Peterburg: Ezro, 1998-

Melamed, E. I. and D. A. Eliashevich. *Arkhivnaia iudaika Rossii, Ukrainy I Belorussii: materialy dlia ukazatelia literatury*. 100 p. Sankt-Peterburg: Izd. Peterburgskogo instituta iudaiki, 2001.

Rossiiskaia evreiskaia entsiklopediia. 2d ed. Moskva: Rossiiskaia akademiia estestvennykh nauk; Rossiisko-izrail'skii entsiklopedicheskii tsentr "EPOS," 1994-

Rumiantsev, A. P. *Voskhod–Knizhki voskhoda: rospis soderzhaniia 1881-1906 gg*. 261 p. Sankt-Peterburg: Gersht, 2001. Index to *Voskhod*.

Rutberg, N. I., I. N. Pidevich, and I. A. Besedin. *Evrei i evreiskii vopros v literature sovetskogo perioda: khronologicheski-tematicheskii ukazatel' literatury, izdannoi za 1917-1991 gg. na russkom iazyke*. 596 p. Moskva: Izd-vo Grant, 2000.

Serhiichuk, Volodymyr. *Pohromy v Ukraini, 1914-1920: vid shtuchnykh stereotypiv do hirkoi pravdy, prykhovuvanoi v radians'kykh arkhivakh*. 542 p. Kyiv: Vyd-vo im. O. Telihy, 1998.

Sholokhova, L. V. *Fonoarkhiv ievreiskoi muzychnoi spadshchyny: kolektsiia fonohrafichnykh zapysiv ievreis'koho folkloru iz fondiv Institutu rukopysu.* 841 p. Kyiv: Natsionalna akademiia nauk Ukrainy, 2001.

Shpitalnik, Sarra. *Evrei Moldovy: deiatel'nost' evreev v kul'ture, nauke, ekonomike Moldovy v XX veke.* 311 p. Kishinev: Evreiskaia Biblioteka im. I. Mangera, 2000.

Sliusarenko, A. G. and A. O. Buravchenkov. *Ukraina v XX stolitti: zbirnyk dokumentiv i materialiv, 1900-1939.* 446 p. Kyiv: [Instytut zmistu i metodiv navchannia], 1997.

Tortshinski, Y. *Kurtser Yidish-Ukrainisher verterbukh = Korotkyi idysh-ukrains'kyi slovnyk.* 206 p. Kyiv: Holovna spetsializovana redaktsiia literatury movamy natsional'nykh menshin Ukrainy, 1996.

2. HISTORY OF EAST-EUROPEAN JEWRY, ANTI-SEMITISM, BIOGRAPHY

Agarunov, IAkov Mikhailovich. *Bolshaia sud'ba malenkogo naroda: vospominaniia.* 153 p. Moskva: Choro, 1995.
Jews and Tats.

Agranovskaia, Marina. *Evrei v Rossii: istoriograficheskie ocherki: 2-ia polovina XIX veka-XX vek.* 256 p. Moskva: Evreiskii universitet v Moskve, 1994.

Agranovskii, G. and I. Guzenberg. *Litovskii Ierusalim: kratkii putevoditel' po pamiatnym mestam evreiskoi istorii i kul'tury v Vilniuse.* 71 p. Vilnius: Lituanus, 1992.

Agranovskii, G. *Stanovlenie evreiskogo knigopechataniia v Litve.* 38 p. Moskva: Evreiskii universitet v Moskve; Ierusalim: Gos. evreiskii muzei Litvy, 1993.

Albats, Evgeniia. *Evreiskii vopros.* 77 p. Moskva: Nezavisimoe izd-vo PIK, 1995.

Alov, A. A. and N. G. Vladimirov. *Iudaizm v Rossii.* 98 p. Moskva: Rossiiskii nauchno-issledovatel'skii institut kul'turnogo i prirodnogo naslediia, 1997.

Alperavicius, Simonas and Izraelis Lempertas. *Jewish Community of Lithuania on the 10th Anniversary of the Revival.* 25 p. Vilnius: Jewish Community of Lithuania, 1999.

Anishchenko, E. K. *Cherta osedlosti: belorusskaia sinagoga v tsarstvovanie Ekateriny II.* 154 p. Minsk: Arti-Feks, 1998.

Asinovskii, S. and E. Ioffe. *Evrei: po stranitsam istorii.* 313 p. Minsk: Zavigar, 1997.

Atamukas, S. *Lietuvos žydų kelias: nuo XIV amžiaus iki XX a. pabaigos.* 431 p. Vilnius: Alma littera, 1998.

Averbukh, Semen. *Nasytilis' my prezreniem* . . . 444 p. Kiev: Glavnaia spetsializirovannaia redaktsiia literatury na iazykakh natsional'nykh menshinstv Ukrainy, 2000.

Beizer, M. *Evrei Leningrada, 1917-1939: natsional'naia zhizn' i sovetizatsiia.* 447 p. Moskva: Mosty kul'tury; Ierusalim: Gesharim, 1999.

Blium, A. V. *Evreiskii vopros pod sovetskoi tsenzuroi, 1917-1991.* 185 p. Sankt Peterburg: Peterburgskii evreiskii universitet, 1996.

Bogomolov, Andrei, Mikhail Parkhimovich, and Petr Sokolov, comps. *Voina po zakonam podlosti.* 477 p. Minsk: Pravoslavnaia initsiativa, 1999. Anti-semitic propaganda.

Borovoi, S. IA. *Evreiskie khroniki XVII stoletiia: epokha "khmel'nichiny."* 287 p. Moskva: Gesharim, 1997.

Borovoi, S. IA. *Vospominaniia.* 383 p. Moskva: Evreiskii universitet v Moskve, 1993.

Borshchagovskii, Aleksandr. *Obviniaetsia krov': dokumental'naia povest'.* 398 p. Moskva: Izdatel'skaia gruppa Progress; Kultura, 1994.

Budnitskii, O. V. *Evrei i russkaia revoliutsiia: materialy i issledovaniia.* 479 p. Moskva; Ierusalim: Gesharim, 1999.

Buianov, M. I. *Delo Beilisa.* 124 p. Moskva: Prometei, 1993.

Chernak, E. I. and IA. M. Kofman. *Evrei v Sibiri: sbornik statei.* 169 p. Tomsk: Izd. Tomskogo universiteta, 2000.

Chernova, L. *Perspektivy vozrozhdeniia evreiskikh obshchin v Vostochnoi Ukraine.* 71 p. Dnepropetrovsk: Dzhoint; Institut sotsial'nykh i obshchinnykh rabotnikov, 1996.

Dal', Vladimir Ivanovich. *Zapiska o ritual'nykh ubiistvakh.* 110 p. Moskva: Vitiaz, 1995.

Dubnow, Simon. *Kratkaia istoriia evreev.* 446 p. Moskva: Svarog, 1996.

Dikii, Andrei. *Evrei v Rossii i v SSSR: istoricheskii ocherk.* 2d ed. 527 p. Novosibirsk: Blagovest', 1994.

Dudakov, S. *Paradoksy i prichudy filosemitizma i antisemitizma v Rossii: ocherki.* 637 p. Moskva: Rossiiskii gosudarstvennyi gumanitarnyi universitet, 2000.

Dvorkin, I. S. and T. D. Vyshenskaia. *Evrei v Srednei Azii: proshloe i nastoiashchee: ekspeditsii, issledovaniia, publikatsii.* 296 p. Sankt Peterburg: Peterburgskii evreiskii universitet, 1995.

Eidel'man, IAkov. *Nezakonchennye dialogi.* 156 p. Moskva: Mosty kul'tury, 1999.

Eliashevich, D. A. *Evrei v Rossii: istoriia i kul'tura: sbornik nauchnykh trudov.* 213 p. Sankt-Peterburg: Peterburgskii evreiskii un-t, 1995.

Eliashevich, D. A. *Evrei v Rossii, istoriia i kul'tura: sbornik nauchnykh trudov.* 393 p. Sankt-Peterburg: Peterburgskii evreiskii universitet, 1998.

Eliashevich, D. A. *Istoriia evreev v Rossii: problemy istochnikovedeniia v istoriografii: sbornik nauchnykh trudov.* 176 p. Sankt-Peterburg: Peterburgskii evreiskii universitet, Institut issledovaniia evreiskoi diaspory, 1993.
Eliashevich, D. A. *Pravitel'stvennaia politika i evreiskaia pechat' v Rossii, 1797-1917: ocherki istorii tsenzury.* 790 p. Sankt-Peterburg: Mosty kultury; Ierusalim: Gesharim, 1999.
Elisavetskii, S. IA. *Berdichevskaia tragediia.* 37 p. Kiev: Akademiia Nauk Ukrainy, 1991.
Elisavetskii, S. IA. *Berdichevskaia tragediia: dokumental'noe povestvovanie.* 111 p. Kiev: NIINTI, 1991.
Elisavetskii, S. IA. *Istoriia evreiskogo naroda: kurs lektsii: uchebnoe posobie.* 431 p. Kiev: Gerkon, 2000.
Engel',Valerii Viktorovich. *"Evreiskii vopros" v russko-amerikanskikh otnosheniiakh: na primere "pasportnogo" voprosa 1864-1913.* 133 p. Moskva: Nauka, 1998.
Erusalimchik, German Il'ich. *Raznye sud'by–obshchaia sud'ba: iz istorii evreev Cheliabinska.* 447 p. Cheliabinsk: Izd. Tatiany Lur'e, 1999.
Esterkin, B. L. *Ievreis'ke naselennia pivdnia Ukrainy: istoriia ta suchasnist'; tezy do naukovoi konferentsii, 19-20 lystopada 1992 r.* 125 p. Zaporizhzhia: [Zaporozhskii gosudarstvennyi universitet], 1992.
Etinger, IA. IA. *Eto nevozmozhno zabyt': vospominaniia.* 270 p. Moskva: Ves' mir, 2001.
Evreiskie obshchiny Sibiri i Dal'nego Vostoka. Nos. 2-7. Krasnoiarsk, 2001.
Evreiskoe naselenie iuga Ukrainy: ezhegodnik: issledovaniia, vospominaniia, dokumenty. 320 p. Khar'kov; Zaporozh'e: Evreiskii mir, 1998.
Flink, Eduard. *Fenomen antisemitizma: evreiskii vopros v tsarskoi Rossii i v Sovetskom Soiuze, 1972-1992 gg.: istoriko-publitsisticheskii ocherk.* 267 p. Moskva: Logos, 2001.
Freidenberg, M. M. *Evrei na Balkanakh: na iskhode srednevekov'ia.* 239 p. Moskva; Ierusalim: Gesharim, 1996.
Freiman, Naum and Sergei IAkovlevich Briman. *Khar'kovskaia evreiskaia obshchina v 1918-1920 gg.: ocherki iz istorii evreev Khar'kova.* 80 p. Khar'kov: Evreiskii mir, 1999.
Gefter, M. IA. *Iz tekh i etikh let.* 481 p. Moskva: Progress, 1991.
Gel'man, Anatolii. *Vozrozhdenie '91: 10 let.* 207 p. Kiev: Adin Shteinzalts; Institut izucheniia iudaizma, 2000.
Gel'man, Boris. *Zabveniiu ne podlezhit': sbornik ocherkov i dokumentov o pamiatnike voinam-evreiam v Sevastopole.* 55 p. Sevastopol: B. Gel'man, 2000.
Gerasimova, I. P., Evgenii Anatol'evich Kimmel, and Genrikh Ioelevich Rutman. *Evrei Belarusi: istoriia i kul'tura: sbornik statei.* Minsk: Otkrytyi universitet Izrailia v Belarusi, 1997-

Goral, Aleksandr. *Evreiskaia istoriia dlia detei.* 378 p. Rostov-na-Donu: Feniks, 2001.

Goldshtein, M. I. *Ocherki istorii evreev Poltavshchiny, 1804-1920 gg.* 67 p. Poltava: Skaitek, 1998.

Gurin-Loov, Eugenia and Gennadii Gramberg. *Eesti Juudi kogukond = The Jewish Community of Estonia.* 31 p. Tallinn: Eesti Juudi kogukond, 2001.

Gusev, Viktor Ivanovich. *Bund, Komfarband, IEvsektsiia KP(b)U: mistse v politychnomu zhitti Ukrainy, 1917-1921 rr.* 227 leaves. Kyiv: [s.n.], 1993.

Hrynevych, V. and L. Hrynevych. *Natsional'ne viiskove pytannia v diial'nosti Soiuzu ievreiv-voiniv KVO, lypen' 1917-sichen' 1918 rr.* 150 p. Kyiv: Natsional'na akademiia nauk Ukrainy, 2001.

IArkov, A. P. *Evrei v Kyrgyzstane.* 176 p. Bishkek: [s.n.], 2000.

IAshunskii, I. V. and Viktor Efimovich Kel'ner. *Rossiiskoe evreistvo i mirovaia voina.* 36 p. Moskva: Obshchestvo Evreiskoe nasledie, 2000.

Ioffe, E. G. and Beniamin Mel'tser. *Dzhoint v Belarusi.* 93 p. Minsk: Magic Book, 1999.

Ioffe, E. G. *Po dostovernym istochnikam: evrei v istorii gorodov Belarusi.* 350 p. Minsk: Chetyre chetverti, 2001. 350 p.

Ioffe, E. G. *Stranitsy istorii evreev Belarusi.* 294 p. Minsk: ARTI-FEX, 1996.

Kabanchyk, I. B. *IEvrei v Ukraini: navchal'no-metodychni materialy do kursu "Istoriia Ukrainy."* 2 vols. L'viv: [s. n.], 1999.

Kabanchyk, I. B. *Evrei v Ukraine: uchebno-metodicheskie materialy.* 2 vols. L'viv: [s. n.], 2000.

Kaganovich, Lazar Moiseevich. *Pamiatnye zapiski rabochego, kommunista-bolshevika, profsoiuznogo, partiinogo i sovetsko-gosudarstvennogo rabotnika.* 570 p. Moskva: Vagrius, 1996.

Kal'nitskii, Mikhail. *Sinagoga kievskoi iudeiskoi obshchiny, 5656-5756: istoricheskii ocherk.* 22 p. Kiev: Institut iudaiki, 1996.

Kara-Murza, S. G. *Evrei, dissidenty i evrokommunizm.* 249 p. Moskva: Algoritm, 2001.
  Antisemitic literature.

Katerli, Nina. *ISK: dokumental'naia povest'.* 318 p. Samara: Izdano Samarskim otdeleniem Rossiiskogo evreiskogo kongressa, 1998.
  Fiction.

Kats, A. S. *Evrei, khristianstvo, Rossiia.* 478 p. Sankt-Peterburg: Novyi Gelikon, 1997.

Kel'ner, Viktor Efimovich, Abraham Jacob Paperna, and G. B. Sliozberg. *Evrei v Rossii, XIX vek.* 557 p. Moskva: Novoe literaturnoe obozrenie, 2000.

Kemerov, M. and S. Pivovarchik. *Evrei Grodno: ocherki istorii i kultury.* 124 p. Grodno: Belorusskii gosudarstvennyi muzei istorii religii; Obshchestvennoe ob"edinenie "Grodnenskii evreiskii obshchinnyi dom Menora," 2000.

Khandros, Borys. *Mestechko, kotorogo net: chast' 1: Shtetl*. 322 p. Kiev: Al'terpres, 2000.
Khonigsman, IA. S., Aleksandr Naiman, and Froim Iakovych Horovs'kyi. *Evrei Ukrainy: kratkii ocherk istorii*. 2 vols. Kiev: Ukrainsko-finskii institut menedzhmenta i biznesa, 1992.
Khonigsman, IA. S. *Liudi, gody, sobytiia: stat'i iz nashei davnei i nedavnei istorii*. 136 p. L'vov: L'vovskoe obshchestvo evreiskoi kultury im. Sholom Aleikhema, 1998.
Kleiner, Izrail. *Vladimir (Zeev) Zhabotyns'kyi i ukrains'ke pytannia: vseliudskist' u shatakh natsionalizmu*. 262 p. Kyiv: Kanads'kyi in-t ukrans'kykh studii, 1995.
Kogan, D. G. *Evrei: navety i deistvitel'nost'*. 130 p. Sankt-Peterburg: [s.n.], 1999.
Kopanskii, IA. M. *Dzhoint v Bessarabii: stranitsy istorii*. 122 p. Kishinev: Liga, 1994.
Kopanskii, IA. M., A. A. Berzoi, and K. L. Zhignia, eds. *Kishinevskii pogrom 1903 goda: sbornik dokumentov i materialov*. 523 p. Kishinev: Izdatel'stvo Ruxanda, 2000.
Korchagin, V. I. *Sionskie Protokoly*. 79 p. Moskva: Vitiaz', 1996.
Korohods'kyi, R. M. *Pole vidchaiu i nadii: almanakh*. 391 p. Kyiv: R. Korohods'kyi, 1994.
Kostyrchenko, G. V. *Tainaia politika Stalina: vlast' i antisemitizm*. 778 p. Moskva: Mezhdunarodnye otnosheniia, 2001.
Kostyrchenko, G. V. *V plenu u krasnogo faraona: politicheskie presledovaniia evreev v SSSR v poslednee stalinskoe desiatiletie*. 397 p. Moskva: Mezhdunarodnye otnosheniia, 1994.
Kosvin, Boris. *Assimilianty i drugie*. 159 p. Khar'kov: Evreiskii mir, 1998.
Kozerod, Oleg. *Perelomnye gody: evreiskaia obshchina Ukrainy v pervoe poslevoennoe desiatiletie, 1919-1929 gg*. 150 p. Khar'kov: Evreiskii mir, 1998.
Kozlov, S. IA. *Evrei Moskvy v 90-e gody XX-go veka: deistvitel'no li proiskhodit religioznyi renessans?* 29 p. Moskva: Rossiiskaia akademiia nauk, Institut etnologii i antropologii, 1999.
Krakhmalnikova, Zoia. *Russkaia ideia i evrei, rokovoi spor: khristianstvo, antisemitizm, natsionalizm: sbornik statei*. 244 p. Moskva: Nauka, 1994.
Kuras, Ivan Fedorovich, N. F. Horovs'ka, and IU. I. Shapoval'. *Pam'iataty zarady zhyttia: materialy kruhloho stolu z pryvodu 40-richchia zahybeli chleniv Ievreis'koho antyfashysts'koho komitetu, Kyiv, serpen' 1992 r*. 227 p. Kyiv: [s.n.], 1993.
Kuzniaeva, S. A. *Evreiskie obshchiny Belarusi v kontse XVIII-nachale XX veka*. 34 p. Minsk: RIP "Petit," 1998.

Lazutka, Stanislav Antonovich and E. Gudavičius. *Privilegiia evreiam Vitautasa Velikogo 1388 goda.* 119 p. Moskva: Evreiskii universitet v Moskve, 1993.
Levashov, Viktor. *Ubiistvo Mikhoelsa.* 475 p. Moskva: Olimp, 1998.
Libinzon, Z. E. and D. I. Belkin. *Evrei Nizhnego Novgoroda.* Nizhnii Novgorod: Nizhegorodskii klub evreiskoi kultury: Izd-vo "Dekom," 1993-
Likhachev, Viacheslav. *Istoriia antisemitizma.* 31 p. Moskva: Evreiskii mir, 2000.
Lokshin, A. *Evrei v Rossiiskoi Imperii XVIII-XIX vekov: sbornik trudov evreiskikh istorikov: uchebnoe posobie dlia uchitelei evreiskikh shkol i studentov evreiskikh universitetov.* 687 p. Moskva; Ierusalim: Evreiskii universitet; Gesharim Press, 1995.
Lukin, V. M., B. N. Khaimovich, and V. A. Dymshits. *Istoriia evreev na Ukraine i v Belorussii: ekspeditsii, pamiatniki, nakhodki: sbornik nauchnykh trudov.* 220 p. Sankt-Peterburg: Peterburgskii evreiskii universitet, 1994.
Melamed, Vladimir. *Evrei vo L'vove: XIII-pervaia polovina XX veka: sobytiia, obshchestvo, liudi.* 263 p. L'vov: Sovmestnoe ukrainsko-amerikanskoe predpriiatie TEKOP, 1994.
Mogarichev, IU. M., I. I. Vdovichenko, and A. G. Gertsen. *Evrei v Krymu: kratkii ocherk istorii iudeiskikh obshchin Kryma = Jews in the Crimea.* 63 p. Simferopol': Tavriia-Plius, 1999.
Naiman, Aleksandr. *Antisemitizm–komu eto vygodno?* 73 p. Kiev: Nauchnoinformatsionnoe predpriiatie "Poisk," 1991.
Naiman, Aleksandr. *Ievreis'ki partii ta ob'iednannia Ukrainy, 1917-1925.* 190 p. Kyiv: Natsional'na akademiia nauk Ukrainy, 1998.
Naumov, Vladimir Pavlovich, A. A. Kraiushkin, and N. V. Teptsov. *Nepravednyi sud: poslednii stalinskii rasstrel: stenogramma sudebnogo protsessa nad chlenami Evreiskogo antifashistskogo komiteta.* 398 p. Moskva: Nauka, 1994.
Novi realii Ukrainy: vidrodzhennia ievreis'koi hromady: ukrains'ko-ievreis'kyi dialoh: Ukraina-SShA-Izrail: stenohrama dyskusii, initsiiovanoi Amerykans'kym Ievreis'kym Komitetom ta Posol'stvom Ukrainy v SShA, Vashynhton, DK, 25 bereznia 1996 roku. 75 p. Kyiv: In-t iudaiky, 1997.
Orlianskii, S. F. and V. S. Orlianskii. *Materialy k istorii evreiskoi obshchiny Aleksandrovska (Zaporozh'ia).* 5 vols. Khar'kov; Zaporozh'e: Evreiskii mir, 1997-1999.
Ostretsov, V. *Chernaia sotnia i krasnaia sotnia.* 48 p. Moskva: Voenno-patrioticheskoe literaturnoe obedinenie "Otechestvo," 1991.
Petrova, Nina Konstantinovna. *Antifashistskie komitety v SSSR, 1941-1945 gg.* 338 p. Moskva: Rossiiskaia akademiia nauk, In-t rossiiskoi istorii, 1999.
Pogorel'skii, Sergei. *Russkie i evrei: shans dialoga.* 95 p. Moskva: Informpechat', 1999.

Pohrebyns'ka, Iryna and Maksym Moiseiovych Hon. *IEvrei v Zakhidnoukrains'kii Narodnii Respublitsi: do problemy ukrains'ko-ievreis'kykh vzaiemyn.* 84 p. Kyiv: Instytut natsional'nykh vidnosyn i politolohii NAN Ukrainy, 1997.

Praisman, Leonid. *Delo Dreifusa.* 157 p. Tallinn: Aleksandra, 1992.

Pudalov, Boris Moiseevich. *Evrei v Nizhnem Novgorode, XIX-nachalo XX veka.* 162 p. Nizhnii Novgorod: Nizhegorodskii gumanitarnyi tsentr, 1998.

Rabinovych, IA. I. *Na zlami vikiv: do 1,000-richchia prozhyvannia ievreiv v Ukraini.* 359 p. Kyiv: IA. Rabinovych, 1998.

Reznik, Genri Markovich et al. *Delo Mendelia Beilisa: materialy Chrezvychainoi sledstvennoi komissii Vremennogo pravitel'stva o sudebnom protsesse 1913 g. po obvineniiu v ritual'nom ubiistve.* 393 p. Sankt-Peterburg: Dmitrii Bulanin, 1999.

Reznik, Semen. *Rastlenie nenavistiu: krovavyi navet v Rossii: istoriko-dokumental'- nye ocherki o proshlom i nastoiashchem.* 193 p. Moskva; Ierusalim: Znanie, 2001.

Romanova, V. V. *Evrei na Dal'nem Vostoke Rossii: II pol. XIX v.-I chetv. XX v.* 252 p. Khabarovsk: Khabarovskii gosudarstvennyi pedagogicheskii universitet, 2000.

Rozenblat, E. S. and I. E. Elenskaia. *Pinskie evrei, 1939-1944 gg.* 311 p. Brest: Brestskii gosudarstvennyi universitet, 1997.

Rozenblat, E. *"Zhizn' i sud'ba" Brestskoi evreiskoi obshchiny, XIV-XX vv.* 84 p. Brest: Belorusskii fond kul'tury, 1993.

Ryvkina, Rozalina Vladimirovna. *Evrei v postsovetskoi Rossii–kto oni? Sotsiologicheskii analiz problem rossiiskogo evreistva.* 239 p. Moskva: URSS, 1996.

Savitskii, E. M. *Bund v Belarusi 1897-1921: dokumenty i materialy.* 608 p. Minsk: BelNIIDAD, 1997.

Selianinov, Aleksandr. *Evrei v Rossii.* 144 p. Moskva: Vitiaz', 1995.

Serebrennikov, A. *Soblazn' sotsializma: revoliutsiia v Rossii i evrei.* 522 p. Parizh: YMCA-Press; Moskva: Russkii put, 1995.

Sharlot, Vladimir Mikhailovich. *Krasnyi poias: "Orlovskii" evreiskii vopros.* 51 p. Samara: SamVen, 1996.

Shenfeld, Ignatii. *Ravvin s Gory Kalvariia.* 259 p. Smolensk: Poligramma, 1994.

Shestopal', M. *IEvrei na Ukraini: istorychna dovidka.* 194 p. Kyiv: Oriiany, 1999.

Shirman, Natan. *Detstvo i iunost': semeinyi arkhiv.* 92 p. Khar'kov: Evreiskii mir, 1999.

Shkurko, E. A. *Ocherki istorii evreev Bashkortostana.* 283 p. Ufa: [s.n.], 1999.

Shulgin, V. V. *"Chto nam v nikh ne nravitsia...": ob antisemitizme v Rossii.* 286 p. Sankt-Peterburg: Khors, 1992.

Skir, Aron IAkovlevich. *Evreiskaia dukhovnaia kul'tura v Belarusi: istoriko-literaturnyi ocherk.* 142 p. Minsk: Mastatskaia litaratura, 1995.
Skurativs'kyi, Vadym. *Problema avtorstva "Protokolov sionskikh mudretsov."* 241 p. Kiev: Insitut iudaiky; Dukh i litera, 2001.
Smilovitskii, Leonid. *Evrei Belarusi: iz nashei obshchei istorii, 1905-1953.* 360 p. Minsk: Arti-Feks, 1999.
Solomonik, E. I. *Evrei Kryma: ocherki istorii.* 127 p. Simferopol': Mosty, 1997.
Solzhenitsyn, Aleksandr Isaevich. *Dvesti let vmeste, 1795-1995.* Moskva: Russkii put, 2001.
Šubas, Mejeris. *Talmudinio mokslo žvaigžde: monografija apie Vilniaus Gaona.* 166 p. Vilnius: Vaga, 1997.
Tager, A. S. *TSarskaia Rossiia i delo Beilisa.* 333 p. Moskva: Terra, 1996.
Tatarinov, S. I. *Evrei Bakhmuta-Artemovska: ocherki istorii, XVIII-XX stoletii.* 83 p. Artemovsk: [s.n.], 2001.
Vaiserman, David. *Kak eto bylo?* 232 p. Birobidzhan: Tipografiia n. 3, 1993.
Zil'bert, Maks. *Fenomen ashkenazskikh evreev.* 59 p. Sankt-Peterburg: Omega, 2000.
Zingeris, E. *Selection of Documents on Jewish Heritage and Problems.* 26 p. Vilnius: Valstybes zinios, 1997.
Zisel's, Iosif. *Esli ia tolko dlia sebia . . .* 365 p. Kiev: Institut iudaiki, 2000.
Zisel's, Iosif. *Nekotorye aspekty migratsii evreev Ukrainy: doklad na vos'moi ezhegodnoi mezhdistsiplinarnoi konferentsii po iudaike.* 43 p. Moskva: Porbel, 2000.

3. HOLOCAUST LITERATURE, WORLD WAR II

Abramovich, Aron. *V reshaiushchei voine: uchastie i rol' evreev SSSR v voine protiv natsizma.* 746 p. Sankt-Peterburg: Dean, 1999.
Agmon, Pinkhas et al. *Vinnitskaia oblast': katastrofa (SHOA) i soprotivlenie: svidetel'stva evreev-uznikov kontslagerei i getto, uchastnikov partizanskogo dvizheniia i podpol'noi bor'by.* 191 p. Tel-Aviv; Kiev: Beit Lokhamei kha-Gettaot, 1994.
Alekseev, Valentin. *Varshavskogo getto bol'she ne sushchestvuet.* 157 p. Moskva: Zvenia, 1998.
Al'tman, I. *Russkaia literatura o Kholokoste: khrestomatiia dlia uchashchikhsia.* 109 p. Moskva: Nauchno-prosvetitel'nyi tsentr "Kholokost," 1997.
Barats, Varvara. *Begstvo ot sud'by: vospominaniia o genotside evreev na Ukraine vo vremia vtoroi mirovoi voiny.* 148 p. Moskva: Art-Biznes-Tsentr, 1993.
Baranouski, IA. I. *Minskae antyfashystskae padpolle.* 254 p. Minsk: Belarus, 1995.

Buianov, M. I. *Kholokost i psikhika.* 100 p. Moskva: Rossiiskoe obshchestvo medikov-literatorov, 1998.

Beilesas, Judelis. *Judkė.* 139 p. Vilnius: Baltos lankos, 2001.

Bekker, Mikhail. *Pamiat' bessmertna.* 319 p. Kishinev: Tsentralnaia tipografiia, 2000.

Botvinnik, Marat. *Pamiatniki genotsida evreev Belarusi.* 324 p. Minsk: Belarusskaia navuka, 2000.

Chaika, T. O. *Holokost v Ukraini: istoriia, psikholohiia, etyka: materialy do navchal'noho kursu: dlia vyshchykh navchal'nykh zakladiv . . . ta 10-11 klasiv serednoi shkoly.* 75 p. Kyiv: Stylos, 2000.

Chernoglazova, R. A. *Judenfrei! Svobodno ot evreev! Istoriia minskogo getto v dokumentakh.* 395 p. Minsk: Asobny Dakh, 1999.

Čiplytė, Joana Viga. *Amžina knygos tauta: Lietuvos žydų gyvenimo puslapiai.* 95 p. Vilnius: Homo liber, 2001.

Davydova, G. R. *Ot Minska do La-Mansha, ili dorogami Kholokosta: dokumental'naia povest'.* 231 p. Minsk: Chetyre chetverti, 2000.

Deko, Oleksandr. *Kedoishim: povist'-khronika Shepetivs'koho hetto.* 110 p. Kyiv: [s.n.], 1995.

Eidintas, A. *Lietuvos žydų žudynių byla: dokumentų ir straipsnių rinkinys = The Case of the Massacre of the Lithuanian Jews.* 823 p. Vilnius: Vaga, 2001.

Elisavetskii, S. IA. *Katastrofa i opir ukrains'koho evreistva, 1941-1944: narysy z istorii Holokostu i oporu v Ukraini = Katastrofa i soprotivlenie ukrainskogo evreistva, 1941-1944.* 423 p. Kyiv: Natsional'na akademiia nauk Ukrainy, Instytut politychnykh i etnonatsional'nykh doslidzhen', 1999.

Erenburg, Michail and Viktorija Sakaitė. *Gyvybę ir duoną nešančios rankos = Hands Bringing Life and Bread.* Vilnius: Valstybinis Vilniaus Gaono žydų muziejus, 1997-

Evrei v Velikoi Otechestvennoi voine: vklad v pobedu: katalog vystavki. 16 p. Moskva: Nauchno-prosvetitel'nyi tsentr "Kholokost," 1995.

Ezergailis, Andrew. *[Holocaust in Latvia, 1941-1944: The Missing Center. Latvian.] Holokausts vācu okupētajā Latvija: 1941-1944.* 591 p. Rīga: Latvijas vēstures in-ta apgāds, 1999.

Feldman, Garri. *Zabveniiu ne podlezhit': sbornik materialov o Kholokoste, perezhitom moimi zemliakami.* 251 p. Zhitomir: "Polissia," 2000.

Gefter, M. IA. and E. I. Vysochina. *Ekho Kholokosta i russkii evreiskii vopros.* 295 p. Moskva: Nauchno-prosvetitel'nyi tsentr "Kholokost," 1995.

Ginaitė-Rubinsonienė, Sara. *Atminimo knyga: Kauno žydų bendruomenė 1941-1944 metai.* 225 p. Vilnius: Margi raštai, 1999.

Girshovich, Leonid. *Obmenennye golovy: roman.* 300 p. Moskva: Tekst, 1995.

Glushkin, Oleg. *Krovotochashchaia pamiat' Kholokosta.* 145 p. Kaliningrad: Regional'nyi obshchestvennyi fond "Shofar," 2001.

Gofman, I. D. *Zhivaia istoriia: veterany vspominaiut boevuiu molodost'.* 117 p. Poltava: Kamelot, 2000.

Gurin-Loov, Eugenia. *Eesti juutide katastroof 1941 = Holocaust of Estonian Jews 1941.* 235 p. Tallinn: Eesti Juudi Kogukond, 1994.

Ioffe, E. G. *Inostrannye evrei v Trostenetskom lagere smerti.* 19 p. Minsk; [s.n.], 2000.

Kapilov, Arkadii. *Ischeznuvshie miry: povest' i rasskazy.* 122 p. Minsk: Dzheikh-Sozh, 1998.

Kaplan, IU. G. *Ekho Bab'ego Iara: poeticheskaia antologiia.* 102 p. Kiev: Firma "RIF," 1991.

Kaplan, IU. G. *Vidlunnia Babynoho IAru: poetychna antolohiia.* Kyiv: Instytut iudaiky, 2001.

Katzenel'son, Itzhak and E. G. Etkind. *Skazanie ob istreblennom evreiskom narode = Dos lied vunem ojsgehargetn jidischn volk.* 239 p. Moskva: IAzyki russkoi kultury, 2000.

Khandros, Borys. *Smertni lysty: dokumental'na povist'.* 123 p. Kyiv: Vyd-vo khudozh. literatury "Dnipro," 1993.

Kharkivs'kyi Prosvitnyts'kyi tsentr "Holokost." *Pamiati trahedii Drobits'koho IAru: materialy naukovoi konferentsii, 16 hrudnia 1998.* 52 p. Kharkiv: Prosvitnyts'kyi tsentr "Holokost," 1999.

Khentova, S. M. *Plamia Bab'ego IAra: trinadtsataia simfoniia D.D. Shostakovicha.* 111 p. Sankt-Peterburg: [s.n.], 1997.

Khonigsman, IA. S. *Katastrofa evreistva Zapadnoi Ukrainy: evrei Vostochnoi Galitsii, Zapadnoi Volyni, Bukoviny i Zakarpat'ia v 1933-1945 gg.* 350 p. L'vov: [s.n.], 1998.

Khonigsman, IA. S. *Katastrofa l'vovskogo evreistva.* 56 p. L'vov: L'vovskoe obshchestvo evreiskoi kul'tury im. Sholom-Aleikhema, 1993.

Klokova, G. V. *Istoriia Kholokosta na territorii SSSR v gody Velikoi otechestvennoi voiny, 1941-1945: posobie dlia uchitelia.* 161 p. Moskva: Nauchno-prosvetitel'nyi tsentr "Kholokost," 1995.

Klovskii, D. D. *Doroga iz Grodno.* 430 p. Samara: Samarskii Dom pechati, 1994.

Koval', Viktor Savych. *Put' k Bab'emu IAru: germanskii antisemitizm: istoriia, teorii, politika.* 54 p. Kyiv: Akademiia nauk Ukraïny, 1991.

Kovba, ZH. M. *Liudianist' u bezodni pekla: povedinka mistsevoho naselennia Skhidnoi Halychyny v roky "Ostatochnoho rozv'iazannia ievreis'koho pytannia."* 268 p. Kyiv: Sfera, 1998.

Kovba, ZH. M. *Liudianist' u bezodni pekla: povedinka mistsevoho naselennia Skhidnoï Halychyny v roky "Ostatochnoho rozv'iazannia ievreis'koho pytannia."* 2d ed., rev. 289 p. Kyiv: Instytut iudaiky; 2000.

Kozak, A. F. *Odessa zdes' bol'she ne zhivet.* 155 p. Samara: Izd. gazety "Tarbut," 1997.

Kuodytė, D. and Stankevičius, Rimantas. *Išgelbėję pasauli... : Žydų gelbėjimas Lietuvoje, 1941-1944.* 371 p. Vilnius: Lietuvos Gyventojų genocido ir rezistencijos tyrimo centras, 2001.

Levin, Roman Aleksandrovich. *Mal'chik iz getto.* 96 p. Moskva: Nauchno-prosvetitel'nyi tsentr "Kholokost," 1996.

Levinsonas, Josifas. *Skausmo knyga = The book of sorrow.* 224 p. Vilnius: Vaga, 1997.

Levitas, Il'ia. *Kniga pamiati: Babii IAr.* 300 p. Kiev: I.M. Levitas, 1999.

Liakhovitskii, IU. M. *Evreiskii genotsid na Ukraine v period okkupatsii v nemetskoi dokumentalistike, 1941-1944.* 289 p. Khar'kov; Ierusalim: Biblioteka gazety "Bensiakh," 1995.

Liakhovitskii, IU. M. *Kholokost, "Evreiskii vopros" i sovremennoe ukrainskoe obshchestvo.* 389 p. Khar'kov; Ierusalim: Biblioteka gazeta "Bensiakh," 1996.

Liakhovitskii, IU. M. *Kholokaust na Ukraine i antisemitizm v perspektive.* 147 p. Khar'kov: Bensiakh, 1992.

Liakhovitskii, IU. M. *Perezhivshie katastrofu: spasshiesia, spasiteli, kollaboranty, martirolog: svidetel'stva, fakty, dokumenty.* 201 p. Khar'kov; Ierusalim: Biblioteka gazety "Bensiakh," 1996.

Liakhovitskii, IU. M. *Poprannaia mezuza: kniga Drobitskogo IAra: svidetel'stva, fakty, dokumenty o natsistskom genotside evreiskogo naseleniia Khar'kova v period okkupatsii, 1941-1942.* Khar'kov: Osnova, 1991-

Margolina, S. M. *Ostat'sia zhit'.* 66 p. Minsk: Natako, 1997.

Marianovskii, M. F., N. A. Pivovarova, and I. S. Sobol. *Kniga pamiati voinov-evreev pavshikh v boiakh s natsizmom, 1941-1945.* Moskva: SEIVV, 1994-

Mikhniuk, V. N. *Niametska-fashystski henatsyd na Belarusi, 1941-1944.* 408 p. Minsk: BelNDTsDAAS, 1995.

Mininberg, L. L. *Sovetskie evrei v nauke i promyshlennosti SSSR v period Vtoroi mirovoi voiny, 1941-1945 gg.: ocherki.* 552 p. Moskva: ITS-Garant, 1995.

Neretina, S. S., I. A. Al'tman, and M. IA. Gefter. *Uroki Kholokosta i sovremennaia Rossiia: materialy kruglogo stola mezhdunarodnogo simpoziuma, Moskva, 6-8 aprelia 1994 g.* 136 p. Moskva: Nauchno-prosvetitelnyi tsentr "Kholokost," 1995.

Petrenko, Vasilii. *Do i posle Osventsima.* 160 p. Moskva: Fond "Kholokost," 2000.

Ryvkin, Mikhail and Arkadii Shul'man. *Porodnennye voinoi: pravedniki narodov mira.* 61 p. Vitebsk: "Olimp," 1997.

Shaikin, I. M. *Rasskazhi synu svoemu . . . : vospominaniia kievlian-veteranov Velikoi Otechestvennoi voiny.* 381 p. Kiev: Evreiskii sovet Ukrainy, 1998.

Shapiro, Gershon and S. L. Averbukh. *Ocherki evreiskogo geroizma.* Kiev: [s.n.], 1994-1997. 3 vols.

Sherman, B. P. *Baranovichskoe getto: Koldychevskii lager smerti: spravka-kharakteristika krupnykh prestuplenii fashistov v gor[ode] Baranovichi i raione v 1941-1944 gg.* 99 p. Baranovichi: [s.n.], 1997.

Shlaen, Aleksandr. *Babii IAr.* 414 p. Kyiv: Abris, 1995.

Shur, Grigorii. *Evrei v Vil'no: khronika 1941-1944 gg.* 224 p. Sankt-Peterburg: Obrazovanie-kul'tura, 2000.

Slutskii, Boris. *Teper' Osventsim chasto snitsia mne.* 124 p. Sankt-Peterburg: Zhurnal Neva, 1999.

Starodinskii, D. Z. *Odesskoe getto: vospominaniia.* 110 p. Odessa: TPP "Khaitekh," 1991.

Sushon, Leonid. *Transnistriia: evrei v adu, chernaia kniga o katastrofe v Severnom Prichernomore po vospominaniiam i dokumentam.* 430 p. Odessa: RIO AO kinokompaniia "Iug," 1998.

Suslens'kyi, IAkiv. *Spravzhni heroi: pro uchast' hromadian Ukrainy u riatuvanni ievreiv vid fashysts'koho henotsydu.* 147 p. Kyiv: Tovarystvo "Ukraïna," 1993.

Sutkus, Antanas. *Pro memoria: gyviesiems Kauno geto kankiniams = To the Living Martyrs of the Kaunas Ghetto.* 36 p. Vilnius: Lietuvos Respublikos Kulturos Ministerija, 1997.

Sverdlov, F. D. *Evrei-generaly vooruzhennykh sil SSSR: kratkie biografii.* 272 p. Moskva: [s.n.], 1993.

TSeitlin, E. L. and I. Guzenberg. *Vilniaus getas: kaliniu sarašai = Vilnius Ghetto: Lists of Prisoners.* 2 vols. Vilnius: Lietuvos Valstybinis Žydų muziejus, 1996-1998.

Veterany "Atikvy vspominaiut": vospominaniia evreev-vinnichan, veteranov Velikoi Otechestvennoi voiny. 47 p. Vinnitsa: [s.n.], 2000.

Vilna Ghetto Posters: Jewish Spiritual Resistance. 12 p. Vilnius: The Vilna Gaon Jewish State Museum, 1999.

Vinokurova, Faina. *Evrei Vinnichiny v period Vtoroi mirovoi voiny: maloizvestnye documenty i novye interpretatsii.* 3 vols. Vynnytsa: Anteks, 2000.

Zabarko, Boris. *Zhivymi ostalis' tolko my: svidetel'stva i dokumenty.* 575 p. Kiev: Instytut iudaiky, 1999.

Zgurskii, V. A. *Pamiat' Bab'ego IAra: [kniga-martirolog].* 95 p. Kyiv: Khvylyna movchannia; Moloda hvardiia, 1991.

Zvonov, M. *Teplyi dozhd' v sentiabre.* 271 p. Riga: [s.n.], 1995. Fiction.

4. EAST EUROPEAN JEWISH CULTURE (YIDDISH LITERATURE IN THE ORIGINAL AND TRANSLATION, FOLKLORE, ART, EDUCATION, THEATER, FICTION, POETRY, JEWISH WIT AND HUMOR)

Averbakh, Fira and Evgeniia L'vova. *Evreiskie shkoly na territorii byvshego Sovetskogo Soiuza.* 113 p. Sankt-Peterburg: Peterburgskii evreiskii universitet, 1996.

Averbakh, L. and I. S. Dvorkin. *Pesni osennikh prazdnikov = Songs of Autumn Festivals.* 67 p. Sankt-Peterburg: Izd. Peterburgskogo evreiskogo universiteta, 1996.
Music score.

Averbakh, L. and I. S. Dvorkin. *Pesni Pesakha = Songs of Passover.* 62 p. Sankt-Peterburg: Peterburgskii evreiskii universitet, 1996.
Music score.

Beiderman, O. A. *Kaboles-ponem: lider.* 44 p. Odesa: Maiak, 1994.

Belenkii, M. S. and M. Fishbein. *Biografiia smekha: ocherk zhizni i tvorchestva Sholom-Aleikhema.* 190 p. Moskva: Khudozhestvennaia literatura, 1991.

Belorusskoe ob"edinenie evreiskikh organizatsii i obshchin. *Sinagogi Belarusi: evreiskii kalendar' na 5756 god (1995-1996).* [Minsk: s.n., 1995?]

Belorusskoe ob"edinenie evreiskikh organizatsii i obshchin. *Dereviannye sinagogi Belarusi: 5757: evreiskii kalendar 1996-1997.* [Minsk: s.n., 1996?]

Beregovskaia, E. M. and M. Beregovskii. *Arfy na verbakh: prizvanie i sud'ba Moiseia Beregovskogo.* 231 p. Moskva: Evreiskii universitet; Ierusalim: Gesharim, 1994.

Beregovskii, M. *Evreiskie napevy bez slov.* 182 p. Moskva: Kompozitor, 1999.
Music score.

Beregovskii, M. and E. M. Beregovskaia. *Purimshpil: evreiskie narodnye muzykal'no-teatral'nye predstavleniia.* 646 p. Kiev: Dukh i Litera, 2001.

Beyder, Khayim. *Anekdoty ot Gershele Ostropolera: klassicheskii evreiskii iumor.* 222 p. Ierusalim: Gesharim; Moskva: Mosty kultury, 2000.

Bukhbinder, Yosl. *Poslednii pervyi sneg: stikhi, proza.* 351 p. Moskva: Sovetskii pisatel', 1991.
Translation from Yiddish.

Burg, Yoysef. *Kvity i sl'ozy: opovidannia. Narysy.* 254 p. Chernivtsi: [s.n.], 1997.
Translation of Yiddish fiction into Ukrainian.

Burg, Yoysef. *Tseviklte stezshkes: dertseylungen.* 29 p. Odesa: Maiak, 1997.

Burshtein, A.-M. Kh., B. I. Burshtein, and A. L. Egorov. *Evreiskie narodnye skazki: izdanie dlia vzroslykh.* 63 p. Moskva: Sovmestnoe sovetsko-avstriiskoe predpriiatie Kh. G. S., 1991.

Dotsenko, Sergei, Irina Belobrovtseva, and Vladimir Khazan. *Mezhdu vostokom i zapadom: evrei v russkoi i evropeiskoi kulture: sbornik statei.* 294 p. Tallinn: Tallinskii pedagogicheskii universitet, 2000.

Dubnova-Erlikh, Sofiia. *Khleb i matsa: vospominaniia, stikhi raznykh let.* 296 p. Sankt-Peterburg: Maksima, 1994.

Epshtein, Solomon Borisovich. *Solomon Borisovich Epshtein: katalog proizvedenii.* 20 p. Sankt-Peterburg: Tsentral'nyi vystavochnyi zal' "Manezh"; Evreiskii obshchinnyi tsentr Sankt-Peterburga, 2000.

Evreiskaia shkola. Sankt-Peterburg: [Institut problem evreiskogo obrazovaniia pri Peterburgskom evreiskom universitete], 1994-[1996?]. Continued by Novia evreiskaia shkola, 1998-

Fain, Tat'iana Anatol'evna, T. Mesamed, and N. B. Aranovich. *Idish, 1 klass: uchebnik.* 127 p. Moskva; Birobidzhan: Ministerstvo obrazovaniia Rossiiskoi federatsii, Institut natsional'nykh problem obrazovaniia, Evreiskii filial, 1993.

Fain, Tat'iana Anatol'evna, T. Mesamed, and N. B. Aranovich. *Kalligrafiia: rabochaia tetrad' po evreiskomu pis'mu dlia uchashchikhsia.* 81 p. Moskva; Birobidzhan: Ministerstvo obrazovaniia Rossiiskoi federatsii, Institut natsional'nykh problem obrazovaniia, Evreiskii filial, 1992.

Feller, M. D. *Poshuky, rozdumy i spohady ievreia, iakyi pam'iataie svoikh didiv, pro ievreis'ko-ukrains'ki vzaiemyny osoblyvo zh pro movy i stavlennia do nykh.* 234 p. Drohobych: Vydavnycha firma "Vidrodzhennia," 1994.

Feller, M. D. *Poshuky, spohady, rozdumy ievreia, iakyi pam'iataie svoikh didiv, pro ukrains'ko-ievreis'ki vzaiemyny, osoblyvo pro neliuds'ke i liudiane v nykh.* 375 p. Drohobych: Vydavnycha firma "Vidrodzhennia," 1998.

Galperin, Teodor. *Kontsert nachinaetsia: evreiskaia tema v avtorskoi pesne.* 66 p. Sankt-Peterburg: Evreiskii obshchinnyi tsentr Sankt-Peterburga; Tsentr evreiskoi muzyki, 2000.

Gastello, Oleg. *Poslednii antisemit: roman.* 172 p. Moskva: Gileia, 1999.

Geizer, Matvei. *Evreiskaia mozaika.* 321 p. Moskva: Prometei, 1993.

Genzeleva, Rita. *Puti evreiskogo samosoznaniia.* 318 p. Moskva: Mosty Kultury; Ierasulim: Gesharim, 1999.

Gerber, S. *Lider un gedanken.* 2 vols. Kiev; San Francisco: S. Gerber, 1990-1994.

Gershtein, A. G. *Minskii gosudarstvennyi evreiskii teatr Sud'ba odnogo teatra.* 95 p. Minsk: Chetyre chetverti, 2000.

Girshin, Mark. *Mozaika.* 422 p. Sankt-Peterburg: Zhurnal "Zvezda," 2000.

Goberman, David Noevich. *Motivy evreiskogo iskusstva v risunkakh Davida Gobermana = Motifs of Jewish Art in the Drawings by David Goberman.* 92 p. Sankt-Peterburg: EZRO, 1996.

Goberman, David Noevich. *Evreiskie nadgrobiia na Ukraine.* Sankt-Peterburg: Iskusstvo, 2001.

Goberman, David Noevich. *Evreiskie nadgrobiia XVIII-XIX vv. na Ukraine i v Moldove: vystavka fotografii.* 15 p. Sankt-Peterburg: Sankt-Peterburgskii Soiuz khudozhnikov Rossii; Evreiskii obshchinnyi tsentr Sankt-Peterburga, 1999.

Goberman, David Noevich. *Zabytye kamni: evreiskie nadgrobiia v Moldove.* 155 p. [Sankt-Peterburg]: Iskusstvo-CPB, 2000.

Goldin, M. *Evreiskaia narodnaia pesnia: antologiia = Jewish Folk Songs: Anthology.* 444 p. Sankt-Peterburg: Kompozitor, 1994.

Goldman, Mikhail. *Na svoei zemle–chuzhie: povest', rasskazy.* 151 p. L'vov: SP "Tekop," 1993.

Grinberg, Aleksandr. *Na nive zdravookhraneniia: evrei-mediki v Moldove.* 106 p. Kishenev: Khesed Ieguda, 1998.

Grozovskii, Mikhail and Evgenii Vladimirovich Vitkovskii. *Svet dvuedinnyi: evrei i Rossiia v sovremennoi poezii.* 518 p. Moskva: Izd-vo AO "Kh.G.S.," 1996.

IAkobson, G. M., D. V. Levin, and V. A. Pantiukhin. *Evreiskaia tematika na markirovannykh pochtovykh kartochkakh SSSR: 1929-1991: katalog-spravochnik.* 39 p. Moskva: [s.n.], 2000.

IAnover, IA. and N. Bakulina. *Masterstvo i vdokhnovenie: sbornik tvorcheskikh rabot.* 227 p. Kiev: TSentr evreiskogo obrazovaniia Ukrainy, 1999. Jewish education in Ukraine.

Ioffe, E. G. and H. Reles. *Mudrye evreiskie skazki.* 271 p. Minsk: Uradzhai, 1999.

Izrailevich, Grigorii. *Grigorii Izrailevich: katalog vystavki.* 31 p. Sankt-Peterburg: Muzei Anny Akhmatovoi v Fontannom dome; Evreiskii obshchinnyi tsentr Sankt-Peterburga, 2001.

Ivanov, V. V. *Mnemozina: dokumenty i fakty iz istorii russkogo teatra XX veka.* Moskva: GITIS, 1996- Includes monograph about Moscow State Yiddish theater GOSET.

Ivanov, V. V. *Russkie sezony: teatr Gabima.* 315 p. Moskva: Artist Rezhisser Teatr, 1999.

Jacovskis, Jokubas. *Žydų anekdotai.* 221 p. Vilnius: Lituanus, 1994.

Jankevičienė, Algė. *Vilniaus Didžioji sinagoga = The Great Synagogue of Vilnius.* 35 p. Vilnius: Savastis, 1996.

Kaplan, Anatolii L. and Joseph Kiblitsky. *Anatolii Kaplan: zhivopis', grafika, keramika, steklo, skul'ptura.* 59 p. [S.-Peterburg]: Palace Edition, 1995.

Kariv, Arkan and IU. Karabchievskii. *Zhizn' Aleksandra Zil'bera: perevodchik.* 365 p. Moskva: Mosty kultury; Ierusalim: Gesharim, 2001.

Kats, Valerii. *"Plius emigratsiia . . .": rasskazy.* 231 p. Moskva: Mosty kultury; Ierusalim: Gesharim, 2001.

Kazinets, V. *Evreiskie anekdoty = Yidishe mayses*. 28 p. [Riga]: [Izd. "Arods"], [1991].

Kazovskii, G. *Khudozhniki Vitebska: Ieguda Pen i ego ucheniki*. 76 p. Moskva: Imidzh, [1991?].

Khait, A. and A. Levenbuk. *1001 evreiskii anekdot: Made in Russia*. 382 p. Moskva: Eksmo-press, 2001.

Kharik, Izi. *Otsel' krichu v griadushchie goda: stikhi i poemy*. 282 p. Minsk: Chetyre chetverti, 1998.

Khavele: Yidish folks-maysele. 12 p. Kyiv: Veselka, 1992. In Yiddish and Ukrainian.

Khazan, Vladimir. *Osobennyi evreisko-russkii vozdukh: k problematike i poetike russko-evreiskogo literaturnogo dialoga v XX veke*. 431 p. Moskva: Mosty kultury, 2001. Includes extensive bibliography.

Kontsept grekha v slavianskoi i evreiskoi kulturnoi traditsii: sbornik statei. 232 p. Moskva: Tsentr nauchnykh rabotnikov i prepodavatelei iudaiki v vuzakh "Sefer"; Mezhdunarodnyi tsentr universitetskogo prepodavaniia evreiskoi tsivilizatsii (Evreiskii universitet, Ierusalim); Institut slavianovedeniia Rossiiskoi akademii nauk, 2000.

Kopytova, G. V. *Obshchestvo evreiskoi narodnoi muzyki v Peterburge-Petrograde*. 71 p. Sankt-Peterburg: EZRO, 1997.

Kostanian, R. and S. Atamukas. *The Jewish State Museum of Lithuania*. 52 p. Vilnius: The Museum, 1996.

Kudish, Efim Iosofovich. *Literaturnoe nasledie Evreiskoi avtonomnoi oblasti: tvorcheskie poiski i nakhodki*. Birobidzhan: [s.n.], 1995-

Kurganov, E. and Henrietta Mondry. *Vasilii Rozanov i evrei*. 269 p. Sankt-Peterburg: Akademicheskii proekt, 2000.

Lavskii, V. V. *Khasidskaia mudrost'*. 276 p. Moskva: Aleteia, 1999.

Lekhaim = Lehayim: iz evreiskogo folklora. 382 p. Minsk: Uradzhai, 2000.

Lemster, Moshe. *Evreiskii dozhd': stikhotvoreniia*. 143 p. Kishinev: Lira, 1997.

Lemster, Moshe. *Evreiskii basnopisets i mudrets Eliezer Shteinbarg*. 241 p. Kishinev: Izdatelstvo Ruxanda, 1999.

Levitina, Viktoriia. . . . *I evrei, moia krov': evreiskaia drama–russkaia stsena*; Jabotinsky, Vladimir. *Ladno*. 343 p. Moskva: Vozdushnyi transport, 1991.

Liampertenė, L. *Evreiskoe schaste: kniga evreiskogo iumora*. 111 p. Vilnius: IAD, 1991.

Lifshitsaite, Nekhama. *Evreiskie pesni: iz repertuara Nekhamy Lifshitsaite: dlia golosa s fortepiano = Yidishe lider: funem repertuar fun Nehameh*

Lifshits: far shtime un klavir. 65 p. [Sankt-Peterburg]: Evreiskii obshchinnyi tsentr Sankt-Peterburga, 2000.

Liki zabytykh predkov: vystavka staroi evreiskoi fotografii. 14 p. Vitebsk: [s.n.], 2000.

Lizen, Aleksander. *Alkhimik: tragikomicheskii roman.* 177 p. L'vov: L'vovskoe obshchestvo evreiskoi kul'tury im. Sholom-Aleikhema, 1999.

Lizen, Aleksander. *Amol iz geven a meylekh: balades.* 29 p. Odesa: Maiak, 1996.

Markish, David. *Evrei Petra Velikogo, ili, Khronika iz zhizni prokhozhikh liudei, 1689-1738: roman.* 333 p. Sankt-Peterburg: Limbus Press, 2001.

Markish, Peretz. *Narechenyi zaviriukhy: virshi i poemy.* 227 p. Kyiv: Sfera, 2000.

Markish, Shimon Peretsovich. *Babel' i drugie.* 234 p. Moskva; Ierusalim: [Gesharim], 1997.

Markish, Shimon Peretsovich. *Rodnoi golos: stranitsy russko-evreiskoi literatury kontsa XIX-nachala XX v.* 463 p. Kyiv: Dukh i litera, 2001.

Mininberg, L. L. *Evrei v rossiiskom i sovetskom sporte, 1891-1991.* 206 p. Moskva: [s.n.], 1998.

Nikolaeva, Elena Viktorovna, Ruslan Kondratiuk, and Nina Shestopalova. . . . *Rodimyi moi krai, kolybel'naia prystan' . . . : ZHitomir v zhizni vydaiushchegosia evreiskogo poeta Khaima Nakhmana Bialika.* 32 p. ZHitomir: Volyn', 1999.

Obshchestvo evreiskoi kultury Respubliki Moldova. *Evrei v dukhovnoi zhizni Moldovy: stranitsy istorii i sovremennost'.* 196 p. Kishinev: Institut natsional'nykh menshinstv (Academia de Ştiinţe a Republicii Moldova), 1997.

Pagirskaja, A. *Žydų valgiai.* 110 p. Vilnius: Yad, 1992.
Jewish cookbook.

Peretz, Isaac Leib. *Narodni opovidannia.* 93 p. Kyiv: Media-Ukraïna, 1994.

Padlipski, A. *Vasil'kovye gody Marka Shagala, ili, Vitebsk v sud'be khudozhnika.* 71 p. Vitebsk: Vitebskii kraevedcheskii fond im. A. Sapunova, 1997.

Polonskii, Pinkhas and M. Kitrosskaia. *Dolg zhivykh: evreiskie traditsii pokhoron i traura.* 178 p. Kishinev: Liga, 1994.

Polyanker, Hirsh. *Bam kval: fun mayne Notits-bikhlekh.* 44 p. Odesa: Maiak, 1995.

Polyanker, Hirsh. *Der oytser: freylekhe un umetike mayses.* 334 p. Kyiv: Holovna spetsializovana redaktsiia literatury movami natsional'nykh menshin Ukraïny, 1996.
Yiddish fiction.

Povartsov, Sergei. *Prichina smerti–rasstrel: khronika poslednikh dnei Isaaka Babelia.* 188 p. Moskva: TERRA, 1996.

Pravda istorii: diialnist' ievreiskoi kul'turno-prosvitnits'koi orhanizatsii "Kulturna liga" u Kyievi, 1918-1925: zbirnyk dokumentiv i materialiv. 207 p. Kyiv: Kyi, 2001.

Raize, E. S. *Evreiskie narodnye skazki: predaniia, bylichki, rasskazy, anekdoty*. 492 p. Sankt-Peterburg: Symposium, 1999.

Reles, H. *V kraiu svetlykh berez*. 395 p. Minsk: E. S. Galperin, 1997.

Reles, H. *Z tykh zha krynits: vershy i paemy*. 156 p. Minsk: Mastatskaia literatura, 1993.

Yiddish poetry translated into Belorussian,

Riabov, G. *Kon Bliednyi evreia Beilisa*. 316 p. Moskva: Detektiv-Press, 2000.

Roizin, Aleksandr. *Mayne lider vi di toybn: lider*. 43 p. Odesa: Maiak, 1994.

Rozin, M. Z. *Ballada o liubvi: evreiskie rasskazy*. 103 p. Minsk: IPP Gosekonomplana Respubliki Belarus', 1993.

Rubina, Dina. *Odin intelligent uselsia na doroge*. 412 p. Sankt-Peterburg: Simpozium, 2000.

Rubina, Dina. *"Vot idet Messiia!"* 346 p. Sankt-Peterburg: RETRO, 2000.

Ryvkin, Mikhail and Arkadii Shul'man. *Iudel' (IUrii) Pen (1854-1937): khudozhnik i pedagog*. 71 p. Vitebsk: Belorusskoe obedinenie evreiskikh obshchin i organizatsii; Tsentr dokumental'nykh issledovanii "Evrei Belorussii: istoriia i sovremennost'," 1994.

Sagalov, Zinovii. *Sed'maia svecha: p'esy*. 308 p. Khar'kov: Tarbut laam, 2001. Play about Mikhoels.

Sandler, Semen. *Idish: uchebnik dlia russkogovoriashchikh* = Yidish: lernbukh far rusish-reyndndike. 522 p. Moskva: Rossiiskii gumanitarnyi universitet; Evreiskaia teologicheskaia seminariia; IVO–Institut evreiskikh issledovanii, 2001.

Sevela, Efraim. *Prodai tvoiu mat'; Viking; Zub mudrosti*. 573 p. Sankt-Peterburg: Kristall, 2000.

Sevela, Efraim. *Monia TSatskes–znamenosets; Popugai, govoriashchii na idish; Pochemu net raia na zemle; Mramornye stupeni*. 574 p. Sankt-Peterburg: Kristall, 2000.

Sevela, Efraim. *Muzhskoi razgovor v russkoi bane; Ostanovite samolet–ia slezu; Mama*. 558 p. Sankt-Peterburg: Kristall, 2000.

Sevela, Efraim. *Legendy Invalidnoi ulitsy; Toiota Korolla*. 557 p. Sankt-Peterburg: Kristall, 2000.

Sholem Aleichem. *Bluzhdaiushchie zvezdy: roman*. 524 p. Moskva: Tekst, 1999.

Sholem Aleichem. *Izbrannoe*. 316 p. Rostov-na-Donu: FEniks, 2000.

Sholem Aleichem. *Mal'chik Motl: povest'*. Moskva: Tekst, 1999.

Shtetl: literaturno-publitsisticheskii sbornik. 61 p. Khmel'nitskii: Oblastnoi blagotvoritel'nyi fond "Khesed-Besht," 2000.

Shulman, Arkadii. Zdes' ostalas' dusha moia. Vitebsk: Mishpokha, 1999. About Jewish art.

Singer, Isaac Bashevis. Fokusnik iz Liublina: roman. 302 p. Sankt-Peterburg: Amfora, 2000.

Singer, Isaac Bashevis. Meshuga. 308 p. Sankt-Peterburg: Amfora, 2001.

Singer, Isaac Bashevis. Na rozsud do moho tata: vybrani opovidannia. 232 p. Kyiv: Holovna spetsalizovana redaktsiia literatury movamy natsional'nykh menshyn Ukrainy, 2000.

Singer, Isaac Bashevis. Posledniaia liubov': rasskazy. 283 p. Moskva: Tekst, 1999.

Singer, Isaac Bashevis. Shosha: roman. 363 p. Sankt-Peterburg: Amfora, 1999.

Singer, Isaac Bashevis. V sude u moego ottsa: roman; Liublinskii shtukar: roman. 485 p. Sankt-Peterburg: Limbus Press, 1997.

Slobodian, Vasyl', Dariia Lonkevych, and Oksana Boiko. Synahohy Ukraïny = Bate ha-keneset ba-Ukrainah. 180 p. L'viv: TSentr IEvropy, 1998.

Stoliar, Z. L. Evreiskaia narodnaia muzyka v Bessarabii i Levoberezhnom Podnestrove, konets XIX–seredina XX vv. 111 p. Kishinev: Liga, 1998.

Stolovich, L. N. Evrei shutiat: evreiskie anekdoty, ostroty i aforizmy o evreiakh. 3d ed. 255 p. Sankt-Peterburg: [Lenizdat], 1999.

Tkach, Zlata. Imia dobroe svoe. 137 p. Kishenev: Liga, 1996. Music score.

Tkach, Zlata. Klingendike oysiyes. 44 p. Keshenev: [s.n.], 1999.

Tkach, Zlata. Shalom-Aleykhem = Shalom-Alechem: sbornik vokal'nykh sochinenii na ivrite, idish i russkom iazykakh. Kishineu: Pontos, 2001.

Tkachev, IU. G. Rasshirenie natsional'nogo obraza mira v russkoi literature XIV-XVII vekov. Vol. 1, Evrei v drevnei russkoi slovesnosti. 132 p. Chernovtsy: Ruta, 2001.

TSegliar, Iakov. IA spivaiu = Ikh zing: ievreiski pisni. 59 p. Kyiv: Kinor, 2001.

TSeitlin, E. L. Dolgie besedy v ozhidanii schastlivoi smerti: iz dnevnikov etikh let. 272 p. Vilnius: Lietuvos valstybinis žydų muziejus, 1996.

TSeitlin, E. L. Žydų muziejus = Evreiskii muzei = The Jewish Museum. 360 p. Vilnius: Lietuvos Valstybinis Žydų muziejus, 1994.

Usova, N. M. IAkov Kruger: (IAnkel Mordukhovich Kruger, 1869-1940): katalog proizvedenii. 37 p. Minsk: Belprint, 2000.

Vilnius Yiddish Institute. The New Vilnius Yiddish Institute at Vilnius University, Lithuania = Der nayer Vilner Yidisher Institut baym Vilner Universitat in Lite. 15 p. Vilnius: Vilnius Yiddish Institute, Vilnius University, [2001?]

Vovsi-Mikhoels, Nataliia. *Moi otets Solomon Mikhoels: vospominaniia o zhizni i gibeli.* 234 p. Moskva: Vozvrashchenie, 1997.

Z arkhiviv Vukhk, Hpy, NKVD, KHB: naukovyi dokumental'nyi zhurnal. Special issue 3/4 (8/9). Kyiv: Sfera, 1998. Soviet Yiddish culture.

Zakharov, Efim and E. Mishnaevskii. *Evreiskie shtuchki.* 316 p. Rostov-na-Donu: Feniks, 2000.

Zapolianskii, Gavriil. *Subbotnie svechi, vremia tsaria Davida: legendy i byli evreiskikh mestechek, pritchi, pritcha o grebtse, geroi Sholom Aleikhema i Mendele Moikher-Sforima, kartiny narodnoi zhizni, Lubok, slavianskie melodii, motivy raznykh let = Shaboss candles.* 183 p. Moskva: P.S., 1992.

5. CONFERENCES, CONGRESSES, SYMPOSIUMS ON EAST EUROPEAN JEWRY

Dubnovskie chteniia: materialy 1-i Mezhdunarodnoi nauchnoi konferentsii "Nasledie Semena Dubnova i izuchenie istorii evreev v stranakh SNG i Baltii," posviashchennoi 140-letiiu so dnia rozhdeniia uchenogo: sbornik statei. 167 p. Minsk: Chetyre chetverti, 2001.

Evrei v meniaiushchemsia mire: materialy 1-i mezhdunarodnoi konferentsii, Riga, 28-29 avgusta 1995 g. 330 p. Riga: Fond "Shamir" im. M. Dubina, 1996.

Evrei v meniaiushchemsia mire: materialy 3-i mezhdunarodnoi konferentsii, Riga, 25-27 oktiabria 1999 g. 540 p. Riga: Fond "Shamir" im. M. Dubina, 2000.

Evrei v Rossii i EAO: vosstanovlenie istoricheskoi pamiati, obrazovaniia i kul'tury: materialy nauchno-prakticheskoi konferentsii, 17 aprelia 1998 g. 44 p. Birobidzhan: Oblastnaia nauchnaia biblioteka im. Sholom-Aleikhema, 1998.

Evreiskaia muzyka: izuchenie i prepodavanie: materialy konferentsii, Moskva, 1996 = Jewish Music: Research and Teaching: Proceedings of the 1996 Moscow Conference. 123 p. Moskva: TSentr nauchnykh rabotnikov i prepodavatelei iudaiki v vuzakh "Sefer"; Rossiiskaia gosudarstvennaia akademiia im. Maimonida, 1998.

Evreiskoe istoricheskoe obshchestvo (Moscow, Russia), Mezhdunarodnaia konferentsiia "Istoricheskie sud'by evreev v Rossii i SSSR: nachalo dialoga" (1989: Moscow, Russia). *Istoricheskie sud'by evreev v Rossii i SSSR: nachalo dialoga: sbornik statei.* Moskva: Evreiskoe istoricheskoe ob-vo, 1992.

International Annual Conference on Jewish Studies (5th: 1998: Moscow, Russia). *Evreiskaia tsivilizatsiia: problemy i issledovaniia: materialy konferentsii.* 319 p. Moskva: [Probel], 1998.

International Conference on Jewish Studies (6th: 1999: Moscow, Russia). *Materialy Shestoi Ezhegodnoi mezhdunarodnoi mezhdistsiplinarnoi konferentsii po iudaike.* 4 vols. Moskva: Probel, 1999.

International Scholarly Conference Devoted to the 80th Anniversary of the Beylis Trial. *Sprava Beilisa–pohliad iz sohodennia: tezy Mizhnarodnoi naukovoi konferentsii do 80-richchia zakinchennia protsesu u spravi Beilisa, Kyiv, 28-29 zhovtnia 1993 r.* 112 p. Kyiv: Instytut natsional'nykh vidnosyn' i politolohii NAN Ukrainy, 1994.

International Symposium "Lessons of the Holocaust and Contemporary Russia." *Ten' Kholokosta: materialy II mezhdunarodnogo simpoziuma "Uroki kholokosta i sovremennaia Rossiia," Moskva, 4-7 maia 1997 g. = Shadow of the Holocaust: Second International Symposium "Lessons of the Holocaust and Contemporary Russia."* 303 p. Moskva: Fond Kholokost, 1998.

Istoriia evreiskikh obshchin Sibiri i Dalnego vostoka: materialy I regionalnoi nauchno-prakticheskoi konferentsii, 4-5 noiabria 2000 goda. 135 p. Tomsk: Izd. Tomskogo universiteta, 2000.

IUdeo-khrystyians'kyi dialoh v Ukraini: stenohrama seminaru, 19-20 kvitnia 1999 roku, m. L'viv. 148 p. L'viv: L'vivska bohoslovs'ka akademiia; Kyiv: Instytut iudaïky, 2000.

Jewish Educational Congress (1991: Vilnius, Lithuania) *"Lietuvos Žydų švietimas ir kultura iki Katastrofos" medžiaga = The Material of Scientific Conference "Education and Culture of the Jews in Lithuania before the Holocaust."* 278 p. Vilnius: Lietuvos kulturos ir švietimo ministerija, 1991.

Mezhdunarodnaia konferentsiia "Bogoslovie posle Osventsima i ego sviaz' s bogosloviem posle GULAGa: sledstviia i vyvody" (2nd: 1998: Saint Petersburg, Russia). *Bogoslovie posle Osventsima i GULAGa i otnoshenie k evreiam i iudaizmu v Pravoslavnoi tserkvi bolshevistskoi Rossii: materialy mezhdunarodnoi nauchnoi konferentsii, Sankt-Peterburg, 26-29 ianvaria 1997 g.* 186 p. Sankt-Peterburg: Vysshaia religiozno-filosofskaia shkola, 1997.

Mezhdunarodnaia konferentsiia "Bogoslovie posle Osventsima i ego sviaz' s bogosloviem posle GULAGa: sledstviia i vyvody" (2nd: 1998: Saint Petersburg, Russia). *Bogoslovie posle Osventsima i ego sviaz' s bogosloviem posle GULAGa–sledstviia i vyvody: materialy vtoroi mezhdunarodnoi nauchnoi konferentsii, Sankt-Peterburg, 26-28 ianvaria 1998 g.* 175 p. Sankt-Peterburg: Vysshaia religiozno-filosofskaia shkola, 1999.

Mezhdunarodnaia nauchnaia konferentsiia "90 let Obshchestvu evreiskoi narodnoi muzyki v Peterburge-Petrograde, 1908-1919 (2001: Saint Petersburg). *Iz istorii evreiskoi muzyki v Rossii.* 172 p. Sankt-Peterburg: Tsentr evreiskoi muzyki, 2001.

Mizhnarodna konferentsiia "IEvreis'ka istoriia ta kul'tura v Ukraini." *Ievreis'ka istoriia ta kul'tura v Ukraini: materialy konferentsii, Kyiv 22-23 lystopada 1993*. 204 p. Kyiv: Asotsiatsiia iudaiky Ukrainy, 1994.

Mizhnarodna konferentsiia "IEvreis'ka istoriia ta kul'tura v Ukraini." *Materialy konferentsii, Kyiv, 8-9 hrudnia 1994*. 232 p. Kyiv: Asotsiatsiia IEvreiskykh orhanizatsii ta obshchyn Ukrainy; Asotsiatsiia iudaïky, Naukovo-Doslidnyi tsentr, 1995.

Mizhnarodna konferentsiia "Ievreis'ka istoriia ta kul'tura v Ukraini." *Materialy konferentsii, Kyiv, 2-5 veresnia 1996*. 334 p. Kyiv: Instytut iudaiky, 1997.

Mizhnarodna konferentsiia "Ievreis'ka istoriia ta kul'tura v Ukraini." *"Shtetl" iak fenomen ievreiskoi istorii: zbirnyk naukovykh prats: materialy konferentsii, [Kyiv], 30 serpnia-3 veresnia 1998 r.* 389 p. Kyiv: Instytut iudaiky, 1999.

Mizhnarodna konferentsiia "Ievreis'ka istoriia ta kul'tura v krainakh Tsentral'noi ta Skhidnoi IEvropy." *Desiat' rokiv ievreis'koho natsionalnoho vidrodzhennia v postradians'kikh krainakh: dosvid, problemy, perspektyvy: zbirnyk naukovykh prats: materialy konferentsii, [Kyiv], 28-30 serpnia 2000 r.* 389 p. Kyiv: Instytut iudaiky, 2001.

Molodezhnaia konferentsiia SNG po iudaike (2nd: 1997: Moscow, Russia). *Tirosh: trudy vtoroi molodezhnoi konferentsii SNG po iudaike.* 188 p. Moskva: Assotsiatsiia studentov iudaiki; TSentr "Sefer," 1998.

Nauchnaia konferentsiia "Evrei Moldovy i istoricheskaia rodina." *Materialy nauchnoi konferentsii, Kishinev, Aprel' 1998 g.* 72 p. Kishinev: Assotsiatsiia evreiskikh organizatsii i obshchin Respubliki Moldova, 1998.

Nauchnaia konferentsiia "Narod Knigi v mire knig." *Materialy nauchnoi konferentsii, Kishinev, Sentiabr' 1997 g.* 42 p. Kishinev: Obshchestvo evreiskoi kul'tury respubliki Moldova, 1997.

Nauchno-prakticheskaia konferentsiia lektorov Narodnykh universitetov evreiskoi kul'tury Vostochnoi Ukrainy. *Materialy Nauchno-prakticheskoi konferentsii lektorov Narodnykh universitetov evreiskoi kul'tury Vostochnoi Ukrainy v Donetske, 27-30 iiunia 1999 g.* 2 vols. Moskva: Izd-vo "Evreiskii mir," 1999-

Nauchno-prakticheskaia konferentsiia "Evrei v Orenburgskom krae" (1997: Orenburg, Russia?). *Evrei v Orenburgskom krae: materialy nauchno-prakticheskoi konferentsii.* 93 p. Orenburg: DIMUR, 1998.

"Vilniaus Gaonas": Conference, Vilnius, Sept. 1997. Vilnius, 1997.

Za mizhnatsional'nu zlahodu proty shovinizmu ta ekstremizmu: materialy naukovo-praktychnoi konferentsii "Podolannia shovinizmu ta ekstremizmu: naivazhlyvisha peredumova mizhnatsional'noi zlahody i hromadians'koho myru v Ukraini," 8-9 zhovtnia 1993 roku. 136 p. Kyiv: Ministerstvo Ukrainy u spravakh natsional'nostei ta mihratsii . . . , 1995.

Zaporozhskie chteniia "Evreiskoe naselenie iuga Ukrainy," 29-30 maia 1997 g.: doklady i soobshcheniia. 230 p. Zaporozh'e: Zaporozhskii gosudarstvennyi universitet; Zaporozhskoe gorodskoe otdelenienie obshchestva "Ukraina-Izrail'," 1997.

Z'izd ievreiskykh orhanizatsii ta obshchyn Ukraïny; Ievreis'ka konfederatsiia Ukraïny. *Materialy z'izdu: pidsumkovi.* 92 p. Kyiv: Ievreis'ka konfederatsiia Ukrainy, 1999.

NOTES

1. Alexander Frenkel's article, "Jewish Book Publishing Today in the Countries of the Former USSR," appears elsewhere in this volume. Ed.

2. At the time of writing, 38 issues had come out.

From Odessa to Odessa: Russian-Jewish Periodicals of Ukraine, 1860-2000

Vladimir Karasik

SUMMARY. Jewish periodicals have been published in Ukraine, in Russian and Ukrainian, over a 140-year time span. They are systematically described here, starting with the first such journal, *Razsviet* (*Rassvet*; Odessa, 1860-61), with accompanying bibliographical analysis. The central part of the article is a table noting all 311 periodicals' characteristics, including titles, cities and dates of publication, main features, and/or subtitles. Their stages of development, regional distribution, and languages of publication are reviewed. It is noteworthy that at the end of 2000, close to 100 Jewish newspapers, magazines, almanacs, and bulletins were active in the republic. The progress of the Jewish press continues in both quantity and quality. *[Article copies available for a fee from The Haworth Document Delivery Service: 1-800-HAWORTH. E-mail address: <docdelivery@haworthpress.com> Website: <http://www.HaworthPress.com> © 2003 by The Haworth Press, Inc. All rights reserved.]*

Vladimir Karasik is affiliated with the Jerusalem Center for Jewish Press, P.O. Box 26369, Jerusalem 91262, Israel (E-mail: karasik@zahav.net.il). He is a researcher on Russian-Jewish periodicals of the world, and is the author of three monographs and dozens of articles on the subject.
The article was translated by Anna Coburn and Zachary M. Baker.

[Haworth co-indexing entry note]: "From Odessa to Odessa: Russian-Jewish Periodicals of Ukraine, 1860-2000." Karasik, Vladimir. Co-published simultaneously in *Slavic & East European Information Resources* (The Haworth Information Press, an imprint of The Haworth Press, Inc.) Vol. 4, No. 2/3, 2003, pp. 119-150; and: *Judaica in the Slavic Realm, Slavica in the Judaic Realm: Repositories, Collections, Projects, Publications* (ed: Zachary M. Baker) The Haworth Information Press, an imprint of The Haworth Press, Inc., 2003, pp. 119-150. Single or multiple copies of this article are available for a fee from The Haworth Document Delivery Service [1-800-HAWORTH, 9:00 a.m. - 5:00 p.m. (EST). E-mail address: docdelivery@haworthpress.com].

http://www.haworthpress.com/store/product.asp?sku=J167
© 2003 by The Haworth Press, Inc. All rights reserved.

KEYWORDS. Databases, Jewish press, magazines, newspapers, Russian periodicals, Ukraine, Ukrainian, Yiddish

After almost half a century of existence, the Russian-Jewish press[1] has spread to dozens of cities in Europe, Asia, America, and Australia. But it all began in Odessa on May 27, 1860, when the very first Russian-language Jewish journal appeared. By comparison, in the year 2000 eight Jewish publications were coming out in Odessa, among them two weekly newspapers boasting record circulation levels for Ukraine and all of Europe. Between these dates and facts lies the story of the Russian-Jewish press in the nineteenth and twentieth centuries.

Our research has proceeded over the course of more than a decade and included, firstly, an analysis and survey of all other work on this topic. We then traveled to the libraries and archives of Russia, Ukraine, Israel, France, and other countries.[2] This work has resulted in the creation of the *REP-2000* (*Russko-Evreiskaia Periodika* [Russian-Jewish Periodicals]) database. It contains detailed descriptions of over 1,500 periodicals from the world over, published between 1860 and 2000.

The Appendix at the end of the article enumerates, for the first time, the 311 Jewish newspapers, journals, bulletins, and almanacs that have been published in Ukraine. The table is arranged chronologically, with opening and closing dates (month and year) given for each title. In addition to its title, place, and dates of publication, each edition's particular specialization is also included. When this is noted in the publication's subtitle it appears within quotation marks. As distinguished from standard bibliographical descriptions, the interested reader may readily use this table to analyze the evolution of periodicals over time, as well as their proliferation throughout regions and cities. This article is consequently limited to five brief conclusions in the form of theses.

THESES

1. Contrasting Periods

As the Appendix reveals, the evolution of the Jewish press may be divided into five periods, and these are characteristic for Ukraine as well as for the Russian Empire and its successors, the USSR and the CIS. This division, shown in Table 1, is a schematic one.

Period I (1860-1916) covers the 20 years of silence after the 1871 pogroms as well as the revolutionary year of 1906. Generally speaking, though, devel-

TABLE 1. Period Breakdown of the Jewish Press in Ukraine (1860-2000)

	Period and years	Length of period (years)	Number of publications started in those years	Median number started each year
I	Half-Century Evolution 1860-1916	57	32	0.6
II	Three Year Revolution 1917-1919	3	67	22.3
III	Soviet Ukraine 1920-1934	15	21	1.4
IV	Half-Century of Silence 1935-1987	53	0	0
V	Years of Rebirth 1988-2000	13	191	14.7
	Summary 1860-2000	141	311	2.2

opment during these decades was gradual, from the very first journal, *Razsviet* (*Rassvet* in new orthography) (Dawn), to the last pre-World War I journal, *Sabakh*.

Period II (1917-1919). The February 1917 revolution brought freedom of the press and a sharp increase in the number of periodical publications. Over the course of nine months, from April to December 1917, a record 40 new titles appeared (nos. 003-072[3]); then, in 1918-1919, another 27. However none of these newspapers, bulletins, and leaflets survived past 1920, and the majority of them existed for only a few months or days.

Periods III-IV (1920-1987)–68 years of Soviet rule. In the 1920s, the Soviet Union encouraged periodicals in the Yiddish language,[4] but prohibited Zionist publications in Hebrew and Russian.[5] In the 1930s, however, the entire Jewish press was obliterated.

Period V (1988-2000) began with the first typewritten bulletins in 1988-1989 (nos. 121-124 in the Appendix), and continued with a large number of newspapers and journals, with circulation levels ranging from the dozens to the tens of thousands.

2. Geography of the Jewish Press

The geography of the Jewish press is closely tied to its history. In the beginning of the eighteenth century, Peter the Great opened his "Window to Europe" through Saint Petersburg. Then, in the nineteenth and twentieth centuries, Odessa became for Russian Jews their "Window to Europe," "Door to America," and "Gateway to the Land of Israel." The ships in the port of Odessa brought not only exotic foreign goods, but also the breath of freedom. The port of Odessa launched and continues to launch ships full of emigrants. Not surprisingly, from 1860 to 1897, the entire Russian-Jewish press in Ukraine emanated from Odessa (nos. 001-005). In the early 1900s, it spread from Kiev to the Crimea, and from the Don Basin to the Carpathians. In 1917, it encompassed the very smallest Ukrainian cities. Of all of these cities, however, the most important centers of the press were Odessa, Donetsk, and Elisavetgrad (renamed Kirovograd in 1939[6]).

At the end of the 1980s a "window to Jewry" opened up in southern and western Ukraine. Between the first and second world wars, Chernovtsy belonged to Romania, and L'vov to Poland. Jews here were better able to preserve their roots, and the Soviet authorities did not succeed in eradicating these roots during the postwar years. That is why it was here that Jewish periodicals began to appear (nos. 121, 125, 134). Then, in the 1990s (as was the case earlier, during the early years of the twentieth century), they spread throughout dozens of large and small cities. Kiev, Dnepropetrovsk, and Khar'kov became the largest new centers of the press. In the second half of the 1990s, Odessa resumed its primacy.

3. Ideals and Titles

The editors of the earliest journals–*Rassvet* (Dawn; no. 001), *Den'* (Day; no. 003), and *Sion* (Zion; no. 002) believed in the emancipation and assimilation of Jews. But these journals and this faith did not survive the ensuing pogroms. After a lengthy hiatus, the first newspaper to come out bore the fitting title *Emigratsiia russkikh evreev* (Emigration of the Russian Jews; no. 004). Throughout the entire twentieth century an abundance of *Workers' Gazettes* and *Proletarian Thoughts* vied with *Jewish Futures* and *Jewish Lifes*. By the end of the century this struggle was over. The Communist idea collapsed, while the Zionist idea remained.

After the samizdat bulletins, the first new Jewish newspaper in Ukraine was the L'vov *Shofar*, in March 1990 (no. 125). Soon thereafter, in Kiev, there appeared *Vozrozhdenie* (Rebirth; no. 126), *Edinenie* (Unity; no. 127), and *Khadashot* (News; no. 123). Throughout Ukraine the familiar Yiddish and Hebrew greetings resounded: *Sholem* (Simferopol'; no. 133), *Shabat Shalom* (Dnepropetrovsk; no. 138), and (separately) *Shabat* (Bershad'; no. 141) and *Shalom* (Khar'kov; no. 146). As if taking a respite from the social and national struggle, Jews dreamed of a placid life and gave their newspapers such peaceable names as *Nadezhda* (Hope) (Korsun'-Shevchenkovskii, 1994; no. 169), *Lebn* (Life) (Konotop, 1994; no. 171), *Obshchina* (Community) (Vinnitsa, 1995; no. 186), *Obshchina i Ty* (The Community and You) (Dnepropetrovsk,

1996; no. 199), *Tkhiia = Tehiyah* (Rebirth) (Chernigov, 1997; no. 223). A clear-cut thesis in the guise of a title was concocted in 1999 in Donetsk: *Nasha zhizn' v diaspore i doma* (Our Life in the Diaspora and at Home; no. 265). The Lubavitcher Hasidim of Dnepropetrovsk greet one other with *Navstrechu Moshiakhu* (Meet the Messiah [immediately!]; no. 279). However, the largest religious publications take a less categorical approach–in Kiev there is *Ot serdtsa k serdtsu* (From Heart to Heart; no. 204), Odessa has *Shomrei Shabos* (Observers of the Sabbath; no. 170) and *Or sameakh* (A Joyous Light; no. 197)–and they remain orthodox while becoming excellent community newspapers. All of the titles mentioned in this paragraph are among the most important publications in Ukraine continuing to appear in 2002.

For the Jewish elderly the charitable voice of the *Hesed* organizations resounds most loudly. [The Hebrew word *hesed*–Russian transliteration: *khesed*–meaning benevolence, or charity, is found in a number of periodical titles found in the Appendix. *Ed.*] And in 2000, for the first time, two journals for Jewish women appeared–*Mir evreiskoi zhenshchiny* (The World of Jewish Women; no. 290) in Lugansk and *A idishe mome* (A Jewish Mother; no. 302) in Donetsk. But above all, publications for Jewish children inspire the greatest hope. The journals *Iunyi Izrail'–tsvetnik Iudei* (Young Israel: Flower of Judah; no. 024) (Lugansk, 1909-1912) and *Kolos'ia* (Ears [of grain]; no. 031) (Odessa, 1913-1918) each survived for five years. More recently, the Jewish school in Kiev produced a newspaper, *Erets Khaverim* (Land of Friends; no. 157), for four years (1993-1997), and it might be revived in 2000. However, the Dnepropetrovsk journal *Eladim* (Children; no. 153), founded in February 1993, will certainly survive its first decade.

In 1860, the publishers of *Rassvet* (Dawn) wanted to liberate Jews from their small town *shtetls* and transform them into ordinary citizens. In 2000, these "ordinary citizens" want to become Jewish again, and give the nostalgic name *Shtetl* to their literary anthology in Proskurov (no. 311)–a city that unfortunately now calls itself Khmel'nitskii. In Kiev, the family club Mishpakha publishes a bulletin with an even more affectionate name: *Shtetele-Mestechechko-Gorodochek* (no. 284).

4. The Language of Russian-Jewish Periodicals

Hebrew is used for instructional purposes in the pages of newspapers, and also as the basis of their titles. Two of the four pages of *Chernovitskie listki = Tshernovitser bleter* (Leaves from Chernovtsy; no. 134) are printed in Yiddish. The Khar'kov *Shalom* (no. 146) published one Yiddish page from 1991 to 1994, as did the L'vov *Shofar* (no. 125) from 1994 to 2002. Another record was set in Odessa: from 1994 to1998, ten issues of the Yiddish literary and artistic journal *Mame-loshn* (Mother Tongue; no. 175) were published.

Beginning with Ukraine's declaration of independence in 1991, the Ukrainian language has been gaining importance everywhere, including in the Jewish press. The majority of periodicals use it along with Russian; different material is printed in different languages. Ukrainian is least used in the Don basin, Khar'kov, Crimea, and in publications for young people. It is used the most in the western districts and in the smaller cities of Ukraine.

Informational and scholarly publications include summaries in English, and sometimes complete English variants of some or all issues.

5. The Third Century

The third century of Russian-Jewish periodicals in Ukraine and in the world commenced in the year 2001. Despite all predictions, Jewish life and the Jewish press in Ukraine have not died out, although many activists now publish their newspapers in Tel Aviv or San Francisco. The most recent period (1988-2000, Period V in Table 1) is unique in its length and stability. Table 2 (column 3) clearly shows that the "birth-rate" of Jewish newspapers and journals has increased without pause since the beginning of the 1990s. In 2000, it reached 30 new titles, a figure that was exceeded only in 1917. Nevertheless, in contrast to the explosion of the revolutionary years, as the years advance the periodicals have experienced a lower "mortality rate" (Table 2, column 4). Therefore the increase in numbers has proved to be enduring. Altogether, we observe a steady and unprecedented increase in these periodicals' "population." In Ukraine, at the turn of the century and the millennium, there were almost 100 active Jewish newspapers and journals, periodical anthologies and almanacs, bulletins and leaflets.

Progress has been not just quantitative, but qualitative as well. *Vinnitskaia Ierusalimka* (Little Jerusalem of Vinnitsa; nos. 191 and 234) is apparently the first publication to transmit its 12 to16 pages worldwide, entirely by e-mail. The Kiev *Evreiskii obozrevatel'* (Jewish Reviewer; no. 304), in its second year of existence, had a most efficient and informative website in Russian and English. The Jewish press of Ukraine lives on.

The study of this press must continue as well (see the Bibliographical Essay, which follows). After more than ten years of research, we have tracked down much and made many corrections, but not everything, to be sure. We are certain that the archives of various countries hold titles that are as yet unknown, along with issues of well-known publications that have yet to be discovered. We invite all researchers, publishers, and readers of Russian-Jewish periodicals to participate in this work. Only through our combined efforts can

TABLE 2. Dynamics of the Jewish Press in Ukraine (1988-2000)

Years	Number of publications at the beginning of the year	Started that year	Ended that year	Increase after that year
1988	0	1	0	+1
1989	1	2	2	+1
1990	2	11	3	+8
1991	10	11	4	+7
1992	17	5	4	+1
1993	18	9	3	+6
1994	24	16	5	+11
1995	35	13	9	+4
1996	39	18	14	+4
1997	43	23	13	+10
1998	53	23	15	+8
1999	61	28	13	+15
2000	76	30	9	+21
2001	97			
Summary for the entire period 1988-2000	Number of publications at the beginning of the period: 0; at the end: 97	Number of publications started in the period: 191	Number of publications ended in the period: 94	Increase in publications in after the period: +97

we write this important chapter in the history of Jewish culture and, simultaneously, the Russian press.

BIBLIOGRAPHICAL ESSAY

Publications about the Russian-Jewish periodical press began earlier than the periodicals themselves. A. Dumashevskii's article, "Nuzhen li zhurnal dlia evreev v nastoiaschee vremia i na kakom iazike dolzhen on izdavat'sia" (Is a Journal for Jews Needed in Present Times, and in Which Language Should It Be Published?), appeared in the journal *Russkii invalid* in 1857. Over the next 150 years, hundreds of monographs, brochures, and articles came out, including encyclopedia entries dating from the 1910s to the twenty-first century. Bibliographical articles appeared not only in scholarly publications. From 1881 to 1911 the widely circulated journals *Voskhod* and *Novyi Voskhod* published valuable documentary surveys. In the 1990s and 2000s, our own series of bibliographical outlines was published in the newspapers *Vesti* and *Tribuna* in Tel-Aviv, *Nash Ierusalim, Evreiskii Obozrevatel'* in Kiev, the journal *Vestnik* in Baltimore, and others.

As a final example, we refer to the article by O. Shkoliarenko, "Sovremennaia evreiskaia pressa Ukrainy," (The Contemporary Jewish Press of Ukraine) in the scholarly collection *Desiat' let evreiskogo natsional'nogo vozrozhdeniia v postsovetskikh stranakh* (Ten Years of Jewish Renaissance in the Post-Soviet Countries) (Kiev, 2001: 252-257), which gives a highly misleading perspective on the subject. In the article's table of newspapers that are still being published, the most important publications of Odessa and L'vov, Khar'kov, and Dnepropetrovsk are left out, followed by the claim "that of 84 newspaper titles that appeared in Ukraine between 1988 and 1999, only 33 continued into the year 2000." Unfortunately, the scholarly nature of a journal does not always guarantee the reliability of bibliographical articles.

The ten most important books on the topic are listed below in chronological order:

1. Iashunskii, I. V. *Evreiskaia periodicheskaia pechat' v 1917 i 1918* (The Jewish Periodical Press in 1917 and 1918). St. Petersburg: 1920 (in Russian). Reprint, Tel Aviv: 1970.
   Described are: 81 publications in Yiddish, 9 in Hebrew, 79 in Russian.
2. *Odesskaia periodicheskaia pressa vremen revoliutsii i grazhdanskoi voiny, 1917-1921* (The Periodical Press of Odessa during the Time of the Revolution and Civil War) (in Ukrainian). Odessa: 1929.
   Publications of all genres and in all languages–from Yiddish and Hebrew, to French–are described.
3. Ivask, U. G. *Evreiskaia periodicheskaia pechat' v Rossii* (The Jewish Periodical Imprints in Russia) (in Russian). Tallinn: 1935.
   First print run of only 300 copies, reprinted in Israel; no details available concerning this edition. The late Estonian artist Uno Ivask (died 1922) left a card catalog of 11,000 titles of the entire Russian press, in all languages, beginning in 1703. The Jewish bibliophile Iulii Gens published part of this material as it related to Russian-Jewish periodicals. It is an exceptionally detailed description (in alphabetical and chronological order) of 83 publications beginning in 1860 and extending up to 1917. Of these, 21 are from Ukraine. Some publications are missing, such as our nos. 004, 018, 019, 025, 026, and others that may be found in our Appendix.
4. Cohen, Y. Y., comp. *Pirsumim yehudiyim bi-Verit ha-mo'atsot = Jewish Publications in the Soviet Union, 1917-1960: Bibliographies*. Edited by Kh. Shmeruk (in Hebrew, English, and Russian). Jerusalem: 1961.

On pages 419-444, 158 publications are listed, mostly based on citations in bibliographical books and articles. Many titles are absent (from Ukraine, our nos. 037, 038, 040, 048, 049, 093-095, 097-100, 116-120).
5. Pinkus, B. and A. A. Greenbaum, comp. *Russian Publications on Jews and Judaism in the Soviet Union, 1917-1967: A Bibliography = Pirsumim rusiyim bi-Verit ha-mo'atsot 'al Yehudim ve-yahadut*. Edited by M. Altshuler (in Hebrew, English, and Russian). Jerusalem: 1970.
On pages 205-236, 162 publications are listed. As with the preceding bibliography, which this work updates, many titles are absent (from Ukraine, our nos. 037, 038, 040, 048, 049, 093, 095, 098, 099, 116-120).
6. Suetnov, Aleksandr. *Samizdat: bibliograficheskii ukazatel'* (Samizdat: Bibliographical Index). 2d ed., with additions (1985-1991) (in Russian). Moscow: 1992.
Supplementary chapter, "Evreiskie izdaniia" (Jewish Publications), by V. Karasik.
7. Karasik, Vladimir. *Evreiskaia pressa na russkom iazyke: Rossiia, 1986-1992: bibliograficheskii spravochnik = Jewish Press in Russian: Russia, 1986-1992: Bibliographic Register* (in Russian and English). Moscow: 1992.
Includes detailed descriptions for Russia (parallel texts, Russian-English), and formulates general criteria for identifying Jewish periodical publications.
8. Karasik, Vladimir. *'Itonim, kitve 'et u-firsumim Yehudiyim, Rusyah, 1960-1994 = Evreiskie periodicheskie izdaniia, Rossiia, 1960-1994 = Jewish Periodicals in Russia, 1960-1994* (in Hebrew, English, and Russian). Tel-Aviv: 1994.
In addition to periodicals from Russia, it includes descriptions of Jewish samizdat publications from the entire USSR during the 1970s and 1980s. Authors and members of editorial boards from cities in Ukraine played an active role in many of these publications.
9. Karasik, Vladimir. *'Itonim, kitve-'et u-firsumim Yehudiyim bi-Verit ha-mo'atsot li-she'avar, 1988-1994 = Jewish Periodicals in the Former USSR, 1988-1994 = Evreiskie periodicheskie izdaniia na territorii byvshego SSSR, 1988-1994* (in Hebrew, English, and Russian). Tel-Aviv: 1995.
Includes detailed descriptions of 135 publications (tables in three languages, illustrated), of which 53 are from Ukraine.
10. Kel'ner, V. E. and D. Eliashevich, *Literatura o evreiakh na russkom iazyke, 1860-1947: bibliograficheskii ukazatel'* (Literature on Jews in

the Russian Language, 1860-1947: Bibliographical Index) (in Russian). St. Petersburg: 1995.
Section XXXL (pages 537-572) is "Organy russko-evreiskoi periodicheskoi pechati, 1860-1945" (Organs of the Russian Jewish Periodical Press, 1860-1945). The table containing a union list of publications worldwide serves as a good basis for future research. Many publications are absent (for Ukraine, our nos. 008, 018, 095, 098, and others). The descriptions of our nos. 016, 019, 020, 027, 029, 039, 041, 042, 044, 051, 068, and other items are inaccurate.

In addition to monographs, there are also several articles worth noting, especially those devoted to the Jewish press on the territory of the former USSR:

1. Beizer, Mikhail. "Contemporary Jewish Periodicals in the USSR," *Jews and Jewish Topics in the Soviet Union and Eastern Europe* 12 (1990): 69-77.
2. Beizer, Mikhail. "Jewish Periodicals in the Former Soviet Union," *Jews and Jewish Topics in the Soviet Union and Eastern Europe, 1990-1991* 19 (1992): 62-77.
3. Beizer, Mikhail and Irina Klimenko. "Jewish Periodicals in the Former Soviet Union, 1992-1993," *Jews in Eastern Europe* 24 (1994): 72-84.
4. Zeltser, Arkadii. "Jewish Periodicals in the Former Soviet Union, 1994-1995," *Jews in Eastern Europe* 30 (1996): 58-83.
5. Frenkel, Alexander and Arkadii Zeltser. "Jewish Periodicals in the Former Soviet Union, 1996-1997," *Jews in Eastern Europe* 1-2 (38-39) (1999): 103-142.

The most complete summary of the Jewish press in the territory of the former USSR is found in the recent article by Alexander Frenkel, Eliyahu Valk, and Arkadii Zeltser, "Jewish Periodicals in the Former Soviet Union, 1998-1999," *Jews in Eastern Europe* 1(44) (2001): 92-146. The first of these authors has spent many years collecting and researching the Russian press. The second and third authors are closely connected with research on Belarus and Latvia. Perhaps because of the authors' specializations, this generally very informative article is weakest in its coverage of Ukraine. The newspaper from Kramatorsk (our no. 183) is not only mistakenly ascribed to the year 1996, but also to Russia! There are also seriously inaccurate descriptions of many publications, in particular for Odessa (our nos. 170, 232, 236, and others).

This bibliographical overview underscores the timeliness of our research, along with the need for it to continue and the importance of enlisting the participation of all interested individuals and organizations.

NOTES

1. "Russian-Jewish (periodical) press" is used as shorthand here to refer to Jewish periodical publications not just in Russian, but also in other languages of the Russian Empire and the USSR. Therefore, in "Russian-Jewish periodicals of Ukraine," we include newspapers published in the Russian and Ukrainian languages, combinations of those languages, or Yiddish. [Russian forms of Ukrainian place names are retained throughout this article and in the accompanying tables, reflecting the predominance of that language in the publications that are described here. *Ed.*]

2. Beyond the limits of this article lies the important but voluminous task of describing the holdings of particular publications, and their distribution among specific collections. We have amassed extensive documentation regarding their locations. Runs of newspapers and journals from all periods, directed at a general readership have turned up almost in their entirety in the repositories of many countries. Rare bulletins from 1917 to 1930, and Jewish samizdat publications from the 1980s may be found in specialized archives or private collections. Publications of the 1990s from small cities in Ukraine may be obtained only from their editors. At the present time, largely thanks to our efforts, the Jewish National and University Library, in Israel, possesses originals or copies of the overwhelming majority of periodical issues of the Russian-Jewish press of the world.

3. Hereafter the publication numbers refer to the Appendix.

4. Many Yiddish newspapers included pages in Russian or Ukrainian. We regard those publications as "Russian-Jewish" if their subject matter is Jewish-national in orientation, e.g., the resettlement of Jews on collective farms or in Birobidzhan (nos. 116-120). However, in the 1920s and 1930s, the communist regime devised another type of periodical publication. In hundreds of factories and small plants in Ukraine and Belarus, the majority of the workers were Jews. Their directors and party committees published factory newspapers for them (so-called *mnogotirazhki* [large-circulation papers]), in two languages–Yiddish and Ukrainian (or Russian, or Belorussian). In Berdichev, Vinnitsa, Vitebsk, and dozens of other cities, an enormous number of newspapers bearing titles such as *Shock Worker, Red Textile Worker*, and *Red Brush-Worker* came out. From our perspective, we might consider including the Yiddish sections of those newspapers, but not the Russian or Ukrainian sections. However, their subject matter is standard Soviet, and not Jewish-national: socialist competition, the struggle against "survivals of capitalism" or "enemies of the people." Therefore, for the purposes of this study we do not regard these publications as "Russian-Jewish."

5. The underground Zionist press in the 1920s and 1930s is the least studied layer of the Russian-Jewish periodical press in the USSR. Quite recently, the archives of the GPU-NKVD-KGB have revealed the titles of Zionist publications under watch by the GPU from 1923 to 1924. See O. IA. Naiman, *IEvreis'ki partii ta ob'iednannia Ukrainy, 1917-1925 = Jewish Parties and Associations in Ukraine, 1917-1925* (Kyiv: Natsional'na akademiia nauk Ukrainy, In-t politychnykh i etnonatsional'nykh doslidzhen', 1998: 154-156. Today we have succeeded in finding only individual issues in collections in various countries. For some bulletins (nos. 103-111) their city, or at least region, of publication is known, as well as the organizations publishing them. For others (nos. 112-115), the GPU could determine only that they were "centrally distributed." We include these titles in the Appendix even though it is not known whether they came out in Ukraine or in Russia. Any clarification will be greatly appreciated.

6. Elisavetgrad was renamed Zinov'evsk (Zinovyevsk) in 1924, and Kirovo in 1936. *Ed.*

APPENDIX: Jewish Periodicals of Ukraine in the Russian and Ukrainian Languages (1860-2000)

No.	TITLE	City	Begin	End (>>> = cont'd in 2001)	Comments (Subtitles are in quotation marks)
001	RASSVET	Odessa	05 1860	05 1861	First Jewish periodical to be published in the Russian language.
002	SION	Odessa	07 1861	04 1862	Continuation of the journal RASSVET.
003	DEN'	Odessa	05 1869	06 1871	Continuation of the journals RASSVET and SION. Shut down after the 1871 pogroms.
004	EMIGRATSIIA RUSSKIKH EVREEV	Odessa	07 1891	07 1891	One-day newspaper. The only issue appeared on July 18, 1891.
005	EZHEGODNIK	Odessa	1894	1897	"Russian-Jewish Literary-Scholarly publication."
006	ROSSIIA I AZIIA	Kiev	1897	1899	The first publication in Kiev dedicated largely to Jewish themes.
007	SIONISTSKOE OBOZRENIE	Elisavetgrad (now Kirovograd)	05 1902	04 1905	First publication in the city.
008	SIONISTSKAIA RABOCHAIA KHRONIKA	Odessa	1903	1903	Publication first discovered in one of the private collections in Israel.
009	SIONISTSKAIA RABOCHAIA GAZETA	Odessa	11 1904	12 1904	Organ of the Odessa committee of the Zionist organization.
010	KADIMA	Odessa	01 1906	09 1906	"Zionist Organ of the South-West region." Later EVREISKAIA MYSL' [1] (see no. 016).
011	RUSSKII EVREI	Odessa	03 1906	06 1906	Journal of a terrorist organization.
012	MOLODAIA IUDEIA	Yalta (Crimea)	04 1906	07 1906	First Russian-Jewish periodical in the Crimea.
013	EVREISKAIA RABOCHAIA KHRONIKA	Poltava	04 1906	06 1906	First publication in the city. Closed by the government. In that same year all three issues were reprinted.
014	MOLOT	Simferopol'	06 1906	07 1906	First publication in the city. Territorialists and social democrats. No. 2 confiscated.
015	NEDELIA RUSSKOGO EVREIA	Elisavetgrad (now Kirovograd)	07 1906	07 1906	"Political-Economic and Literary Journal."

016	EVREISKAIA MYSL' [1]	Odessa	10 1906	07 1907	Published in place of the weekly KADIMA (see no. 010), with new enumeration.
017	EVREISKII GOLOS	Odessa	10 1906	09 1907	Earlier (June-September 1906) appeared in Bialystok. Territorialist organ.
018	KAGAL	Khar'kov	08 1907	08 1907	First publication in Khar'kov. Not mentioned in reference guides.
019	IZVESTIIA EVREISKOGO TERRITORIALIST'SKOGO OBSHCHESTVA "ETO"	Kiev	10 1907	01 1908	Publication absent from or not fully described in reference guides.
020	EVREISKII MEDITSINSKII GOLOS	Odessa	02 1908	12 1911	Publication absent from or not fully described in reference guides.
021	NOVAIA IUDEIA	Odessa	04 1908	07 1908	Monthly.
022	LETUCHII LISTOK BUNDA	Odessa	05 1908	05 1908	One known issue, on hectograph.
023	EVREISKAIA BUDUSHCHNOST'	Odessa	01 1909	07 1909	Monthly newspaper.
024	IUNYI IZRAIL' (with suppl. EVREISKAIA DETSKAIA BIBLIOTEKA)	Lugansk	1909	1912	"The Only Weekly Illustrated Journal for Jewish Children." First publication in the city.
025	EKATERINOSLAVSKII REMESLENNIK	Ekaterinoslav (now Dnepropetrovsk)	07 1910	09 1910	First publication in the city. "Ekaterinoslav. Society for the Aid of Poor Jewish Artisans."
026	NA EVREISKIE TEMY	Kiev	02 1911	07 1911	Bund Journal.
027	TSVETNIK IUDEI	Lugansk	01 1912	1914	"Weekly Illustrated Journal for Jewish Children."
028	EVREISKOE OBOZRENIE	Odessa	05 1912	05 1912	One issue appeared.
029	EVREI	Odessa	07 1912	02 1914	Weekly. 11/27-12/10/1912: Changed to daily newspaper ODESSKAIA ZHIZN' (see no. 030).
030	ODESSKAIA ZHIZN'	Odessa	11 1912	12 1912	Daily. (11/27-12/10/1912) Changed from weekly EVREI (see no. 029).
031	KOLOSYIA	Odessa	01 1913	01 1918	Journal for Jewish children.
032	SABAKH	Lutsk (now Volyn' oblast')	04 1914	04 1914	Only known publication from the city. One issue appeared.

APPENDIX (continued)

No.	TITLE	City	Begin	End (>>> = cont'd in 2001)	Comments (Subtitles are in quotation marks)
033	IUNYI IZRAIL'	Elisavetgrad (now Kirovograd)	04 1917	07 1917	"Organ of the Elisavetgrad Jewish Students' Club."
034	MOLODAIA IUDEIA	Odessa	04 1917	09 1917	Publication of the Odessa Zionist student-youth organization "Histadrut."
035	EVREISKAIA MOLODAIA MYSL'	Kiev	04 1917	07 1917	First youth publication in the city.
036	EVREISKAIA MYSL' [2]	Odessa	04 1917	06 1917	Later EVREISKAIA MYSL' [3] (see no. 067), with different enumeration and different publishers.
037	IZVESTIIA TAVRICHESKOGO I ODESSKOGO KARAIMSKOGO DUKHOVNOGO PRAVLENIA	Evpatoriia (Crimea)	05 1917	11 1917	First periodical publication in the Crimea.
038	SVOBODNOE SLOVO	Kherson	05 1917	07 1917	First publication in the city.
039	ET LIBNOT (ET LI-VENOT)	Kiev	05 1917	10 1917	Heading only Hebrew and Latin.
040	EVREISKII SOTSIALIST	Lugansk	05 1917	05 1917	Organ of the United Socialist Jewish Workers Party.
041	VESTNIK FEODOSIISKOI ORGANIZATSII OB'EDINENNOI EVREISKOI SOTSIALISTICHESKOI PARTII	Feodosiia (Crimea)	06 1917	06 1917	Only known publication in the city.
042	EVREISKOE SLOVO	Aleksandrovsk (now Zaporozh'e)	06 1917	08 1917	First publication in Zaporozh'e.
043	EVREISKAIA MOLODEZH	Guliai-Pole (now Zaporozh'e oblast')	06 1917	08 1917	Only known Russian-Jewish publication in Guliai-Pole.
044	NASHE SLOVO	Khar'kov; Ekaterinoslav (now Dnepropetrovsk)	06 1917	03 1918	Organ of Bund, part of the issue shared with RSDRP.
045	NASH GOLOS	Odessa	06 1917	08 1917	Organ of Bund. Later RABOCHII PONEDEL'NIK (see no. 073).

132

046	DOMOI V SION	Kremenchug (now Poltava oblast')	06 1917	06 1917	First publication in the city. Later MOLODOI IZRAIL' (see no. 052).
047	IZVESTIIA EKATERINOSLAVSKOGO RAIONNOGO KOMITETA SIONISTSKOI ORGANIZATSII	Ekaterinoslav (now Dnepropetrovsk)	06 1917	10 1917	From 06/25 to 10/4, five issues released.
048	BIULLETEN' POLTAVSKOGO KOMITETA OB'EDINENNOI EVREISKOI SOTSIALISTICHESKOI PARTII	Poltava	06 1917	06 1917	Only one issue known.
049	PROBUZHDENIE	Novogeorgievsk (Kirovograd oblast')	06 1917	06 1917	Earlier, the city was called Krylov and Aleksandriia. In the 1950s the city was flooded to create the Kremenchug reservoir.
050	SVOBODNYI PUT'	Odessa	07 1917	10 1917	Organ of the party "Poalei-Tsion."
051	PROLETARSKAIA MYSL'	Kremenchug (now Poltava oblast')	07 1917	09 1917	Organ of the party "Poalei-Tsion."
052	MOLODOI IZRAIL'	Kremenchug (now Poltava oblast')	07 1917	08 1917	Continuation of the publication DOMOI V SION (see no. 046), with numeration retained.
053	VECHERNIAIA GAZETA NOMER TRI	Odessa	07 1917	08 1917	Pre-election Bund publication ("Spisok no. 3").
054	ZEMLIA I VOLIA	Lugansk	07 1917	07 1917	Pre-election pamphlet of SRs and United Socialist Jewish Workers Party.
055	EVREISKAIA ZHIZN'	Elisavetgrad (now Kirovograd)	08 1917	08 1917	Only one known issue.
056	NOVAIA IZRAIL'SKAIA ZHIZN'	Kiev	08 1917	08 1917	"Biweekly Nonpartisan Newspaper." Only issue appeared on August 25.
057	PALESTINA	Odessa	08 1917	02 1918	"Journal dedicated to questions of Palestinian Colonization."
058	EVREISKII IZBIRATEL'	Elisavetgrad (now Kirovograd)	09 1917	11 1917	From 09/13 to 11/21 8 issues appeared.

APPENDIX (continued)

No.	TITLE	City	Begin	End (>>> = cont'd in 2001)	Comments (Subtitles are in quotation marks)
059	IZVESTIIA KOMITETA KONOTOPSKOI ORGANIZATSII "BUNDA"	Konotop (Chernigov gub.; now Sumy oblast')	09 1917	09 1917	First publication in the city.
060	EVREISKII PUT'	Ekaterinoslav (now Dnepropetrovsk)	11 1917	12 1917	"Zionist Newspaper."
061	EDINENIE	Odessa	11 1917	11 1917	Publication of the party "Poalei-Tsion."
062	EVREI-IZBIRATEL'	Zhitomir; Poltava	11 1917	11 1917	Pre-election newspaper, "Idishe Folkspartey." Published in Poltava.
063	MAKKABI	Odessa	11 1917	04 1919	"Organ of All-Russia Society of Jewish Sporting Clubs."
064	EVREISKAIA ZARIA	Aleksandriia (now Kirovograd oblast')	12 1917	12 1917	First publication in the city.
065	K VOSTOKU	Berdiansk (now Zaporozh'e oblast')	12 1917	12 1917	First publication in the city. Journal of the Zionist student organization ("Histadruth").
066	EVREISKOE IUNOSHESTVO	Kiev	12 1917	01 1918	Journal of the Central Committee of the All-Russia Union of Jewish Secondary School Students.
067	EVREISKAIA MYSL' [3]	Odessa	12 1917	01 1920	Continuation of EVREISKAIA MYSL' [2] (see no. 036), with different enumeration and different publishers.
068	ZARIA	Lokhvitsy (now Poltava oblast')	12 1917	12 1917	Only known publication in this city. One issue released.
069	KADIMA	Rovno	12 1917	12 1917	Only known publication in this city. One issue released.
070	NASH PUT'	Ekaterinoslav (now Dnepropetrovsk)	1917	1917	One known issue. Date not known.
071	GOLOS IZRAILIA	Kamenets-Podol'skii	1917	1917	First publication in the city. One issue released. Date unknown.
072	SVOBODNAIA EVREISKAIA OBSHCHINA	Kiev	1917	1917	Three known pamphlets. Dates unknown.

134

073	RABOCHII PONEDEL'NIK (later RABOCHII EZHENEDEL'NIK)	Odessa	01 1918	01 1918	Earlier NASH GOLOS (see no. 045), later RABOCHII EZHENEDEL'NIK (see no. 075).
074	GOLOS EVREIA-VOINA	Kiev	01 1918	01 1918	One issue released.
075	RABOCHII EZHENEDEL'NIK (former RABOCHII PONEDEL'NIK)	Odessa	02 1918	09 1918	Earlier RABOCHII PONEDEL'NIK (see no. 073), enumeration retained.
076	VESTNIK MIRA	Kiev	03 1918	03 1918	Publication of the Mildmay Mission to the Jews (Christian missionaries).
077	SION I VOLIA	Kiev	04 1918	05 1918	"Organ of Zionist National Thought."
078	PALESTINA–EVREIAM	Odessa	04 1918	04 1918	Daily newspaper of the Zionist organization in Odessa.
079	RABOCHAIA MYSL'	Odessa	05 1918	05 1918	"Organ of Odessa Committee of United Socialist Jewish Workers Party."
080	BRAT BRATU	Odessa	05 1918	05 1918	One edition. "Society for the Aid of Poor and Sick Jews of the city of Odessa 'Ezras Kholim.'"
081	EVREISKAIA OBSHCHINA	Simferopol'	07 1918	12 1918	Publication of the District Community Council (Va'ad).
082	EVREISKAIA BUDUSHCHNOST'	Kiev	09 1918	09 1918	"Organ of Zionist Socialist Thought."
083	BIULLETEN' OBSHCHESTVA REMESLENNOGO I ZEMLEDELCHESKOGO TRUDA SREDI EVREEV V ROSSII	Kiev; Petrograd (Russia)	09 1918	12 1919	Publication of the organization ORT. No. 1, 3–Petrograd, no. 2–Kiev.
084	NARODNOE DELO	Khar'kov	11 1918	12 1918	"Weekly organ of Jewish Social Thought."
085	STUDENCHESKAIA ZHIZN'	Ekaterinoslav (now Dnepropetrovsk)	1918	1918	"Society Journal of Mutually Reliant Students and Free-Listening Jewish Foreign Comrades."
086	ZARIA	Khar'kov	04 1919	09 1919	"Organ of Jewish National Thought."
087	EVREISKAIA TRUDOVAIA KHRONIKA	Khar'kov	05 1919	12 1919	Organ of Zionist workers' faction "Tseirei Tsion."
088	BIULLETEN' SEKRETARIATA EVREISKOI SOTSIAL-DEMOKRATICHESKOI RABOCHEI PARTII "POALEI TSION" NA UKRAINE	Kiev	07 1919	07 1919	Only one known machine-printed issue.

APPENDIX (continued)

No.	TITLE	City	Begin	End (>>> = cont'd in 2001)	Comments (Subtitles are in quotation marks)
089	BIULLETEN' PALESTINSKOGO EMIGRATSIONNOGO BIURO PRI VREMENNOM MERKAZE SIONISTSKOI ORGANIZATSII V TAVRICHESKOI GUBERNII	Simferopol'	08 1919	09 1919	Two issues released (August 22 and September 25).
090	VOSKHOD	Elisavetgrad (now Kirovograd)	08 1919	11 1919	"Weekly newspaper dedicated to Jewish interests."
091	EVREISKAIA PROLETARSKAIA MYSL'	Kiev; Khar'kov; Moscow (Russia)	08 1919	12 1926	Publication began in Kiev. As of 12/30/1920–Khar'kov; from February 1921–Moscow.
092	EVREISKAIA ZHIZN'	Khar'kov	09 1919	10 1919	Publication of the Jewish cooperative, "Kalkolo."
093	VESTI O PALESTINE	Uman (now Cherkassy oblast'l)	10 1919	10 1919	First publication in the city. Only one known issue from 2(15) October.
094	NASH GOLOS	Kiev	10 1919	10 1919	Only one known issue.
095	KOMMUNISTICHESKOE SLOVO	? [underground]	11 1919	11 1919	Publication first discovered by us in one of the archives in Jerusalem.
096	EVREISKOE SLOVO	Kherson	12 1919	02 1920	No. 1-8 published by the forces of Denikin. No. 9 (02/05/1920) confiscated by the Soviet government.
097	EVREISKII MIR	Odessa	12 1919	01 1920	"Nonpartisan organ of Jewish Democratic Thought."
098	PROLETARSKAIA MYSL' (?)	? [underground]	1919	1919	Publication first discovered in one of the archives in Jerusalem.
099	BIULLETEN' KERCHENSKOGO KOMITETA SIONISTSKOI ORGANIZATSII	Kerch (Crimea)	1919	1919	Only known publication in this city. Dates unknown.
100	VESTNIK EVREISKOI ZHIZNI	Simferopol'	04 1920	10 1920	Publication of the Zionist organization (with the forces of Vrangel').
101	KOMMUNISTICHESKAIA MYSL'	Chernigov	1920	12 1920	First publication in the city. Printed on wrapping paper. Date of origin unclear.
102	IUNYI PECHATNIK	Vinnitsa	1922	1922	First publication in the city. Languages: Russian, Yiddish.

103	EVREISKOE RABOCHEE DVIZHENIE V PALESTINE (?)	? (Vinnitsa oblast') [underground]	1923?	1923?	[A. Naiman, 1998, from 154]: press of Zionist-Socialists of Podolia.
104	K VOPROSAM SUSHCHNOSTI SIONISTSKO-SOTSIALISTICHESKOGO SOIUZA MOLODEZHI	? (Vinnitsa oblast') [underground]	1923?	1923?	[A. Naiman, 1998, from 154]: press of Zionist-Socialists of Podolia.
105	SIONISTSKO-SOTSIALISTI-CHESKAIA MYSL' (?)	? (Vinnitsa oblast') [underground]	1923?	1923?	[A. Naiman, 1998, from 154]: press of Zionist-Socialists of Podolia.
106	IUNYI BORETS (?)	? (Vinnitsa oblast') [underground]	1923?	1923?	[A. Naiman, 1998, from 154]: press of Zionist-Socialists of Podolia.
107	GOLOS TRUDA (?)	Piriatin (Poltava oblast')	1924?	1924?	[A. Naiman, 1998, from 156]: Zionist press (STP and "Right" he-Haluts).
108	GOLOS PODPOL'IA (?)	Priluki (Chernigov oblast')	1924?	1924?	[A. Naiman, 1998, from 156]: Zionist press (STP and "Right" he-Haluts).
109	NASHI TSELI	Priluki (Chernigov oblast')	1924?	1924?	[A. Naiman, 1998, from 156]: Zionist press (Only All-Russia Organization of Zionist Youth).
110	NASH GOLOS (?)	Khar'kov	1924?	1924?	[A. Naiman, 1998, from 156]: Zionist press (SSP).
111	REVOLIUTSIONNAIA MYSL' (?)	Khar'kov	1924?	1924?	[A. Naiman, 1998, from 156]: Zionist press (SSF "Dror").
112	PROLETARSKAIA MYSL' (?)	? [underground]	1924?	1924?	[A. Naiman, 1998, from 156]: "central" Zionist press.
113	PUT' SKAUTMEISTERA (?)	? [underground]	1924?	1924?	[A. Naiman, 1998, from 156]: Discovered in one of the archives. Machine printed, hectograph.
114	TRUMPELDORETS (?)	? [underground]	1924?	1924?	[A. Naiman, 1998, from 156]: "central" Zionist press.
115	YUGEND	? [underground]	1924?	1924?	[A. Naiman, 1998, from 156]: "central" Zionist press.
116	ODNODNEVNAIA GAZETA OZET	Kremenchug (now Poltava oblast')	05 1929	05 1929	First Ukrainian publication of the Society for Jewish Construction Workers.
117	NOVYI PUT'	Cherkassy	05 1929	05 1929	"Daily newspaper of the Shevchenkov District Board of OZET."
118	OZETOVETS	Sevastopol'	09 1934	09 1934	First known Jewish periodical publication in the city. One issue released.
119	ZA SOTSIALISTICHESKUIU POMOSHCH' EVREISKOI AVTONOMNOI OBLAST'I	Khar'kov	11 1934	11 1934	"One-day edition of the Khar'kov State Soviet OZET . . . "

APPENDIX (continued)

No.	TITLE	City	Begin	End (>>> = (cont'd in 2001)	Comments (Subtitles are in quotation marks)
120	ZA SOTSIALISTICHESKII BIROBIDZHAN	Kremenchug (now Poltava oblast')	11 1934	11 1934	"Daily newspaper of the Kremenchug OZET."
121	INFORMATSIONNYI BIULLETEN' CHERNOVITSKOGO EVREISKOGO OBSHCHESTVENNO-KULTURNOGO FONDA (from 1990–SHOFAR)	Chernovtsy	08 1988	09 1993	First new publication in Ukraine. Machine printed, rotoprint. Until no. 6: "Informational bulletin of the Fund for the assistance and preservation of the Chernovtsy Jewish cemetery."
122	BENSIAH	Khar'kov	05 1989	1997	First new publication in Khar'kov. Released irregularly.
123	KHADASHOT [1]: Bulletin	Kiev	09 1989	11 1989	First new publication in Kiev. Printed by hand and by machine. Three issues released.
124	KOL HADASH	Kiev	11 1989	11 1989	Bulletin of the Zionist organization "Irgun Tsioni." One issue released.
125	SHOFAR	L'vov	03 1990	>>>	First new Jewish newspaper in Ukraine. First issue printed 7/03/1990.
126	VOZROZHDENIE (09.1990-10.1994 Title VOZROZHDENIE'91)	Kiev	03 1990	>>>	First new Jewish newspaper Kiev. Issue 1, "March," first printing 3/04/1990.
127	EINIKAIT–EDINENIE	Kiev	03 1990	>>>	In 1990–Bulletin, from 1991–newspaper. Frequency: 2-5 issues per year.
128	BIULLETEN': Information Supplement to the magazine GALUT	Dnepropetrovsk	04 1990	05 1990	First new publication in the city–before GALUT (see no. 131). Two issues released.
129	IGERET	Kiev	06 1990	12 1992	Publication of the Union of Jewish Youth, "BEITAR."
130	INFORMATSIONNYI BIULLETEN' "MAKKABI"	Kiev	07 1990	07 1990	Machine printed, Xerox. One known issue.
131	GALUT	Dnepropetrovsk	08 1990	08 1990	One known issue. Earlier released as BIULLETEN' (see no. 128).

132	ALEF	Donetsk	10 1990	11 1995	First publication in the city.
133	SHOLEM	Simferopol'	10 1990	>>>	First new publication in the Crimea, one of the first in Ukraine.
134	CHERNOVITSKIE LISTKI–TSHERNOVITSER BLETER	Chernovtsy	11 1990	>>>	Two pages, 4-8, in Yiddish, under the subheading TSHERNOVITSER BLETER.
135	SHOLEM	Kherson	12 1990	03 1991	First new publication in the city after 70-year hiatus (see no. 096).
136	MOI IZRAIL'	Chernovtsy	01 1991	>>>	Supplement to newspaper, CHERNOVITSKIE LISTKI (see no. 134).
137	BOKER–UTRO–RANOK	Nikolaev	02 1991	10 1991	First Jewish periodical publication in the city.
138	SHABAT SHALOM	Dnepropetrovsk	04 1991	>>>	First new Jewish newspaper in the city. Included supplements (nos. 243-245, 289).
139	EVREISKIE VESTI [1] (Newspaper)	Kiev	04 1991	>>>	One of the first new Jewish newspapers in Ukraine.
140	SHATIL–ROSTOK	Tul'chin (Vinnitsa oblast')	04 1991	04 1991	Only publication in the city and first in Vinnitsa oblast' after 70 year hiatus.
141	SHABAT	Bershad' (Vinnitsa oblast')	08 1991	>>>	First publication in the city. Since 1998 included supplement KALEIDOSKOP (see no. 242).
142	KHADASHOT [2]: Newspaper	Kiev	08 1991	>>>	Subheading, "News of Jewish Organizations in Ukraine," repeats no. 123.
143	KHASHAKHAR: Supplement to Newspaper "ATV"	Khar'kov	09 1991	09 1991	One issue released.
144	EVREISKOE AGENTSTVO GALICHINY	L'vov	10 1991	>>>	Pages of the Jewish Agency in the newspaper SHOFAR (see no. 125).
145	VESTNIK "LIUDI OSTAIUTSIA LIUD'MI"	Chernovtsy	10 1991	1996	Anthology of documents and evidence from eyewitnesses of the catastrophe in Ukraine.
146	SHALOM	Khar'kov	12 1991	>>>	One of the first new Jewish newspapers in Ukraine.
147	UKRAINA-IZRAIL' [1]	Kiev	01 1992	02 1993	"Journal of literature, art, and politics." Two issues released.
148	MENORA: Pages in newspaper "Odesskii Vestnik"	Odessa	02 1992	1992	First new publication in Odessa. Irregular, 1-2 pages.
149	EVREISKIE VESTI [2] (Bulletin)	Kiev	03 1992	03 1992	One issue released. Machine printed, rotoprint.

APPENDIX (continued)

No.	TITLE	City	Begin	End (>>> = cont'd in 2001)	Comments (Subtitles are in quotation marks)
150	GEULA [1] (Magazine)	Dnepropetrovsk	06 1992	06 1992	"Journal for Those Who Want to Improve the World."
151	ALEVAI !	Dnepropetrovsk	10 1992	1993	"Children's Jewish Newspaper."
152	NOVOSTI EVREISKOI OBSHCHESTVENNOI I KUL'TURNOI ZHIZNI	Kiev	01 1993	03 1995	Machine-printed bulletin (see also nos. 154, 160, 163).
153	ELADIM	Dnepropetrovsk	02 1993	>>>	Illustrated Jewish children's journal.
154	INFORMATSIONNYI BIULLETEN' EVREISKOGO SOVETA UKRAINY	Kiev	03 1993	1994	Machine printed. Contents similar to no. 152. In Russian and English.
155	NOAR	Kiev	04 1993	11 1994	"Kiev City Jewish Youth Club 'Bet ha-No'ar.'"
156	IGERET	Nikolaev	07 1993	1997?	Publication of the Union of Jewish Youth "BEITAR."
157	ERETS KHAVERIM: Jewish School Newspaper	Kiev	10 1993	04 1997	Known supplements (see nos. 193, 207). Renewed in 1998 (see no. 250).
158	HA-MELITS (KHA-MELITS)	Odessa	11 1993	05 1995	Until June 1994–Informational Bulletin, From July 1994–newspaper.
159	BNEI AKIVA–UKRAINA	Kiev	1993	1994	Bulletin of the Youth movement of religious Zionists.
160	EVREISKII KALEIDOSKOP	Kiev	1993	1995	Machine printed. Contents similar to nos.152, 154.
161	EVREISKAIA STRANITSA (in newspaper MELITOPOL'SKIE VEDOMOSTI)	Melitopol' (Zaporozh'e oblast')	02 1994	1995	First Jewish publication in the city. Pagination and enumeration irregular or lacking.
162	SLOVO	Melitopol' (Zaporozh'e oblast')	07 1994	1995	Founder of the Jewish council. Contents sometimes Christian.
163	KHRONIKA EVREISKOI ZHIZNI UKRAINY	Kiev	09 1994	02 1995	Machine printed. Contents similar to nos. 152, 154, 160.
164	EVREISKAIA ISTORIIA I KUL'TURA V UKRAINE	Kiev	10 1994	>>>	Continuation of the scholarly anthology (conference materials), not numbered.

165	SIMKHA	Odessa	10 1994	03 1995	"Bulletin of the Jewish Youth Club 'Gesher'." (see also no. 125).
166	LEKHAIM	Kremenchug (Poltava oblast')	11 1994	01 2000	First new publication in the city (see nos. 046, 051, 052, 116, 120).
167	IGERET	Krivoi Rog (Dnepropetrovsk oblast')	11 1994	11 1994	First publication in the city. Bulletin of the Union of Jewish Youth "BEITAR." One known issue.
168	GEULA [2] (Weekly)	Dnepropetrovsk	11 1994	>>>	"Jewish Weekly Published by the Jewish Religious Society of Dnepropetrovsk."
169	NADEZHDA	Korsun-Shevchenkovskii (Cherkassy oblast')	12 1994	>>>	"Bulletin of the Religious Association of Jewish Organizations in Small Cities of Ukraine."
170	SHOMREI SHABOS	Odessa	12 1994	>>>	Until 02/1995–special issue of newspaper HA-MELITS (see no. 158), then weekly newspaper.
171	LEBN	Konotop (Sumy oblast')	12 1994	>>>	First new publication in the city.
172	SHOLOM	Zhitomir	1994	08 1996	First new publication in the city (see no. 062). Month of origin unknown.
173	AVIV	Kiev	1994	1996	Almanac of the religious organization "Aish ha-Torah."
174	POLE VIDCHAIU I NADII (Ukrainian; Russian title: POLE OTCHAIANIIA I NADEZHDY)	Kiev	1994	1994	Almanac of Ukrainian-Jewish relations.
175	MAME-LOSHN	Odessa	1994	1998	Only new almanac (journal) in Yiddish. Summary and translation in Russian.
176	EVREISKOE NASELENIE IUGA UKRAINY	Zaporozh'e; Khar'kov	1994	>>>?	Known issues: Zaporozh'e,1994; Khar'kov, 1998 ("Yearly").
177	MABAT ANOAR	Kiev	01 1995	09 1996	"All-Ukraine Jewish youth newspaper."
178	GEULA [1]	Khar'kov	01 1995	>>>	Publication of Khar'kov religious society of orthodox Judaism.
179	EGUPETS = IEHUPETS	Kiev	03 1995	>>>	Artistic and journalistic almanac. Languages: Ukrainian and Russian.
180	SHAKHAR	Kiev	03 1995	09 1995	Flyer of the Youth Club "Shakha" of the Israeli Cultural Center.

APPENDIX (continued)

No.	TITLE	City	Begin	End (>>> = cont'd in 2001)	Comments (Subtitles are in quotation marks)
181	ANAHNU (title till 06/1995: ALIAH)	Kiev	05 1995	06 1996	"Informational Bulletin of the Jewish Agency–'Sokhnut Ukraina'."
182	SHALOM ALEIKHEM [1]	Kamenets-Podol'skii (Khmel'nitskii oblast')	08 1995	12 1999	From 2000, the newspaper came out in the city of Khmel'nitskii (see no. 310).
183	YAHAD	Kramatorsk (Donetsk oblast')	09 1995	05 1996	First publication in the city. Student publication of Jewish Sunday school.
184	MENORA	Slaviansk (Donetsk oblast')	09 1995	>>>	In 1996-1999–only Jewish publication in all of Donetsk oblast'.
185	GAN ISROEL	Zhitomir	11 1995	08 1996	"Children's newspaper of the Zhitomir Jewish Religious Society."
186	OBSHCHINA	Vinnitsa	12 1995	>>>	First publication in the city after 73-year hiatus (see no. 102).
187	GILEL	Kiev	12 1995	12 1999	Published by the Solomon International University and Jewish Students' Cultural Center.
188	DAIDZHEST-E	Khar'kov	12 1995	>>>	Publication Khar'kov oblast' committee, "Drobitskii Iar'."
189	DER YID (Title of issue 1: GAZETA)	Khmelnitskii (formerly: Proskurov)	12 1995	1995?	First Russian-Jewish publication in the Khmel'nitskii (until 1954: Proskurov).
190	IGERET	Vinnitsa (?)	01 1996	1996?	Publication Union of Jewish youth "BEITAR." One known issue.
191	INFORMATSIONNYI LISTOK (later: VINNITSKAIA IERUSALIMKA)	Vinnitsa	01 1996	01 1998	Later VINNITSKAIA IERUSALIMKA (see no. 234).
192	IZRAIL'SKII KUL'TURNYI TSENTR	Khar'kov	02 1996	04 1996	Later version: NASHI NOVOSTI (see no. 214).
193	MIST–BRIDGE–GESHER	Kiev	07 1996	09 1996	Supplement of the organization "Aish ha-Torah" in the newspaper ERETS KHAVERIM (see no. 157).
194	GMILUS HESED [1] (Bulletin)	Odessa	03 1996	1996	Later GMILUS HESED [2] (see no. 233) with different numbering, summary, subtitle.

195	ODESSKAIA EVREISKAIA GAZETA	Odessa	04 1996	03 1997	12 issues released in 12 months.
196	SHMA ISRAEL	Kiev	05 1996	11 1996	"Bulletin of the Only Judaic Religious Society in Ukraine."
197	OR SAMEAKH	Odessa	06 1996	>>>	Weekly newspaper of the school "Or Sameakh" and synagogue on Evreiskii Street 25.
198	GOLOS OBSHCHIN–THE VOICE OF THE COMMUNITIES	Kiev	07 1996	1997	Bulletin of the Jewish Council of Ukraine and the European Jewish Congress.
199	OBSHCHINA I TY	Dnepropetrovsk	09 1996	>>>	"Bulletin of the Institute for Community and Social Workers in Dnepropetrovsk."
200	GOLOS HESED AVOT	Kiev	10 1996	10 1996	One bulletin of two pages released.
201	KHESED AVOT OT VSEI DUSHI	Kiev	10 1996	>>>	Includes pages of the Kiev Institute for Community and Social Workers.
202	NOAR GILEL	Khar'kov	10 1996	1997	Publication of the student organization HILEL'.
203	BET HAYENU–SHKOLA	Dnepropetrovsk	11 1996	1997?	"Printing Organ of the Jewish Secondary School no. 144" (Chabad-Lubavitch).
204	OT SERDTSA K SERDTSU	Kiev	12 1996	>>>	"Monthly publication of the Jewish religious society Chabad-Lubavitch."
205	SHALOM	Kremenchug (Poltava oblast')	12 1996	1998?	"Bulletin of Kremenchug City Jewish Religious Community, and the Cultural-Educational Society 'Shalom'."
206	BAT-KOL	Kiev	1996	1997?	Newspaper for "Messianic Jews."
207	MASHGIAKH RUKHANI	Kiev	1996	1996	Suppl. to the newspaper. ERETS KHAVERIM (see no. 157).
208	MIR I MY (?)	Khar'kov	1996?	1996?	One of the publications of the Israeli Cultural Center known only by report.
209	KADIMA	Odessa	02 1997	05 1997	Publication of the organization "Bnei Akiva." Known only by report.
210	RASSVET–SHAKHAR	Sevastopol'	03 1997	>>>	First Jewish newspaper in the city. Named after the Odessa journal RASSVET (see no. 001).
211	KRYMSKIE KARAIMY	Simferopol'	03 1997	03 1997	One known issue. First newspaper in the Crimean peninsula for 80 years (see no. 037).
212	IGERET	Odessa	05 1997	07 1997	Publication of the Union of Jewish youth "Beitar."

APPENDIX (continued)

No.	TITLE	City	Begin	End (>>> = cont'd in 2001)	Comments (Subtitles are in quotation marks)
213	GILEL-L'VOV	L'vov	09 1997	11 1998	Publication of the student organization "Beit-Gilel".
214	NASHI NOVOSTI	Khar'kov	09 1997	>>>	Publication of the Israeli Cultural Center of Khar'kov. Earlier version: see no. 192.
215	EVREISKII MIR	Kiev	09 1997	10 1998	Informational Bulletin of the Jewish Fund of Ukraine (see also nos. 216, 217).
216	JEWISH WORLD (in English)	Kiev	09 1997	10 1998	English language version of the bulletin EVREISKII MIR (see no. 215).
217	Di YIDISHE VELT (in Yiddish)	Kiev	09 1997	10 1998	Yiddish version of the bulletin EVREISKII MIR (see no. 215).
218	BBYO-NEWS: Bulletin of the children's organization Bnai Brit Ukrainy	Kiev	10 1997	10 1997	Published by 9th-grader in the Jewish school. He also put out the bulletins VIRAZH, PRIKOLY, as well as no. 250.
219	GOROD REBE	Dnepropetrovsk	11 1997	12 1997	Publication of Dnepropetrovsk Yeshiva of Chabad-Lubavitch.
220	VESTNIK SIMFEROPOL'SKOGO EVREISKOGO OBSHCHESTVA "YAD EZRA"	Simferopol'	11 1997	04 1998	Later-KHAVERIM (see no. 235).
221	EVREISKII MIR: Vostochno-Ukrainskaia organizatsia "Tarbut Iaam"	Khar'kov; Zaporozh'e	12 1997	>>>	Practically identical to the bulletin EVREISKII MIR (Moscow).
222	ISTOKI: Vestnik Narodnogo universiteta evreiskoi kul'tury v Vostochnoi Ukraine	Khar'kov	12 1997	>>>	Scholarly anthology on Jewish themes. Semiannual.
223	TEHIA	Chernigov	12 1997	>>>	Second newspaper in Chernigov (see also nos. 101, 253, 257).
224	EVREISKAIA MYSL' SKVOZ' VEKA	Dnepropetrovsk	1997	>>>	Scholarly anthology on Jewish themes (conference proceedings). Annual.
225	SIMKHA NEWS (?)	Dnepropetrovsk	1997?	1997?	Publication of the Center of Children's Creative Works. Known only through report.

№	Title	City	Date1	Date2	Notes
226	SHARSHERET	Dnepropetrovsk	1997	07 1999	"Jewish Youth Newspaper with the Jewish Agency ('Sokhnut')."
227	V.E.K.–Vseukrainskii Evreiskii Kongress	Kiev	1997	>>>	"Weekly of the All-Ukraine Jewish Congress."
228	ISRA-ALON (also titles IZRAIL'SKII BIULLETEN', IZRAIL'SKII KUL'TURNYI TSENTR)	Kiev	1997	>>>	Suppl. to the newspaper, VOZROZHDENIE (see no. 128). Includes suppl. MUSAF (see no. 277).
229	UKRAINA-IZRAIL' [2]: Vestnik Obshchestva Druzhby	Kiev	1997	>>>	Journal of the Society of Friendship "Ukraina-Izrail'," in Ukrainian only.
230	GEULA [2]	Khar'kov	1997	>>>	"Special Weekly Issue" (weekly chapters of the Torah).
231	YAHAD	Dnepropetrovsk	01 1998	>>>	Journal of the Israeli Cultural Center's youth club "Yakhad."
232	ATIKVA (Issues 1,2–TIKVA)	Odessa	03 1998	>>>	Bulletin of the Jewish Agency's youth club "Gesher" (see no. 165).
233	GMILUS HESED [2] (Newspaper)	Odessa	03 1998	>>>	Differs from GMILUS HESED [1] (see no. 194) in numbering and editorship.
234	VINNITSKAIA IERUSALIMKA (former INFORMATSIONNYI LISTOK)	Vinnitsa	04 1998	>>>	Continuation of INFORMATSIONNYI LISTOK (see no. 191) with same numbering.
235	KHAVERIM	Simferopol'	04 1998	>>>	Earlier–VESTNIK SIMFEROPOL'SKOGO EVREISKOGO OBSCHESTVA "YAD EZRA" (see no. 220).
236	KAHOL VE-LAVAN	Odessa	08 1998	>>>	Publication of the Israeli Cultural Center.
237	KADIMA	Sevastopol'	10 1998	>>>	News of the Jewish Agency in Crimea (partly based on IKTs materials in Odessa). Till September 2000: within newspaper RASSVET (see no. 210).
238	SOKHNUTON	Kiev	11 1998	11 1998	Bulletin of the Jewish Agency ("Sokhnut") in the region of Kiev.
239	KESHET–RADUGA	Odessa	11 1998	>>>	Informational Bulletin of the Jewish Agency.
240	SOKHNUT-UKRAINA: KHAR'KOVSKOE PREDSTAVITELSTVO	Khar'kov	1998	09 1998	7 issues known. Continued by: MAKHAR (see no. 241).
241	MAKHAR–KOL HA-SOKHNUT (2nd title–in Hebrew)	Khar'kov	11 1998	>>>	Continues: SOKHNUT-UKRAINA: KHAR'KOVSKOE PREDSTAVITEL'STVO (see no. 240).

APPENDIX (continued)

No.	TITLE	City	Begin	End (>>> = cont'd in 2001)	Comments (Subtitles are in quotation marks)
242	KALEIDOSKOP	Bershad' (Vinnitsa oblast')	12 1998	>>>	Youth suppl. to the newspaper SHABAT (see no. 141).
243	VESTNIK EVREISKOGO OBSHCHINNOGO TSENTRA	Dnepropetrovsk	12 1998	>>>	Suppl. to SHABAT SHALOM (see no. 138).
244	VESTNIK SOKHNUTA	Dnepropetrovsk	12 1998	>>>	Suppl. to SHABAT SHALOM (see no. 138).
245	VZGLIAD NA IZRAIL'	Dnepropetrovsk	12 1998	02 2000	Suppl. of Israeli Center to SHABAT SHALOM (see no. 138). Later–See No. 289.
246	ALEF	Zaporozh'e	1998	1998	"Newspaper of the Zaporozh'e City School-Gymnasium 'Alef.'" One known issue.
247	YIDISHE YEDIES	Kiev	1998	1999	Newspaper of the Jewish Council of Ukraine, in Yiddish.
248	EVREISKOE AGENTSTVO UKRAINA I MOLDOVA	Kiev	1998	07 1998	Only no. 4 known, under the title PEDAGOGICHESKII TSENTR-UL'PAN.
249	EVREIS'KA ISTORIIA TA KULTURA V KRAINAKH TSENTRAL'NOI TA SKHIDNOI IEVROPY (Title in Ukrainian only)	Kiev	1998	1998?	Continuation of the scholarly anthology. Languages: Ukrainian, Russian. Nos. 1, 2 (1998) are known.
250	ERETS KHAVERIM OBNOVLENNAIA [2]	Kiev	1998	>>>	Continuation of ERETS KHAVERIM (see no. 157) with different editor and different numbering.
251	SOKHNUT-UKRAINA	Krivoi Rog (Dnepropetrovsk oblast')	1998?	1999	Known only issues after April 1999.
252	VESTNIK "SOKHNUTA": MELITOPOL'SKII VYPUSK	Melitopol' (Zaporozh'e oblast')	1998	2000	6 issues known.
253	STRANICHKA "SOKHNUTA"	Chernigov	1998	1998	After two issues (autumn 1998): independent newspaper SOKHNUTON (see no. 257).
254	NOVOSTI "SHALOM"	Evpatoriia (Crimea)	1999	>>>	First new publication in the city after 82-year hiatus (see no. 037).

255	SHALOM, KHAVERIM!	Dnepropetrovsk	01 1999	>>>	Newspaper of Dnepropetrovsk department V.E.K. (see also no. 227).
256	BARUKH ASHEM (till Issue 49–BARUKH GASHEM)	Donetsk	01 1999	>>>	"Weekly Newspaper." In fact, chapters of the Torah (see also no. 265).
257	SOKHNUTON	Chernigov	02 1999	>>>	Publication of the Jewish Agency. Second part of the publication–BUKVAR'-OLE (see no. 285).
258	EDINSTVO (later YAHAD)	Sumy	03 1999	12 1999	Later the newspaper YAKHAD (see no. 288), with new numbering.
259	YAHAD	Dneprodzerzhinsk (Dnepropetrovsk oblast')	04 1999	1999?	Only known Russian-Jewish periodical publication in the city.
260	SHABAT SHALOM–UKRAINA	Dnepropetrovsk	04 1999	04 1999	Newspaper of the center "Or-Avner Chabad-Lubavitch." One issue released.
261	GOLOS HESEDA	Zaporozh'e	05 1999	>>>	Informational Bulletin of the Zaporozh'e charitable fund "Hesed Mikhael."
262	MISHPAHAT BET HA-SEFER	Khar'kov	05 1999	05 1999	Religious publication of the Jewish school. One issue known.
263	ATIKVA	Poltava	07 1999	>>>	First new publication in the city after 82-year hiatus (see nos. 013, 048).
264	BIULLETEN' ASSOTSIATSII EVREISKIKH BIBLIOTEK VOSTOCHNOI UKRAINY	Dnepropetrovsk; Lugansk	09 1999	>>>	Association in Dnepropetrovsk. Edited and printed in Lugansk.
265	NASHA ZHIZN' V DIASPORE I DOMA	Donetsk	09 1999	>>>	Monthly newspaper (see also nos. 256, 296).
266	EVREISKII MERIDIAN (in Russian)	Kiev	09 1999	>>>	"Informational Newspaper of the Jewish Confederation of Ukraine" (see also nos. 267, 304).
267	JEWISH MERIDIAN (in English)	Kiev	1999	>>>	English variant of newspaper EVREISKII MERIDIAN (see no. 266).
268	NER [1]: Newspaper	Lugansk	09 1999	>>>	First publication of the city in 82 years (see nos. 024, 027, 040, 054). Suppl.: see no. 307.
269	NASHA GAZETA	Kiev	10 1999	1999?	Monthly children's Jewish newspaper of the school "Simkha-Khabad."
270	TIKVA	Kirovograd	10 1999	>>>	First new publication of the city after 80-year hiatus (see no. 090).

APPENDIX (continued)

No.	TITLE	City	Begin	End (>>> = cont'd in 2001)	Comments (Subtitles are in quotation marks)
271	KHESED ARYE	L'vov	10 1999	>>>	Original format: 15 × 41 cm. (A5 × 2).
272	INFORMATSIONNYI BIULLETEN' VNUTRENNEGO POL'ZOVANIIA	Uman (Cherkassy oblast')	11 1999	>>>	Added title: EVREISKOE AGENTSTVO "SOKHNUT."
273	RADUGA (?)	Donetsk	1999?	1999?	Publication known only from the press. Student journal, from the Donetsk Jewish school?
274	VESTNIK MEZHDUNARODNOGO SOLOMONOVA UNIVERSITETA	Kiev	1999	>>>	Issues on mathematics, sociology, history (including Jewish history) are known.
275	EST' OTVET	Kiev	1999	1999	Bulletin of the organization "Aish ha-Torah" and of the Jewish school-gymnasium. One known issue—"autumn 1999."
276	MOST	Kiev	1999	>>>	Publication of the Jewish Agency "Sokhnut-Ukraina."
277	MUSAF	Kiev	1999	>>>	Literary-journalistic suppl. to ISRA-ALON (see no. 228). One known issue—"Suppl. to 7(16)."
278	INFORMATSIONNYI BIULLETEN'	Smela (Cherkassy oblast')	1999	>>>	Known issues: 23 (April 2000) and 30 (in 2000).
279	NAVSTRECHU MOSHIAKHU (Issue 1–Title "??")	Khar'kov	1999	>>>	"Yeshiva ktana. Khabad Liubavich Or Avner."
280	SHALOM	Cherkassy	1999	>>>	First new publication in Cherkassy after 70-year hiatus (see no. 117).
281	MIGDAL D'OR	Khar'kov	1999?	1999?	Religious publication, known only from reports.
282	KHESED-LEIB	Ivano-Frankovsk (former Stanislav)	2000?	>>>	Only known publication in the city.
283	NASH DOM	Odessa	01 2000	>>>	Internet Newspaper of the boys school "Or Sameakh."
284	SHTETELE-MESTECHECHKO-GORODOCHEK	Kiev	01 2000	>>>	Literary and humorous bulletin of the Family Club "Mishpakha."
285	BUKVAR'-OLE	Chernigov	01 2000	>>>	Part 2 of the newspaper SOKHNUTON (see no. 257)–pages 9-12 are paginated alef-dalet.

286	DNEPROPETROVSKAIA EVREISKAIA OBSHCHINA	Dnepropetrovsk	02 2000	"Informational Digest."
287	MIGDAL'-TIMES [1]: Bulletin	Odessa	02 2000	Two issues released. Continued by: MIGDAL'-TIMES [2] (see no. 297).
288	YAHAD	Sumy	02 2000	Continuation of bulletin EDINSTVO (see no. 258), with new numbering.
289	IZRAIL' DALEKII I BLIZKII	Dnepropetrovsk	03 2000	Suppl. to the newspaper SHABAT SHALOM (see no. 258). Earlier–VZGLIAD NA IZRAIL' (see no. 245).
290	MIR EVREISKOI ZHENSHCHINY	Lugansk	03 2000	Publication of the Jewish Women's Club "Khaia Mushka."
291	KHESED SHUSHANA	Chernovtsy	03 2000	Original format 15 × 41 cm. (A5 × 2).
292	ALEF-KHRONIKA	Dnepropetrovsk	04 2000	"Informational newspaper. Chronicle of the Jewish society in Dnepropetrovsk."
293	GINGER	Dnepropetrovsk	05 2000	Youth newspaper. One issue known.
294	TKUMA	Dnepropetrovsk	05 2000	News of the scholarly enlightenment center, focused on Holocaust studies.
295	BIULLETEN' ASSOTSIATSII OBSHCHINNYKH TSENTROV S.N.G.	Dnepropetrovsk; Moscow (Russia)	05 2000	One "pilot" issue. Mock-up prepared in Dnepropetrovsk.
296	VESTNIK DONETSKOGO SOKHNUTA	Donetsk	05 2000	Newspaper within the newspaper NASHA ZHIZN' V DIASPORE I DOMA (see no. 265).
297	MIGDAL'-TIMES [2]: Magazine	Odessa	07 2000	Earlier bulletin: see no. 287.
298	KIEV EVREISKII	Kiev	08 2000	"Informational Bulletin of the Kiev Jewish center "Kinor."
299	EKHO	Uzhgorod	08 2000	First Russian-Jewish newspaper in the city. Pages numbered from right to left.
300	KOMPAS-MATSPEN	L'vov	09 2000	"Informational Bulletin of the Jewish Agency of Galicia." Before the first issue (Sept. 2000) there was an undated special issue, MI KOL' KHALEV [= MI-KOL HA-LEVI] (2000?).
301	MADREGOT	Khar'kov	09 2000	Newspaper of the city charitable fund "Zabota–Ma'alot Hesed."
302	A IDISHE MOME	Donetsk	10 2000	"Women's Journal." Included in the exhibit "Jewish press-2000" in Moscow.

APPENDIX (continued)

No.	TITLE	City	Begin	End (>>> = cont'd in 2001)	Comments (Subtitles are in quotation marks)
303	V RADOSTI	Kiev	10 2000	>>>	Monthly children's Jewish newspaper of the school "Simkha-Khabad."
304	EVREISKII OBOZREVATEL'	Kiev	10 2000	>>>	Suppl. to the newspaper EVREISKII MERIDIAN (see no. 266). Independent publication since Sept. 2001.
305	OBSHCHINA	Kiev	10 2000	10 2000	Special issue "Rosh ha-Shanah 5761" in some Jewish newspapers in Kiev.
306	OTKRYTAIA DVER'–OPEN DOOR	Kiev	10 2000	>>>	"Religious Publication of the United Society of Progressive Judaism in Ukraine."
307	NER [2]: Special Issue NEDELNAIA GLAVA	Lugansk	10 2000	>>>	Supplement to the newspaper NER (see no. 268). List of brochures on Jewish themes, on some pages.
308	VMESTE–INEINEM	Cherkassy	12 2000	>>>	Newspaper of the society and fund "Hesed Dorot."
309	OSHIBKA 2000	Dnepropetrovsk	2000	2000	Daily newspaper of the KVN command (popular game for humorists and wits).
310	SHALOM ALEIKHEM [2]	Khmel'nitskii (former Proskurov)	2000	>>>	In 1995-1999 the newspaper came out in the city Kamenets-Podol'skii (see no. 182).
311	SHTETL: Literaturno-publitsisticheskii sbornik	Khmel'nitskii (former Proskurov)	2000	>>>	Publication of Khmel'nitskii oblast' charitable fund "Hesed Besht."

Bibliographical Projects in Polish-Jewish Studies Since 1989

Stephen D. Corrsin

SUMMARY. Over the last two decades, interest in the field of Polish-Jewish studies has grown, in Poland as well as in North America, Western Europe, and Israel. One aspect of this is that bibliographic projects have begun, with the goal of tracking and making generally available information about publications in this field. This article describes in particular the ongoing project that the author manages with the Israeli journal *Gal-Ed: On the History of the Jews in Poland*, which includes plans to make available as an online resource the information in the printed installments of the bibliography. *[Article copies available for a fee from The Haworth Document Delivery Service: 1-800-HAWORTH. E-mail address: <docdelivery@haworthpress.com> Website: <http://www.HaworthPress.com> © 2003 by The Haworth Press, Inc. All rights reserved.]*

KEYWORDS. Bibliography, online resources, Polish-Jewish studies, Poland

In the 1989-1990 volume of *Judaica Librarianship*, the journal of the Association of Jewish Libraries, Zachary M. Baker published a brief article which

---

Stephen D. Corrsin is Head of Acquisitions, Wayne State University Library System, 5150 Anthony Wayne Drive, Detroit, MI 48102 USA (E-mail: ag5153@mail.wayne.edu).

[Haworth co-indexing entry note]: "Bibliographical Projects in Polish-Jewish Studies Since 1989." Corrsin, Stephen D. Co-published simultaneously in *Slavic & East European Information Resources* (The Haworth Information Press, an imprint of The Haworth Press, Inc.) Vol. 4, No. 2/3, 2003, pp. 151-167; and: *Judaica in the Slavic Realm, Slavica in the Judaic Realm: Repositories, Collections, Projects, Publications* (ed: Zachary M. Baker) The Haworth Information Press, an imprint of The Haworth Press, Inc., 2003, pp. 151-167. Single or multiple copies of this article are available for a fee from The Haworth Document Delivery Service [1-800-HAWORTH, 9:00 a.m. - 5:00 p.m. (EST). E-mail address: docdelivery@haworthpress.com].

http://www.haworthpress.com/store/product.asp?sku=J167
© 2003 by The Haworth Press, Inc. All rights reserved.
10.1300/J167v04n02_09

can serve as a useful touchstone for the study of the recent bibliography of the Jews in Poland: "The Chosen Book: Reinventing the Jew in Absentia: Recent Judaica Publishing Trends in Poland." When this paper appeared, Poland was experiencing a great (and peaceful) revolution: the end of nearly half a century of communist rule, and the transition to an undeniably democratic and open state, society, and economy. Baker, then Head Librarian of the YIVO Institute for Jewish Research in New York, begins, "One of the most striking developments in the Judaica publishing world during the past decade [the 1980s] has been the appearance in Poland of scores of books and journals devoted to Jews and Judaism."

Baker refers to the key factor that makes this development all the more "striking": the poverty of the Polish Judaica literature published in the preceding decades, since the end of the Second World War and the imposition of communist rule in Poland. He states, "After having been all but written out of Polish history since 1945, Poland's Jews are now finding themselves being reincorporated into the Polish literary, cultural, and historical consciousness."[1] Baker links the specific phenomenon of the great increase in the number of Judaica titles published in the 1980s in Poland to wider trends in Polish society and politics since the end of the Second World War and the Holocaust. An additional point, which he does not discuss, is that since circa 1980 there has also been a significant upswing in interest and a "proliferation of Judaica publications" in Israel, the United States, and elsewhere in Europe, concerning Jewish history in Poland.

The study of writings and publications on or by the Polish Jews must be placed in the context of the larger, tragic history of the Jewish community of Poland in the twentieth century, as well as in the larger framework of Polish and East-Central European history in general. Modern Poland–as separate lands or provinces, partitioned among Russia, Germany, and Austria from the late eighteenth century until the end of the First World War, and then as the Second Polish Republic in the interwar years–was home to the largest Jewish community in Europe, which was, moreover, extraordinarily diverse. On the eve of the Second World War, it included over three million people, approximately ten percent of the population of Poland. In the course of the war and Holocaust, most of this community was killed. The survivors, including some tens of thousands who had survived in hiding or in the German ghettos and concentration camps, and more who had survived either in the Soviet Union or elsewhere (for instance, those serving in the Polish army formations based in Britain), totaled several hundred thousand. Those survivors who returned to Poland, or who emerged from hiding, found their situations extraordinarily difficult. It is enough to mention the wave of individual violence, as well as large-scale pogroms directed against the Polish Jews in Kielce and elsewhere in 1945-1946. Most of them emigrated in the late 1940s, leaving a small community numbering perhaps some tens of thousands, with little opportunity to organize or express itself under the conditions of high Stalinism and subsequent modest liberalization that prevailed in Poland in the 1950s to 1960s. The last significant wave of Jewish emigration and expulsions from Poland took place in 1968, during the upsurge of officially sanctioned anti-Semitism in the Soviet bloc following the victory of Israel in the Six Day War of 1967. Taken in all, the losses during the Holocaust and the Second World War, and then the postwar emigrations and expulsions of the remnants of Polish Jewry, led to a situation in which, by the 1970s, the Jewish community of Poland had practically ceased to exist. It consisted of a few thousand openly self-identified Jews, or individuals of acknowledged Jewish ancestry. The only significant scholarly organization was the Jewish Historical Institute (Żydowski Instytut Historyczny) in Warsaw. To young scholars in any country interested in entering the field up to the early 1980s, the prospects of making a career in the field of Polish-Jewish studies, or even just of research and publishing in the area, must have seemed very bleak.

Beginning in the early to mid-1980s, however, the field of Polish-Jewish studies showed signs of renewed life. And since the end of communist rule in Poland in 1989, there has been a significant renaissance–though compared to many other fields of Jewish studies, this renaissance is, and is likely to remain, modest. In Poland itself, the process of change and growth was gradual but noticeable through the 1980s, despite the difficult conditions of martial law that prevailed. Most generally, the Polish authorities found that the old anti-Semitic card–when in crisis, rouse the majority populace against the Jews–no longer worked. There was also a significant wave of new interest in and appreciation of Poland's Jewish heritage on the part of the dissidents and the Polish underground. To quote the conclusion of Baker's 1989-1990 article, "Given the obsession that so many Poles have with their country's fate, the present-day rediscovery of the Jewish skeletons in their nation's closet may mark only the beginning of a long voyage of [Polish] self-exploration."[2] This point–that the increase in Polish interest in the country's Jewish heritage is a matter of "self-exploration"–is a very important one.

These and other factors led to a situation in which, once communist rule ended in Poland in 1989, a great expansion of academic institutionalization of the field was possible, including research, publishing, the establishment of institutes and programs, and conferences. The now-venerable Żydowski Instytut Historyczny has continued and expanded its work, and more recently founded bodies at other research institutions, and universities have developed ambitious and exciting programs as well.

Outside of Poland in the same period, important markers of the rising scholarly interest in the field included the series of international conferences held on the general topic of the history and culture of the Jews in Poland, beginning at Columbia University in 1983. The serial *Polin*, published first at Oxford, from 1986, and subsequently at Brandeis University, and the Israeli biannual *Gal-Ed: On the History of the Jews in Poland*, which had begun to appear at Tel Aviv University in the 1970s, have served as high-quality, focused academic markets for the products of Western European, American, Canadian, and Israeli scholarship. Both have published substantial amounts of work from Poland as well. In Poland, the *Biuletyn* (Bulletin) of the Żydowski Instytut Historyczny has been replaced by the *Kwartalnik Historii Żydow* (Jewish History Quarterly). Also, the Polish Society for Jewish Studies (Polskie Towarzystwo Studiów Żydowskich), founded in 1996, now publishes the semiannual *Studia Judaica*.

The scope of my present report begins in the early 1990s, when Professor David Engel, of New York University and the Diaspora Research Institute of Tel Aviv University, asked me to prepare an ongoing bibliography of new publications in the field of Polish-Jewish history. This bibliography would appear as a regular feature in *Gal-Ed: On the History of the Jews in Poland*, which publishes both English- and Hebrew-language contributions, of which Dr. Engel has been an editor for many years. The bibliography has, so far, appeared in three installments in *Gal-Ed*, in volumes 14 (1995), 15-16 (1996-1997), and 17 (1998). The fourth is in the process of preparation, and will appear in the 19th volume of *Gal-Ed*. It was also planned that the bibliography would be made available in online form by the Diaspora Research Institute. The initial attempt to make the bibliography readily available online had only limited success. But we expect to proceed with this plan again, placing the cumulated bibliography on the web in an academic computing environment, since this is an obvious direction in which to proceed.

In this paper, I will discuss the development of this bibliography over the past decade, in the context of the rise in interest in Polish Jewish studies in a number of countries. The essential idea behind any bibliographical effort, of course, is that the bibliography should serve as a resource that can be of significant usefulness to scholars and students. Ours is, further, a relatively obscure field, with researchers working in many countries and languages, factors that complicate any research effort considerably. Future prospects, in particular finding an online home, should make the bibliography significantly more useful to a wider audience. The conclusion to this essay will discuss prospects for such continued and extended work. The development of the bibliography has also provided many lessons for these sorts of undertakings, though I would not claim for it the status of a model project, by any means (unless the word "model" is used to denote anything that teaches one useful or at least usable lessons).

One important point to note is that my concern is with Polish-Jewish studies, which can be broadly defined as research and publications on the history and culture of the Jews in Poland. I am not specifically focusing on items published *in Poland*, on Jews, Judaism, and Jewish topics–which perhaps is the way "Polish Judaica" might profitably be defined.

OVERVIEW OF THE FIELD

The field of Polish-Jewish studies is modest in size, certainly when compared to the neighboring fields of the histories and cultures of the Jews in Germany and Austria, or Russia and the Soviet Union. Nonetheless, several useful bibliographical projects in the field of Polish-Jewish studies have appeared in the last twenty years or so.

One can begin with the Israeli facsimile reprint of Majer Balaban's *Bibliografia historii Żydów w Polsce i w krajach ościennych za lata 1900-1930 (Bibliography on the History of the Jews in Poland and in Neighboring Lands: Works Published during the Years 1900-1930).*[3] Balaban (1877-1943), an outstanding interwar figure in the field of Jewish history who died in the Holocaust, clearly meant to continue this project, as indicated by the fact that this publication is listed as volume or fascicle (*zeszyt*) 1. The Israeli facsimile has a new introduction (in Hebrew) by Ezra Mendelsohn of the Hebrew University. The facsimile also features new Hebrew and English title pages. Mendelsohn himself published an important bibliography, in Hebrew, at the same time as this republication of Balaban's work. It covered the entirety of East-Central Europe rather than Poland alone: *Yehude mizrah-merkaz eiropa ben shete milhamot-ha-olam: bibliyografyah nivheret (The Jews of East-Central Europe between the Two World Wars: A Selected Bibliography).*[4]

A few years later, in 1984, Gershon David Hundert and Gershon C. Bacon published an especially important work, which remains very useful for summarizing the field: *The Jews in Poland and Russia: Bibliographical Essays.*[5] Both individual authors have continued to publish bibliographical materials, including (by Hundert) annual bibliographies in volumes of 9-11 of *Polin*, covering the years 1993-1995.

A problematic effort, for scholarly purposes of limited use, appeared in 1986: Jerzy J. (George) Lerski and Halina T. Lerski, *Jewish-Polish Coexistence, 1772-1939: A Topical Bibliography.*[6] It evidently has the goal of documenting especially the positive sides of Polish-Jewish relations and coexistence in the Polish lands: a noble effort, but not a truly scholarly one. It has a major methodological and editorial flaw, which, regardless of other concerns, which makes it practically unusable for identifying and locating publications in languages other than English. The compilers state:

> In view of the large number of entries and the fact that the book is being published in the United States, it was decided to translate all titles from the 11 languages represented into English and to indicate the original language . . . only in parenthesis, for example: (H) for Hebrew or (P) for Polish . . . Professional bibliographers may question these decisions of the authors, but the options were taken to complete this bibliography in one not over-large volume. (p. 3)

In fact, this decision went far beyond questionable: it renders the compilation nearly useless for items that did not appear in English.

One narrowly defined bibliographical project is especially worthy of mention. This is Zachary Baker's compilation of memorial books from the Polish lands: "Bibliography of Eastern European Memorial (Yizkor) Books." The most recent version appeared as an appendix in the second, expanded edition of Jack Kugelmass and Jonathan Boyarin (editors and translators), *From a Ruined Garden: The Memorial Books of Polish Jewry*.[7] These *yizkor* books, typically post-Holocaust collections prepared by the survivors on the history, people, and destruction of the Jewish communities of Eastern and East-Central Europe, with materials in Yiddish, Hebrew, and other tongues, are an extraordinarily important resource for those studying the history of the European Jews in the first half of the twentieth century. The primary approach in Baker's listing is geographical by community. While he includes all parts of the greater Eastern European region, a very large share of the communities represented consists of those that were in historic, or interwar, Poland.

Another ongoing bibliographical project from Poland is worthy of special mention. As noted above, the interest of Poles in their country's Jewish heritage rose through the 1980s. Among the efforts that this interest led to was the establishment of an ongoing bibliographical project at Jagiellonian University in Kraków. It was based at the University's Research Center for Jewish History and Culture in Poland (Międzywydziałowy Zakład Historii i Kultury Żydów w Polsce), long led by Professor Jozef Gierowski. The bibliographic project, *Studia Polono-Judaica: Series Bibliographica*, directed by Krzysztof Pilarczyk of the University, appears to be finished after eight volumes published in 1992-2000, though there are still gaps in the overall numbering of the series. A new series, *Studia Judaica Cracoviensia: Series Bibliographica*, has replaced it, under the auspices of the University's Judaic Studies Department (Katedra Judaistyki).

The most significant volumes in the earlier series are, *Przewodnik po bibliografiach polskich judaików* (Guide to Bibliographies of Polish Judaica) and *Judaika polskie z XVI-XVIII wieku: materiały do bibliografii*[8] (Polish Judaica of the Sixteenth and Seventeenth Centuries: Materials for a Bibliography). Both are edited by Pilarczyk. The latter bibliography was planned to appear in two parts as volume 4 of the series, *Studia Polono-Judaica: Series Bibliographica*, but only the first part, covering "publications in non-Jewish languages," has actually appeared; the second part, intended to cover primarily Hebrew, and "to a lesser degree [publications] in the Aramaic language and Yiddish," has not yet been published. Other volumes in the series, meant to cover contemporary publications in Poland touching on Jewish topics, in an extremely comprehensive fashion, have appeared but seem of more limited value; greater selectivity would probably have led to more useful bibliographies. In any case, these annual listings of *Judaika wydane w Polsce* (Judaica Published in Poland) can serve as a monument to an impressive amount of collecting work. This effort has been succeeded by the new *Bibliografia historii i kultury Żydów w Polsce* (Bibliography of the [sic] Jewish History and Culture in Poland). Its first volume, with publications dating from 1994, was edited by Stefan Gąsiorowski. In its introduction, Gąsiorowski refers to

> the Editors' intention to take stock of books and articles in Jewish studies that refer to Poland, published both in this country and abroad, while continuing with the list of Polish publications on foreign Judaica.[9]

For an ongoing, expressly scholarly effort, one can also use the journal, *Studia Judaica*, which has published a series of review articles on recent Israeli and Polish publications in the field, by, respectively, Shaul Stampfer and Stefan Gąsiorowski. In addition, the *Biuletyn Żydowskiego Instytutu Historycznego*, and now the *Kwartalnik Historii Żydów*, have published regular installments of "Żydzi w Polsce: materiały do bibliografii," compiled by Wanda Kochowska and Urszula Grygier.[10]

One more volume in a related series needs special mention, edited by Katarzyna Muszyńska. These are the proceedings of an international conference held in Kraków in 1988, organized by the above-mentioned Research Center of the Jagiellonian University: *Bibliographies of Polish Judaica: International Symposium*. The papers, primarily contributions by Polish scholars, are presented entirely in English in this volume. The editor refers to the ambitious ideas with which the conference was held: "The goal of this working conference was the presentation and summing up of the current state of research on the bibliography of Polish Judaica as carried out in Poland and abroad, as well as the joint working out of plans for further work." She notes that a key long-term goal is "the compilation of the 'Bibliography of Polish Judaica,' which will be invaluable for all students and enthusiasts of the history and culture of Polish Jews and will cover the whole thousand-year history of the Jewish presence in Poland."[11] The present status and future prospects of such a huge–and perhaps unattainable–goal, which would require the application of very considerable resources in what remains fundamentally a minor field in Poland, is unclear.

THE GAL-ED *BIBLIOGRAPHY PROJECT*

The first installment of *Gal-Ed*'s bibliography, in its 1995 volume, begins with the following statement of proposed contents:

> This bibliography lists books, articles, dissertations, and films bearing imprint dates between 1990-94 on the history and culture of the Jews of Poland. It represents the first fruits of what is hoped will be an ongoing bibliographic data base project under the auspices of *Gal-Ed*...
> Only publications in English, Polish, Hebrew, German, French, and Yiddish have been included. The list has been confined to scholarly publications; for the most part, material from newspapers or magazines... does not appear. Reviews... have been excluded entirely. Holocaust memoirs have been listed, with some exceptions, only if they were published by university or major trade publishers. Facsimile reprints of earlier publications have been included, as have translations of previously published works and new editions of older books in which the editorial matter or scholarly apparatus has been updated. New printings of previously published editions, however, have been omitted.[12]

What has been the result of this collection program? We now have a published bibliographical file of over 2,200 records (*Gal-Ed*, vol. 14: items 1-867; vols. 15-16: items 868-1585; vol.17: items 1586-2218). The beginning point is that we have included only items with an imprint or publication date after 1989. This year was chosen in part because of the momentous changes which took place in Poland in that year, but also for the sake of convenience: having a distinct starting date makes the work more manageable. We have included only items in the six languages listed above, which are the most important ones for the field. No doubt significant works in (for example) Lithuanian, Ukrainian, and Italian have been missed, but one can hope that these are few. We have avoided addressing the vexed and vexing question, "Where is Poland?" in our collecting policy, and have tried to take a broad and inclusive approach.

Thus, territories within present-day Poland have been included, as well as a great deal of material from the historic Polish lands.

The question of the scholarly level of materials included in the bibliography is, obviously, not at all a simple one. Judgments vary enormously. In such cases, it is often simplest to say what is *not* included. For example, besides those exclusions mentioned above, we decided from the beginning to leave out such items as many self-published Holocaust narratives, master's degree writings, and fiction in any form. We also excluded articles from more general interest magazines, or news and opinion periodicals as much as possible, "even intellectual reviews or public affairs journals such as *Polityka, Commentary,* or *New York Review of Books.*" One might add *Almanach Żydowski,* to use as an example a semi-popular serial the contents of which have been excluded (though in fact it is not unusual for scholars to publish general interest pieces in that annual). It is obvious that choices are difficult and there has been a significant amount of inconsistency in selecting items for inclusion. There is also no question that many publications and other items at non-scholarly levels have been listed. So it must be asked: have we been successful in covering the greater part of the field, particularly with respect to scholarly publications, without being overwhelmed by popular publications? That judgment must be left to others, but the fact that no significant criticisms have been offered of our approach as a whole, or cries of outrage about particular items included or excluded, is encouraging.

It should also be noted that the original idea was that every item should be examined, *de visu*. This is a fine principle for bibliographical work, and it quickly proved impracticable. Instead, we have come to rely for information chiefly on such indexing sources as *RAMBI* (the Hebrew acronym for the *Index of Articles on Jewish Studies*[13]), *Historical Abstracts, ABSEES,* the *Bibliografia Historii Polski* (Bibliography of the History of Poland), and the *Bibliografia Zawartości Czasopism* (Bibliography of Periodical Contents); online catalogs of major universities that have programs in the field of Polish-Jewish studies; the sales catalogs of several book vendors who specialize in selling to academics and to university libraries;[14] and also publishers' catalogs. The OCLC online bibliographical network, the greatest contemporary shared resource of its kind, has proved of extraordinary usefulness, indeed a necessity–but chiefly for confirmatory purposes or to find more details about books and journals the existence of which is known or suspected from other sources.

One particularly problematic issue concerns formats of the materials included. As noted above, when beginning the work in the early 1990s, it was decided to include films (or, more properly, video recording formats). Not much has been done, in fact, because it has not been easy to identify those that might be of interest, much less those of scholarly character and quality. More of these deserve inclusion, particularly documentaries or historical videos. Another important non-print resource would be microform collections of resources (newspapers, archives, etc.) that can readily be classed as recent publications, and are therefore deserving of inclusion in the bibliography. Several microform publishers specialize precisely in these sorts of historical materials, and have undertaken large-scale retrospective projects in the last decade, as libraries and archives in east central and eastern Europe have opened much more to researchers.

But it is the rapid progress of web publications that requires that we rethink some of our premises. It seems obvious that web resources–whether digitalized older materials, online-only books or journals, informational sites, and the like–should be listed. The first question is how these materials, which are as varied in their contents and level as are publications and resources in print or other formats, should be judged. This remains an open question.

The nature of the records in the bibliography, once the individual items have been selected, is the next matter for discussion. An example will be provided at the end of this section. But for now, it is most important to focus on the main access points in the records, for users of the bibliography. The introduction to the first installment in *Gal-Ed* states about the records:

> Records in all languages are interfiled in Polish alphabetical order by author(s) or editor(s) or, failing this, by title. The actual format ... represents a compromise between the standard *Anglo-American Cataloging Rules* (2d ed., rev.) (*AACR2*) and the more flexible practices typically used by scholars. A particular problem is presented by proper names. It is impossible to be entirely consistent and appropriate when one is dealing with works and languages encompassing many centuries of history. With respect to places, Polish forms (Wilno, Lwów, Kraków, Gdańsk) have been employed ... The exceptions are Warsaw, Auschwitz, Silesia, and Pomerania, all of which appear in their well known English forms. Most authors' and other personal names appear in the forms provided by the Library of Congress Name Authorities File. Sometimes these standard forms do not match an author's name as it appears at the head of a particular book or article. In other cases, chiefly involving Israeli authors, a compromise has been sought between Library of Congress standards and forms which might make more sense to scholars.[15]

Clearly this covers a great many topics of intense and long-standing debate among librarians, particularly the choice of heading for individual entries, the forms of these headings (names and places), and other authorities-related matters.

Whenever I am involved in bibliographic description and analysis–having been trained and worked for many years as a cataloger in libraries–I think in *AACR2* terms. That massive compilation, most readily comparable to the Talmud as an edited storehouse of a vast range of past wisdom intended to guide present and future conduct, has been the standard–albeit a constantly revised one–for library cataloging in the English-speaking world. In the course of working on this bibliography, however, I found myself modifying my practices under the influences of the peculiar customs of the field of historical scholarship, as well as practical concerns in the development and maintenance of a tightly focused, subject-specific bibliography. Areas that reflect this particularly well are the following: the question of the heading for each entry; the related topic of the "filing" of entries, that is, placing them in order; the forms of names, generally regarded as "authorities" work in libraries; and questions of subject analysis and indexing. It should be added that, as I have worked in the past year or two to convert the entire bibliography to machine-readable status, it has become clear that many of the practices and ideas that apply to the print version need to be reexamined and, perhaps, revised.

First, the choice of the "heading" that serves as the "main entry." For the purposes of the printed bibliography, it can be briefly defined as, the element–that is, the name, word, or phrase–under which the individual entry is listed. When *AACR2* was introduced, one of the dramatic changes in practice that it made was to push catalogers away from using the names for editors, etc., for main entries when no individual, personal author was available. But in planning the work for *Gal-Ed*, I found myself pulled backwards: historians and other scholars will, I felt, look for the names of the editors rather than titles. All but a few of the records, therefore, have a personal name at the head, whether author or editor. How will this be changed by the conversion of the bibliography to online? It is often said that in an online environment, the choice of main entry becomes irrelevant. That may well be true, but if the print version remains the "master," then its needs take precedence and we will still have a choice of heading for the main entry.

The next matter is the "filing rules." (The use of this phrase illustrates how the idea of the card catalog still can dominate, at least terminologically.) We made a decision to follow Polish alphabetical order, which is a little different from English-language usage. This may seem an odd choice, but considering that the greatest share of entries are in Polish it is quite reasonable. Two other points should be noted here: Hebrew-alphabet entries are interfiled with those in the Roman alphabet; and each installment of the bibliography follows its own alphabetical and numbering sequence. The decisions to proceed in this fashion were dictated by practicality.

With regard to the forms of names, the paragraph quoted above from the first installment of the bibliography concludes with a plea for understanding. Noting that our approach relies chiefly on the Name Authorities File of the Library of Congress, with some modification, we state: "This practice has resulted in some inconsistencies . . . ; it is hoped that these will not prove too obtrusive or offensive to the authors involved." The questions of the preferred forms of names–personal, corporate, and geographical–and also of topical subjects are and can be expected to remain among the most complex and contentious areas of library theory and practice. I do not wish at this point to go into detail: the matter is all too familiar to librarians, and all too arcane for everyone else. Ultimately, like many matters involving the choices of names and languages, questions involving name authorities in bibliographical or library work can be highly political. A couple of examples will suffice to show that the questions involved are, at least, highly complex, and not be readily or casually resolved.

Isaac Bashevis Singer (1904-1991) was born and raised in the partitioned Polish lands and grew to adulthood in the independent Second Polish Republic. His native language was Yiddish, but since his family came from scholarly and religious backgrounds he was also fluent in Hebrew–at least the Ashkenazic variety traditional among the Eastern and Central European Jews. As a popular writer in interwar Poland, he published in Yiddish, and continued to do so after he moved to the United States. As his fame grew, more and more of his work was translated into English. He cooperated with, or supervised these translations, sometimes revising the originals, which raises the question as to the degree to which these were original works in English rather than translations into that language. Moreover, it is a common complaint of Singer scholars that translations into other languages have often been done from the English versions rather than the Yiddish originals. Before he won great fame as "Isaac Bashevis Singer"–and eventually the Nobel Prize, giving his acceptance speech in Yiddish–his works had other forms of his name on the title pages. The Library of Congress lists his authorized heading as: "Singer, Isaac Bashevis." It notes the following variations, mostly transliterated from Yiddish: "Bashevis, Isaac"; "Singer, Itzhak Bashevis"; "Bashevis, Yitshak"; "Bashevis-Zinger, Yitshak"; "Singer, I. B. (Isaac Bashevis)"; and "Bashevis-Singer, Isaac." (There seems little doubt that they missed a few.[16])

Singer's case is unusual primarily for his fame. His is by no means the most complex instance which can be offered in the realm of name authorities–not even close, in fact. As concerns our bibliography, however, it is not at all unusual for Israeli scholars in particular to publish in two or more languages; that is, to compose works in multiple languages, not merely to write in one language and then, for the most important few, see them translated into others. In the complex situation of language choice and usage that the entries in our bibliography represent, the most reasonable thing to do is follow a widely accepted and readily available source–in our case, the Library of Congress Name Authorities File–and live with the consequences, disagreements, and misunderstandings that will result in any such matter. This is also familiar to librarians specializing in the fields of Slavic, East European, and Eurasian studies. Of course, to complicate matters, many of the names that appear in the *Gal-Ed* bibliography do not appear in the LC Name Authorities File, in OCLC, or anywhere in American library collections. Names that appear only in the Hebrew alphabet are especially problematic, as is the matter of cataloging in and transliteration from Hebrew or Yiddish. In the final analysis, one does the best one can to come up with reasonable solutions, and one learns to live with the criticisms.

The areas of indexing and subject analysis provide the last access points included in the printed version of the bibliography. The print version includes three separate indexes: topical, chronological, and general.

The Topical Index attempts to deal with the problem that an alphabetical listing of hundreds of entries can be difficult to search for broad subject areas. It lists entries under the following headings (entries may appear under more than one): Surveys and general works; Bibliography, historiography, scholarship; Jewish communities; Politics, diplomacy, and legal status; Demography and economic conditions; Social conditions and life; Cultural life and intellectual life; Religion; Education, children, youth; Literature, linguistics, folklore; Relations between Jews and non-Jews; Polish Jews abroad; Holocaust; Memoirs, autobiographies, diaries, etc.; Documents; Films, photographs, and recordings; and, Collected studies.

The Chronological Index divides the history of the Polish Jews into the following periods: Pre-Partition (up to 1795); Partition (1795-1918); Interwar (1918-1939); Holocaust and World War II (1939-1945); and Postwar (since 1945). In the next installment, the Postwar period will be closed out as 1945-1989, and a new, Post-Communist (since 1989) period will be added. The practice with the printed bibliography has been to include up to two periods per entry. When three or more periods seem possible, the catchall term, "General and multiperiod" has been used. However, since so many works cover large stretches of the twentieth century, it has been decided to initiate a new chronological heading for that as well, when there are three or more periods covered: e.g., "Interwar," "Holocaust and World War II," and "Postwar."

The General Index covers the widest range of names and subjects. This index lists all personal names that appear (including those of the authors and editors), organizations mentioned in entries, places, and a number of topical subject headings of much greater specificity than in the actual Topical Index. The names that appear in the General Index are presented, as much as possible, in the forms provided by the Name Authorities File. The topical subjects, however, are established rather on the fly, at need. While the ideal of a prearranged thesaurus is an excellent one, it quickly proves to be impracticable. There is, however, a great deal of consistency among the installments of the bibliography, and the fact that the "General Index" has been prepared with a high degree of consistency by individuals knowledgeable in the field, helps as well.

The following is a sample record, entry no. 126, which appeared in the first installment of the bibliography. In fact, only the portion through the indicated pagination was printed in the actual entry. The subsequent topical, chronological, and general index fields all appeared separately, in their respective sections at the end of the entire bibliography; they display below in square brackets.

CORRSIN, STEPHEN D.

'Language Use in Cultural and Political Change in pre-1914 Warsaw: Poles, Jews, and Russification.' *Slavonic and East European Review* 68 (no.1, 1990): 69-90. [Topical Index: Cultural and intellectual life; Literature, linguistics, folklore. Chronological Index: Partition period. General Index: Warsaw.]

MOVING TO THE ONLINE FORMAT

In the first installment of the print bibliography, it was stated that an important priority would be placing and maintaining the bibliography online. As stated earlier, the initial attempt, at the website of the Diaspora Research Institute of Tel Aviv University, did not prove practical.

Since 2000, we started to try another tack, of a more homemade variety. The first step (now largely complete) has been to convert the previous three installments into a single online file–or rather, several large files. This has largely been an adventure in re-keying, because the original files either no longer existed, or did not exist in compatible forms; further, it seemed like a good way to correct and revise the inconsistencies and (mostly) minor errors that had appeared. The bibliography now exists as several fairly generic text files, with a few quirks.

The first noteworthy issue is that the simplest way to begin was to separate the Roman and Hebrew alphabet materials. Approximately 15% of the total is in the Hebrew alphabet, that is, citations for items that were originally published in Hebrew or Yiddish. Since the bibliography uses the original titles in their original forms, rather than transliterated or translated ones, the simplest thing to do was to have separate files. The separate main Roman and Hebrew files are linked by their original record numbers, however, making a single unified file an easy matter.

The second issue is that of software. The *Nota Bene Lingua Workstation* is now being used for the next installment of the bibliography. This is appropriate because of its multilingual, multialphabetical capabilities. However, it remains to be seen whether it will be most useful for a complete web version. That is now being investigated. We are also looking for a suitable home for the web bibliography. While in theory, this could be anywhere, experience shows that it is generally a good idea for the bibliographer to be in physical proximity to the website's host institution. Further, while consistency and compatibility with the print installments are important concerns, in creating and maintaining a master web version it may be possible to upgrade significantly the bibliography's–one will have to say, the database's–contents and searching capabilities. There are fascinating possibilities and we can hope that the decision and conversion processes will be complete by the end of 2003.

CONCLUSION

The obvious question to conclude with is this: what is the future of this bibliographical project? The first aspect of the general question is this: will there be sufficient interest among scholars for this work to continue to be useful? It is difficult to predict the future of Polish-Jewish studies and many factors must enter into any such attempt. The Jewish community of Poland has revived to a very modest degree, but it seems unlikely that it will again provide a significant pool of scholars. The increase of interest, and the institutionalization of scholarship on Jewish topics at Polish universities is impressive, but the field of Polish-Jewish history is likely to remain of minor interest, at best, in Poland, once the initial wave of "self-exploration" appears complete or at least sufficient.

The field of Polish-Jewish studies is also likely to remain of minor interest in Israel, where "diaspora" studies have always had a lesser draw, and in North America and Western and Central Europe. I would predict that the level of research and publishing in this area will level off soon and then decline somewhat, but it will not disappear by any means: it will remain a modest field of interest to a limited number of scholars and readers.

That said, it remains true for the *Gal-Ed* bibliography that the most important area for work right now and in the immediate future is to continue to publish (in print or online) information on newly published materials. This includes expanding the collection methods to cover more non-print resources, particularly web items and microform (or digital) collections. The second key initiative is to convert the existing print bibliography to machine-readable form, in a systematic way, improving and correcting it as necessary, and making it readily available in online form. A much more distant goal is to provide retrospective entries as well: to cover the field in decades previous to the 1990s, in other words. But for the time being that must remain, at least in the context of the work for the journal *Gal-Ed*, a project for (many) rainy days.

NOTES

1. Zachary M. Baker, "The Chosen Book: Reinventing the Jew in Absentia: Recent Judaica Publishing Trends in Poland," *Judaica Librarianship* 5 (no.1, 1989-1990): 62.
2. Baker, 65.
3. Majer Balaban, *Bibliografia historii Żydow w Polsce i w krajach ościennych za lata 1900-1930* (Bibliography on the History of the Jews in Poland and in Neighboring Lands: Works Published during the Years 1900-1930) (Warsaw: Towarzystwo Szerzenia Wiedzy Judaistycznej, 1939; reprint, Jerusalem: World Federation of Polish Jews, 1978).
4. Ezra Mendelsohn, *Yehude mizrah-merkaz eiropa ben shete milhamot-ha-'olam: bibliyografyah nivheret* (The Jews of East-Central Europe between the Two World Wars: a Selected Bibliography) (Jerusalem: Merkaz Zalman Shazar le-ha'amakat ha-toda'ah ha-historit ha-yehudit, 1978).
5. Gershon David Hundert and Gershon C. Bacon, *The Jews in Poland and Russia: Bibliographical Essays* (Bloomington: Indiana University Press, 1984).
6. Jerzy J. (George) Lerski and Halina T. Lerski, *Jewish-Polish Coexistence, 1772-1939: A Topical Bibliography* (New York: Greenwood Press, 1986).
7. Jack Kugelmass and Jonathan Boyarin, eds. and trans., *From a Ruined Garden: The Memorial Books of Polish Jewry*, 2d expanded ed. (Bloomington: Indiana University Press, 1998). Baker's compilation appears on pp. 273-339. Earlier versions of the bibliography appeared in this work's first edition (New York: Schocken, 1982), and subsequently in 1989 and 1992, in publications of the Jewish Genealogical Society.
8. Krzysztof Pilarczyk, comp., *Przewodnik po bibliografiach polskich judaików* (Guide to Bibliographies of Polish Judaica). Kraków: Uniwersytet Jagielloński, Międzywydziałowy Zakład Historii i Kultury Żydów w Polsce, 1992); Krzysztof Pilarczyk, comp., *Judaika polskie z XVI-XVIII wieku: materiały do bibliografii* (Polish Judaica of the Sixteenth and Seventeenth Centuries: Materials for a Bibliography, Pt. 1). (Kraków: Uniwersytet Jagielloński, Międzywydziałowy Zakład Historii i Kultury Żydów w Polsce, 1995.

9. Stefan Gąsiorowski, ed., *Bibliografia historii i kultury Żydów w Polsce* (Bibliography of the [sic] Jewish History and Culture in Poland) (Krakow: Uniwersytet Jagielloński, Katedra Judaistyki, 2002): [11].

10. See also Michał Czajka, "Bibliografia zawartości *Biuletynu Żydowskiego Instytutu Historycznego*, 1950-2000," *Kwartalnik Historii Żydów* 199 (no.3, 2001): 393-531).

11. Katarzyna Muszyńska, ed., *Bibliographies of Polish Judaica: International Symposium* (Kraków: Uniwersytet Jagielloński, Międzywydziałowy Zakład Historii i Kultury Żydów w Polsce, 1993): [7].

12. Stephen D. Corrsin, "Works on Polish Jewry, 1990-1994: A Bibliography," *Gal-Ed* 14 (1995): 131.

13. *Reshimat ma'amarim be-mada'e ha-yahadut* = *Index of Articles on Jewish Studies*. Jerusalem: Magnes, 1966- ; also freely available over the web, at <http://jnul.huji.ac.il/rambi/>.

14. I would like to thank especially Mr. and Mrs. Jerzy Kulczycki, the owners of Orbis Books, London, England; and the staff of "Lexicon" Księgarnia Wysyłkowa, Warsaw, Poland, for sending me their catalogs promptly upon request.

15. Corrsin, 131-32.

16. See Library of Congress Name Authorities File ARN 299502. One further point should be noted: the date and other identifying information has been left out of the bibliography's headings, as a matter of practicality–or if one prefers, a desperate shortcut. Regarding Singer, it should be noted that in his regular contributions to the Yiddish newspaper *Forverts* he published under a variety of additional pseudonyms, most notably: Segal, D.; Varshavski, Yitshak. See: David Neal Miller, *Bibliography of Isaac Bashevis Singer, 1924-1949* (New York: Peter Lang, 1983).

Resources on the Genealogy of Eastern European Jews

Zachary M. Baker

SUMMARY. This article presents a progress report on grassroots efforts to document the Eastern European Jewish genealogical heritage. Most of the resources that are described here were developed by and for genealogists of Jewish ancestry. Until the end of the Cold War, access to Eastern European vital records was often difficult and at times not possible. Because of that, Jewish genealogists focused on ancillary sources such as immigration records and community memorial books. Since then, these have been augmented by an impressive array of guidebooks, serials, and electronic resources (websites, databases). *[Article copies available for a fee from The Haworth Document Delivery Service: 1-800-HAWORTH. E-mail address: <docdelivery@haworthpress.com> Website: <http://www.HaworthPress.com> © 2003 by The Haworth Press, Inc. All rights reserved.]*

KEYWORDS. Archives, databases, Eastern Europe, gazetteers, genealogy, Jews, websites, web sites

---

Zachary M. Baker is the Reinhard Family Curator of Judaica and Hebraica Collections, Stanford University Libraries. He was previously Head Librarian, YIVO Institute for Jewish Research, New York, where he worked closely with a large genealogical constituency. He is the author of numerous articles in genealogical newsletters and journals.

Address correspondence: Zachary M. Baker, Green Library 321–ASRG, Stanford University, Stanford, CA 94305-6004 USA (E-mail: zbaker@stanford.edu).

[Haworth co-indexing entry note]: "Resources on the Genealogy of Eastern European Jews." Baker, Zachary M. Co-published simultaneously in *Slavic & East European Information Resources* (The Haworth Information Press, an imprint of The Haworth Press, Inc.) Vol. 4, No. 2/3, 2003, pp. 169-184; and: *Judaica in the Slavic Realm, Slavica in the Judaic Realm: Repositories, Collections, Projects, Publications* (ed: Zachary M. Baker) The Haworth Information Press, an imprint of The Haworth Press, Inc., 2003, pp. 169-184. Single or multiple copies of this article are available for a fee from The Haworth Document Delivery Service [1-800-HAWORTH, 9:00 a.m. - 5:00 p.m. (EST). E-mail address: docdelivery@haworthpress.com].

http://www.haworthpress.com/store/product.asp?sku=J167
© 2003 by The Haworth Press, Inc. All rights reserved.

Over twenty years ago I spent an afternoon sitting at a microfiche reader in the Map Division at the Library of Congress. As I pored over a detailed map of the district in southern Poland where my maternal grandparents were born, I could not help but eavesdrop on a disembodied conversation between one of the Map Division's librarians and a persistent researcher at the other end of a telephone line. The librarian was responding to an interrogation about Eastern European geography until, finally, he paused and asked his interlocutor, "Excuse me, are you by any chance a Jewish genealogist?" The association that the map librarian was making between Eastern Europe and "Jewish genealogists" amused me. Evidently the frequency with which he was fielding questions of this sort had caused a pattern to form in his mind. And that day I, too, was one of those Jewish genealogists.

This article presents a progress report on grassroots efforts to document the Eastern European Jewish genealogical heritage. Over the past twenty-five years genealogists have produced a remarkable array of printed and (more recently) electronic guides, gazetteers, and finding aids aimed at identifying published and unpublished materials that serve their research needs, along with the repositories in Eastern European countries and elsewhere that house those materials. Most of the informational resources that are described here were developed by and for genealogists of Jewish ancestry. Nevertheless, genealogical research does not proceed in a vacuum, and some of the resources mentioned are of a more general character. The others, though tailored to a specifically Jewish audience, are relevant to additional constituencies as well: genealogists, historians, archivists, librarians, and even travel agents.

For family historians of all stripes geographical awareness is indeed one of the keys to successful research. The most relevant archival documents for genealogical research—above all vital records (births, marriages, deaths)—if extant are usually housed in municipal and regional repositories in or near the specific localities where they were created. Individuals of Eastern European background are confronted by an array of obstacles in tracing their ancestry. The violent disruptions, wars, frequent border changes, and political repressions of the twentieth century have placed formidable barriers to genealogical research. Archival *fonds* are often scattered, with the result being that local historical research may require examination of documents in archives situated in different countries. Published guides and widely accessible finding aids for genealogical research in Eastern Europe have frequently been inadequate or altogether lacking.

For American Jews of Eastern European descent the political rupture of the Cold War followed on the heels of the eradication of Jewish communities throughout Central and Eastern Europe during World War II. These factors, combined with large-scale emigration into the 1920s, the suppression of communal autonomy under Soviet rule, and periodic outbreaks of state-sponsored anti-Semitism after 1945, created an enormous sense of distance from a region that little more than a century ago accounted for 80 percent of the world's Jewish population–and a sizable proportion of the region's overall population (as high as 18 percent in some districts, and a plurality of the urban population in most[1]). Memories of the Old Country persist among the dwindling cohort of émigrés and Holocaust survivors, but for their descendants Eastern Europe came to represent a vast historical void.

In the United States popular interest in genealogy was energized in the mid-1970s by Alex Haley's book *Roots* and the television series that was based on it. At that time almost no reference tools were available to address the still inchoate research needs of the Jewish genealogical constituency. Access to Eastern European vital records was often difficult and at times not possible; in addition, primary sources were in languages that many researchers could not read. A great deal of improvisation in research strategies was required, and several guidebooks were published to meet the market demand and help novice and advanced researchers alike. These reference books, in addition, identify materials of general research value.[2]

Because the Old World was *terra incognita* for most American Jewish genealogists, one common misconception that developed was that thousands of Eastern European localities had, with the catastrophic destruction of their Jewish communities, been "wiped off the map." And indeed, this perception was underscored by the difficulties that many genealogists encountered in identifying and locating cities and towns whose Yiddish names–which were preserved in their families' oral traditions, albeit in often garbled versions–did not correspond to forms encountered on maps and in gazetteers. How could one possibly "get from Amshinov to Mszczonów without moving an inch"?[3] Until the publication of *Where Once We Walked: A Guide to the Jewish Communities Destroyed in the Holocaust* (1991), genealogists had to rely on a witches' brew of geographical reference sources in order to identify their ancestors' places of residence. These included both standard and specialized atlases and gazetteers, along with Jewish-oriented publications such as Yad Vashem's *Blackbook of Localities*, Chester Cohen's *Shtetl Finder*, and Berl Kagan's *Hebrew Subscription Lists*.[4]

Where Once We Walked, a gazetteer of more than 22,000 localities throughout Europe where Jews resided before World War II, is one of the many essential reference works to appear under the imprint of Avotaynu, a genealogical publishing house located in northern New Jersey. Each entry includes the locality's official place name as of 1991 along with variants, country, prewar Jewish population, distance from the nearest large city, geographical coordinates, and bibliographical references. In contrast to some gazetteers, narrative is kept to a strict minimum in *Where Once We Walked*. This volume marked the inauguration of the now widely used Daitch-Mokotoff Soundex System, a six-digit code that matches letters and letter combinations to sequences of numerals. This Soundex system (named after its creators, Randy Daitch and Gary Mokotoff) is modeled on one that was devised by the National Archives for federal census records, and is specifically adapted to Slavic and Yiddish phonology. In *Where Once We Walked* it is employed in a special "Listing of Town Names," where it serves as a very effective medium for the matching of garbled names with official toponyms.[5]

Before the Berlin Wall fell, Jewish genealogical researchers were largely restricted to resources that might best be described as ancillary to tracing their Eastern European lineages. The genealogist's field of vision was perpetually clouded in the center and clearer on the periphery–a kind of "research glaucoma." In the absence of easy access to Eastern European vital records (unless one was fortunate enough to be descended from ancestors who resided in those localities whose mid-nineteenth century records were microfilmed by the Latter Day Saints' Family History Library during the 1960s[6]) genealogists focused their attentions on immigration records,[7] specialized genealogies–especially for rabbinical lineages[8]–and community memorial books published since the Holocaust.

The memorial book genre is especially noteworthy for its genealogical, memoiristic, ethnographic, and local historical detail. Its antecedents in Jewish literature include Rhineland martyrologies from the era of the Crusades and chronicles of the massacres that accompanied the Cossack uprising of Bohdan Khmel'nyts'kyi (1648-1654).[9] The first Jewish community memorial books to be issued in modern times came out in response to the 1919 pogroms in the Podolian towns of Proskurov (later renamed–ironically, from a Jewish perspective–Khmel'nyts'kyi, Ukraine) and Fel'shtin. Like almost all of the post-1945 memorial books, the Proskurov and Fel'shtin volumes were published far away from the communities that they commemorate, under the sponsorship of émigré *landsmanshaft* organizations (mutual aid societies that are founded on the basis of home town origin).[10]

The format of the post-Holocaust memorial books gradually came to fit into a regular pattern. Chapters about the early and modern history of the towns and their Jewish communities were usually accompanied by personal recollections by non-professional authors, and testimonies concerning the Holocaust period. Lists of names of Holocaust victims are often (but not always) included in these volumes, representing their most salient genealogical aspect. For English speakers, the best introduction to the memorial book genre is the anthology *From a Ruined Garden*, edited by the anthropologists Jack Kugelmass and Jonathan Boyarin. The 1998 edition includes the most up-to-date bibliography of the approximately 700 Eastern European Jewish memorial books (covering at least double that number of cities and towns) that have been published to date.[11]

Most of the early memorial books were in Yiddish; by the 1960s their languages of publication were often a medley of Hebrew and Yiddish. Since the 1970s the predominant language of these books has been Hebrew. (Immediately after World War II many memorial books were published in Germany, the United States, and Argentina; by the mid-1950s Tel Aviv became the most frequent imprint.) English sections–most of them rather brief–were often included within these volumes. Occasionally, translations of entire volumes have appeared.[12]

Approximately 75 percent of all memorial books are for localities within the interwar boundaries of the Polish Republic. Many are for communities that were situated in the *kresy*–regions that now belong to Belarus and Ukraine. Very few, however, are for cities and towns located east of the pre-1939 Soviet frontier. Memorial books continue to be published, albeit in small numbers; the ones that have come out in recent years tend to be for towns outside of historic Poland, in areas on the western periphery of the former Soviet Union such as Moldova and Carpatho-Ruthenia, as well as Hungary, Slovakia, and Transylvania.

Interest in memorial books among genealogists remains strong, even though so many other genealogical resources have become available. The JewishGen website, which is described below, includes library listings for memorial books and links to translations (usually only of portions of these books). A veritable cottage industry of memorial book translating has emerged in recent years.

Until Eastern European archives became more readily accessible, as we have noted, Jewish genealogists were compelled to rely upon those records that were available in Western repositories. These included LDS microfilms of Jewish vital records for Poland and Hungary, a set of World War I-vintage Russian consular records,[13] and *landsmanshaft* archives.[14] In the United States, specialized institutions such as the Dorot Jewish Division of The New York Public Library, the Library of the United States Holocaust Memorial Museum, and the YIVO Institute for Jewish Research, came to play pivotal roles as centers for genealogical research. The Jewish Genealogical Institute at the new Center for Jewish History, in New York (where YIVO and other Jewish research organizations are now housed), represents an attempt to provide a central address and clearinghouse for Jewish genealogical research. In Israel, the Yad Vashem Holocaust memorial (Jerusalem) and the Douglas E. Goldman Jewish Genealogy Center at the Diaspora Museum (Beth Hatefutsoth, Tel Aviv) fill a similar function.

In the late 1970s (very shortly after popular interest in family history emerged), a loose confederation of Jewish genealogical societies came into existence across the U.S. and in other countries. In addition to holding regular meetings locally, these societies convene an International Seminar on Jewish Genealogy each summer, under the aegis of the International Association of Jewish Genealogical Societies <www.jewishgen.org/ajgs/>. Many of these societies publish newsletters, which often contain an array of useful information for researchers. For example, the Winter 2001/2002 issue of *Dorot: The Journal of the Jewish Genealogical Society* (New York) includes an announcement about a new online archival guide to documents in Eastern Europe (which is described below) and an article about the genealogical value of Tsarist legal decrees.[15] Atop the pyramid of Jewish genealogical journals stand two publications: the pioneering *Toledot: The Journal of Jewish Genealogy*, edited by Arthur Kurzweil and Steven W. Siegel (New York: 1977-1982), and *Avotaynu: The International Review of Jewish Genealogy*, edited by Gary Mokotoff and Sallyann Amdur Sack (Teaneck, NJ: 1985-).

Avotaynu (the title is Hebrew for "Our Ancestors") is indexed in *RAMBI: The Index of Articles on Jewish Studies* <jnul.huji.ac.il/rambi/>. Given the Eastern European background of most of the world's Jewish population, it is not surprising to encounter many articles in this journal that relay researchers' findings in Central and Eastern Europe. Here are a few recent citations, culled from *RAMBI*:

> Dmitry Z. Feldman, "Archival Sources for the Genealogy of Jewish Colonists in Southern Russia in the 19th Century," *Avotaynu* 15, no. 2 (1999): 14-17.
> David B. Hoffman, "Researching 18th-Century Census and Tax Lists from the Grand Duchy of Lithuania," *Avotaynu* 17, no. 3 (2001): 7-9.
> Barbara R. Krasner, "Breaking New Ground: The Story of Jewish Records Indexing—Poland Project," *Avotaynu* 17, no. 1 (2001): 7-14.
> Edward David Luft, "German and Polish Archival Holdings in Moscow," *Avotaynu* 17, no. 4 (2001): 11-13.
> Sallyann Amdur Sack, "Can Jewish Genealogists Successfully Research 18th-Century Poland?" *Avotaynu* 16, no. 3 (2000): 16-18.

In addition to its journal and the *Where Once We Walked* gazetteer, Avotaynu has published several key reference books of Eastern European interest. These include how-to manuals (e.g., *How to Document Victims and Locate Survivors of the Holocaust*, by Gary Mokotoff; *Finding Your Jewish Roots in Galicia: A Resource Guide*, by Suzan F. Wynne), archival guides (e.g., *Jewish Vital Records, Revision Lists And Other Jewish Holdings in the Lithuanian Archives*, by

Harold Rhode and Sallyann Amdur Sack), the English translation of a memorial book (*Kaminits Podolsk and Its Environs*), and several massive works on onomastics, by Alexander Beider (*A Dictionary of Jewish Surnames From the Russian Empire*; *A Dictionary of Jewish Surnames From the Kingdom of Poland*; and *A Dictionary of Ashkenazic Given Names*). Avotaynu also maintains an online store <www.avotaynu.com/> through which one may order journal subscriptions, books by various publishers, microfiche, maps, CD-ROMs, videos, and JPEG images (mostly of old postcards, including many for Eastern European towns).

Travel accounts are a frequent feature of *Avotaynu* and other Jewish genealogical journals and newsletters. The authors of these articles focus on different aspects of the Eastern European tourist experience: general travel conditions, encounters with local residents, visits to cemeteries, and archival research–to name a few main topics. Until the late 1980s research on Jewish historical topics was virtually taboo in the then-Soviet Union, for locals and foreigners alike, and the practical effect of this was that archives were virtually closed for scholarship in Jewish Studies.[16] With the onset of *perestroika* cracks began to appear in the formerly monolithic façade, to the benefit of genealogical researchers as well, who were now able to conduct ad hoc archival surveys and publish them in *Avotaynu*. (An early example of this is Alex E. Friedlander's pathbreaking 1990 article "Jewish Vital Statistic Records in Lithuanian Archives."[17])

The fall of the Berlin Wall and the demise of the Soviet Union led to vastly increased travel opportunities and dramatically improved access to vital records and other collections of value for genealogical and historical research. Jewish tourism to Eastern Europe takes a variety of forms, including group or individual travel to ancestral cities and towns, pilgrimages to gravesites of famous Hasidic rabbis, trips to "sites of memory" (former concentration camps and Holocaust memorials)–sometimes within the framework of the ideologically freighted March of the Living[18]–and visits to local and regional archival branches in quests for documentation of family roots. A typical itinerary can include any or all of these destinations. Jewish mass tourism to Eastern Europe is a phenomenon that has attracted the attention of journalists and ethnographers alike.[19] This tourist trade has become so well entrenched that there are now travel agencies and entire websites catering to the needs of Jewish genealogists. The omnibus Jewish genealogical website, JewishGen <www.jewishgen.org/>, for example, offers as one of its SIGs (special interest groups) the JewishGen ShtetlSchleppers® <www.jewishgen.org/ShtetlSchleppers/>, with dozens of organized tours traveling to Central and Eastern Europe each year.

The end of Communist rule coincided with the emergence and development of the Internet, which has proved such a boon in so many research arenas. Electronic mail has sped up communication worldwide, and indexing projects and the creation of online finding aids now make it possible to conduct research from home that would formerly have required long-distance travel or a time-consuming exchange of correspondence. Through the Ellis Island database <www.ellisislandrecords.org/>, to take a general example, one can readily locate arrival records for immigrants to the United States. Only a few short years ago it would have taken weeks or days to obtain results that are now available within seconds.

The JewishGen website offers layer upon layer of information relating to Eastern Europe in general, and the genealogy of Eastern European-descended Jews in particular. The site's resources are far too numerous to list here, and we will therefore confine ourselves to just a few notable examples under some of the main categories into which the home page is subdivided:

- **Learn**
  The **JewishGen InfoFile Index**, under this heading, functions much like a site map. **Topics** and **Countries** are listed alphabetically, in separate sections, at the top of the page, followed by **JewishGen Operational Files** (discussion groups, SIGs, frequently asked questions) and **InfoFiles, by Topic** (alphabetical list of subject headings), **InfoFiles, by Country**, and **Data Files**.
- **Research**
  JewishGen Databases is subdivided into general and geographical databases. Under **Poland**, for example, is found **The Oshpitzin Yizkor Database**, compiled by Rabbi Joseph Schachter, and containing 5,406 entries for Jews who lived in the town of Oshpitsin–the Yiddish name for Oświęcim (Auschwitz), Poland–between 1919 and 1941. The Daitch-Mokotoff Soundex system may be used for name searches.
- **Projects and Activities**
  ShtetLinks leads to extensive background information on and SIGs for hundreds of localities. The **Yizkor Book Project** provides links (among other things) to translations, necrologies, and library holdings of community memorial books. The **JewishGen ShtetlSchleppers®** are also found under this heading.
- **Special Interest Groups**
  These are subdivided regionally and by country. The heading **Belarus**, for example, provides links to **Shtetls of Belarus, Belarus Surname Index, Archival Resources, Travel**, and much more. The page includes a period map of the five Tsarist *gubernii* that covered most of present-day Belarus (Grodno, Minsk, Mogilev, Vilna, Vitebsk) along with links to multiple levels of information about each *guberniia*.

- **Hosted Organizations**
  Among **JewishGen-hosted Projects**, for example, is **Jewish Records Indexing–Poland (JRI-PL)**, "a project to index all the Jewish vital records in Poland."

JewishGen offers a prime example of the ways in which genealogists put their voluntarism to work, in cooperation with professionally staffed research organizations (publicly funded archives and libraries in North America, Europe, and Israel; Jewish-sponsored institutions; and the LDS Family History Library), individuals (academicians, librarians, archivists, translators, community leaders, "web sovereigns"), and commercial enterprises (publishers such as Avotaynu). The resultant synergies are powerful indeed.

Finally, in light of the centrality of archives for genealogical research, we turn our attentions to Miriam Weiner's efforts to bring Eastern European archival resources closer to genealogists in the West. Ms. Weiner, who is both a licensed private investigator and a Board-certified genealogist (two highly complementary credentials!), has since the mid-1980s carved out a distinctive niche in the delivery of personalized services to individual genealogists and in the creation and dissemination of comprehensive finding aids.

"Routes to Roots" <www.routestoroots.com/>, which offers various services for a fee, could be described as Ms. Weiner's "commercial arm." Routes to Roots "specialize[s] in Jewish research in the archives of Eastern Europe, can visit ancestral towns on your behalf or can arrange a customized visit for you and your family to the 'old country.'" The countries and regions for which she offers these services are Belarus, Moldova/Bessarabia, Poland, Ukraine, and Galicia/Austro-Hungary. Note the overlapping categories: Contemporary Moldova encompasses most of Tsarist Bessarabia, and the Austro-Hungarian region of Galicia is today split between Poland and Ukraine. Use of the historic names for these regions reflects the family traditions of many Jewish genealogists.[20]

In the course of her visits to Eastern European archives, Ms. Weiner systematically collected information on genealogical records in hundreds of repositories, which eventually resulted in the publication of two indispensable archival guides: *Jewish Roots in Poland: Pages from the Past and Archival Inventories* (1997), and *Jewish Roots in Ukraine and Moldova: Pages from the Past and Archival Inventories* (1999). The Miriam Weiner Routes to Roots Foundation and the YIVO Institute for Jewish Research jointly published both volumes; the first one was issued in cooperation with the Polish State Archives and the second, with the cooperation of the Ukrainian State Archives and the Moldovan National Archives.

In addition to extensive inventories of vital records (births, marriages, deaths) for thousands of cities and towns, the two guides contain historical and geographical chapters on hundreds of localities, along with maps and historical and present-day photographs–including photographs of archival repositories and some of the documents that reside within them. The Poland volume also "provides updated information on the holdings of Warsaw's famous Jewish Historical Institute [Żydowski Instytut Historyczny] and the concentration camp archives at Majdanek and Auschwitz-Birkenau." In a nutshell, each of these books constitutes "a combination reference book, travel guide, Holocaust book and genealogical handbook," which "could not even have been attempted before the collapse of communism in the former Soviet Union and Eastern Europe."[21]

After the Ukraine/Moldova volume came out, Ms. Weiner shifted her focus to the dissemination of information over the Internet, via the Routes to Roots Foundation website <www.rtrfoundation.org/>. Her RTR Foundation was established in 1994, initially to support the publication of the Poland and Ukraine/Moldova surveys. Its home page lists the following goals:

- Survey, study, research, inventory and document Jewish material, archives and Judaica in Eastern European archives;
- Foster and promote the study and preservation of Jewish genealogical material;
- Assemble, catalogue, publish and disseminate information from research and study of Jewish materials;
- Compile, maintain and update library and/or archive of collections of Jewish historical, cultural and genealogical information;
- Sponsor educational lectures and seminars.

The RTR Foundation website offers consolidated access to archival inventories for vital records in five countries (Belarus, Lithuania, Moldova, Poland, and Ukraine), through the Eastern European Archival Database. It also includes the introductions and chapters by archivists that appeared previously in the Poland and Ukraine/Moldova guides, along with maps and links to other websites. The Database, which is accessible gratis, "will be updated periodically based upon new information received directly from the archives or from individuals (which will then be verified by the appropriate archives)."[22] Searches are done by place name, according to "Exact Match," "D[aitch]-M[okotoff] Soundex," or "Begins With." The geographical–and geopolitical–scatter of Eastern European vital records is indicated by a search under Lazdijai (a Lithuanian border town that was my paternal grandfather's birthplace). This search yields references to archival inventories for the following *types* of records: Army/Recruits, Birth, Death, Immigration, Marriage, and Divorce. These records are held by repositories in the following *cities*: Białystok, Suwałki, Vilnius, Warsaw. Most of the pre-1918 records for Lazdijai are housed in Polish archives, probably because until then it was situated in the Tsarist *guberniia* of Suwałki; the city of Suwałki has belonged to the Polish Republic since 1918.

"Eastern European Archival Database" is a slightly misleading name in that it is limited to *genealogical* records for the *Jewish* population of Eastern Europe. It is neither a general archival database for that part of Europe nor a genealogical database for all of its religious and ethnic groups. Nevertheless, from this brief description it should be apparent that it is a very powerful tool. The RTR Foundation website contains useful links to other sites that are likely to be of interest to genealogists seeking to trace their Jewish ancestry. Among these are:

- Archives in Eastern Europe (Belarus, Lithuania, Poland, Ukraine) and worldwide;
- National Archives (Washington);
- Library of Congress (Washington), New York Public Library;
- Family History Library (Salt Lake City);
- Federation of East European Genealogical Societies;
- Polish Roots: The Polish Genealogy Source.[23]

Avotaynu, JewishGen, and The Miriam Weiner Routes to Roots Foundation offer clear evidence of what a highly motivated user community is capable of achieving. Whether the experiences, skills, and accomplishments of genealogists–Jewish or otherwise–can be replicated in, or indeed are even transferable to, other realms of archival documentation for Eastern Europe is a question worth pondering. Meanwhile, genealogists continue to develop an impressive array of research tools that make life considerably easier for the librarians and archivists who field a never-ending stream of genealogical inquiries.[24]

SELECTED RESOURCES MENTIONED IN THIS ARTICLE

Print

Avotaynu: The International Review of Jewish Genealogy. Teaneck, NJ, 1985- .
   Plus the following Avotaynu monographic publications:
      Alexander Beider. *A Dictionary of Ashkenazic Given Names*. Teaneck, NJ: Avotaynu, 2001.

_____. *A Dictionary of Jewish Surnames From the Kingdom of Poland.* Teaneck, NJ: Avotaynu, 1996.

_____. *A Dictionary of Jewish Surnames From the Russian Empire.* Teaneck, NJ: Avotaynu, 1993.

Gary Mokotoff. *How to Document Victims and Locate Survivors of the Holocaust.* Teaneck, NJ: Avotaynu, 1995.

Gary Mokotoff and Sallyann Amdur Sack. *Where Once We Walked: A Guide to the Jewish Communities Destroyed in the Holocaust.* Teaneck, NJ: Avotaynu, 1991.

Harold Rhode and Sallyann Amdur Sack. *Jewish Vital Records, Revision Lists And Other Jewish Holdings In the Lithuanian Archives.* Teaneck, NJ: Avotaynu, 1996.

Suzan F. Wynne. *Finding Your Jewish Roots in Galicia: A Resource Guide.* Teaneck, NJ: Avotaynu, 1998.

Jack Kugelmass and Jonathan Boyarin, eds. *From a Ruined Garden: The Memorial Books of Polish Jewry.* New York: Schocken, 1983. 2nd ed.: Bloomington: Indiana University Press, 1998. Both editions include the "Bibliography of Eastern European Jewish Memorial Books," compiled by Zachary M. Baker.

Arthur Kurzweil and Miriam Weiner, eds. *The Encyclopedia of Jewish Genealogy*, vol. 1. Northvale, NJ: Jason Aronson, 1991.

Sallyann Amdur Sack and Suzan Fishl Wynne. *The Russian Consular Records Index and Catalog.* New York: Garland, 1987.

Rosaline Schwartz and Susan Milamed. *A Guide to YIVO's landsmanshaftn Archive: From Alexandrovsk to Zyrardow.* New York: YIVO Institute for Jewish Research, 1986.

Miriam Weiner. *Jewish Roots in Poland: Pages from the Past and Archival Inventories.* Secaucus, NJ: The Miriam Weiner Routes to Roots Foundation and the YIVO Institute for Jewish Research, 1997.

_____. *Jewish Roots in Ukraine and Moldova: Pages from the Past and Archival Inventories.* Secaucus, NJ: The Miriam Weiner Routes to Roots Foundation and the YIVO Institute for Jewish Research, 1999.

Electronic

Avotaynu: <www.avotaynu.com>.
Daitch-Mokotoff Soundex System: <www.jewishgen.org/infofiles/soundex.txt>.
Ellis Island database: <www.ellisislandrecords.org/>.
Family History Library (Salt Lake City): <www.familysearch.org/Eng/Library/FHL/ frameset_library.asp>.
Federation of East European Family History Societies: <feefhs.org/>.
GeoNet Names Server: <http://164.214.2.59/gns/html/index.html>.

JewishGen: <www.jewishgen.org>.
March of the Living: <www.marchoftheliving.org/>.
Polish Roots™: *The Polish Genealogy Source*: <www.polishroots.org/>.
RAMBI: The Index of Articles on Jewish Studies: <jnul.huji.ac.il/rambi/>.
Routes to Roots: <www.routestoroots.com/>
and The Miriam Weiner Routes to Roots Foundation: <www.rtrfoundation.org/>.

NOTES

1. "Russia: Census Statistics," in *The Jewish Encyclopedia*, vol. 10 (New York: Funk and Wagnalls, 1905): 529-534. According to the 1897 Russian census, no fewer than six Tsarist *gubernii* had Jewish populations comprising over 15 percent of the total: Warsaw (18.12%), Grodno (17.28%), Siedlce (15.84%), Piotrków (15.83%), Minsk (15.77%), and Łomża (15.69%). In 13 other *gubernii* the proportion of Jews to the total population exceeded 10 percent. Similarly high percentages were encountered in Galicia, Bukovina, Carpatho-Ruthenia, and parts of Hungary.

2. Dan Rottenberg, *Finding Our Fathers: A Guidebook to Jewish Genealogy* (New York: Random House, 1977; reprints 1986, 1995); David Kranzler, *My Jewish Roots: A Practical Guide to Tracing and Recording Your Genealogy and Family History* (New York: Sepher-Hermon Press, 1979); Arthur Kurzweil, *From Generation to Generation: How to Trace Your Jewish Family History and Genealogy* (New York: William Morrow, 1980; various reprint editions); Arthur Kurzweil and Miriam Weiner, eds., *The Encyclopedia of Jewish Genealogy*, vol. 1 (Northvale, NJ: Jason Aronson, 1991).

3. Zachary M. Baker, "Eastern European 'Jewish Geography': Some Problems and Suggestions," in *Toledot: The Journal of Jewish Genealogy* 2, no. 3 (1978/1979): 9-14; Edward Stankiewicz, "Yiddish Place Names in Poland," in *The Field of Yiddish: Studies in Language, Folklore, and Literature* 2, ed. Uriel Weinreich (The Hague: Mouton, 1965): 158-181.

4. Among the standard geographical tools are the *Columbia Lippincott Gazetteer of the World*, ed. Leon E. Seltzer (New York: Columbia University Press, 1952); the *Słownik geograficzny Królestwa polskiego i innych krajów słowiańskich* (Warszawa: Nakładem Filipa Sulimierskiego i Władysława Walewskiewgo, 1880-1902; reprints 1975, 1986-87); and country gazetteers published by the United States Board on Geographic Names (now available via the GeoNet Names Server: <164.214.2.59/gns/html/index.html>). Jewish-oriented geographical reference works include Gary Mokotoff and Sallyann Amdur Sack, *Where Once We Walked: A Guide to the Jewish Communities Destroyed in the Holocaust* (Teaneck, NJ: Avotaynu, 1991); *Blackbook of Localities Whose Jewish Population Was Exterminated by the Nazis* (Jerusalem: Yad Vashem, 1965); Chester G. Cohen, *Shtetl Finder: Jewish Communities in the 19th and Early 20th Centuries in the Pale of Settlement of Russia and Poland, and in Lithuania, Latvia, Galicia, and Bukovina, and with Names of Residents* (Los Angeles: Periday, 1980; reprint 1989); and Berl Kagan, *Sefer haprenumerantn: vegvayzer tsu prenumerirte hebreishe sforim un zayere hotmim fun 8,767 kehilot in Eyrope un*

tsofn-Afrike = *Hebrew Subscription Lists* (New York: Library of the Jewish Theological Seminary of America, 1975).

5. The conversion table for the Daitch-Mokotoff Soundex System is found in a number of Avotaynu publications, including *Where Once We Walked*: 419-424, and at the following URL: <www.jewishgen.org/infofiles/soundex.txt>. As an example of how this system works, let us take the Yiddish name of the town in southern Poland where some of my ancestors came from, Rozvadov (stress on the first syllable). In the Daitch-Mokotoff Soundex System vowels are ignored within words, so the numerical equivalent of the consonants RZVDV is 94737. Since each Soundex heading requires six digits, a zero is added at the end of this particular sequence, yielding 947370 for RZVDV. In the Soundex index to *Where Once We Walked*, 947370 results in the following place-name spellings: Rozvadov, Rozvaduv, Rozvidev, Rozwadow. These are for the following localities: Lalovo (village, Moldova), Rozvadov (village, Ukraine, near L'viv), and Rozwadów (town, Poland–now part of Stalowa Wola; residence of many of my maternal forebears), and in the main, alphabetical section of the gazetteer there are cross-references from variant spellings to official ones.

6. Lists of Jewish vital records for Hungary, Poland, and Germany, which were microfilmed by the LDS Family History Library, were published in *Toledot: The Journal of Jewish Genealogy* ("Hungarian Jewish Records at the Genealogical Society of Utah," vol. 1, no. 3 [Winter 1977-78]; "Polish Jewish Records at the Genealogical Society of Utah," vol. 1, no. 4 [Spring 1978]; "German Jewish Records at the Genealogical Society of Utah," vol. 2, no. 1 [Summer 1978]), and then reprinted in Arthur Kurzweil and Miriam Weiner, *Encyclopedia of Jewish Genealogy*, vol. 1: 178-215.

7. See Arlene Eakle and Johni Cerny, eds., *The Source: A Guidebook of American Genealogy* (Salt Lake City: Ancestry Publishing Co., 1984); Estelle Guzik, *Genealogical Resources in the New York Metropolitan Area* (New York: Jewish Genealogical Society, 1989); Christina K. Schaefer, *Guide to Naturalization Records of the United States* (Baltimore: Genealogical Publishing Co., 1997); Michael Tepper, *American Passenger Arrival Records: A Guide to the Records of Immigrants Arriving at American Ports by Sail and Steam* (Baltimore: Genealogical Publishing Co., 1988).

8. Examples of comprehensive rabbinical genealogies include: Nathan Zebi Friedmann, *Otsar ha-rabanim* = *Otzar harabanim; Rabbis' Encyclopedia: Rabbinate Era from 970-1970*. ([Bnei-Brak?]: Agudat Otsar Harabanim, 1975); Raphael Halperin, *Atlas 'ets hayim* ([Bene Berak?]: Hotsa'at Hekdesh Ruah Ya'akov, [1978]- ; at least 18 volumes have appeared); and Neil Rosenstein, *The Unbroken Chain: Biographical Sketches and the Genealogy of Illustrious Jewish Families from the 15th to the 20th Century* (New York: Shengold, 1976; 2nd ed., New York: CIS, 1990, 2 vols.). There is also a 5-volume encyclopedia by Meir Wunder, *Me'ore Galitsyah: entsiklopedyah le-hakhme Galitsyah* = *Meorei Galicia: Encyclopedia of Galician Rabbis and Scholars* (Jerusalem: Makhon le-hantsahat Yahadut Galitsyah, 1978-1997).

9. The most famous such chronicle is by Nathan Nata Hanover, *Yeven metsulah* (Venice: [s.n.], [1653]; and many subsequent editions in Hebrew). An English translation is also available: *Abyss of Despair (Yeven metzulah): The Famous 17th Century Chronicle Depicting Jewish Life in Russia and Poland during the Chmielnicki Massacres of 1648-1649*, trans. Abraham J. Mesch (New York: Bloch, 1950; reprint 1983).

10. Daniel Soyer, *Jewish Immigrant Associations and American Identity in New York, 1880-1939* (Cambridge: Harvard University Press, 1997).

11. Jack Kugelmass and Jonathan Boyarin, eds., *From a Ruined Garden: The Memorial Books of Polish Jewry* (New York: Schocken, 1983; Bloomington: Indiana University Press, 1998). Both editions include the "Bibliography of Eastern European Jewish Memorial Books," compiled by Zachary M. Baker. That bibliography, in turn, is based on the "Bibliographical List of Memorial Books Published in the Years 1943-1972," by David Bass, in *Yad Vashem Studies* 9 (1973): 273-321.

12. *Sefer Skalah*, ed. Max Mermelstein (New York: Irgun yots'e Skalah, 1978), is a fully trilingual–English, Hebrew, Yiddish–volume. The *Memorial Book Szydlowiec*, edited by Berl Kagan (New York: Shidlowtzer Benevolent Association in New York, 1989), is a complete translation of the *Shidlovtser yizker bukh*, which first came out in New York, 1974. *Luboml: The Memorial Book of a Vanished Shtetl*, edited by Nathan Sobel (Hoboken, N.J.: KTAV, 1997), was translated from the *Sefer yizkor li-kehilat Luboml*, which was issued in Israel circa 1974. These examples of English-language memorial books, however, are the exceptions rather than the norm.

13. Sallyann Amdur Sack and Suzan Fishl Wynne, *The Russian Consular Records Index and Catalog* (New York: Garland, 1987).

14. Rosaline Schwartz and Susan Milamed, *A Guide to YIVO's landsmanshaftn Archive: From Alexandrovsk to Zyrardow* (New York: YIVO Institute for Jewish Research, 1986).

15. "New Eastern European Archival Database"; Michael Steinore, "Exploring the Details of Czarist Decrees," in *Dorot: The Journal of the Jewish Genealogical Society* 23, no. 2 (Winter 2001/2002): 10-11, 18-20.

16. Very few American and European specialists in Russian and Soviet Jewish history conducted research *in situ* until the end of the 1980s, and after 1967 the entire Soviet Union was off-limits to Israelis (where most scholarship on Eastern European Jewry was being written after 1948).

17. Alex E. Friedlander, "Jewish Vital Statistic Records in Lithuanian Archives," in *Avotaynu* 6, no. 4 (1990): 4-12.

18. The March of the Living, which has taken place each spring since 1988, brings as many as 6,000 Jewish teenagers (almost half from North America) to sites of Jewish martyrdom in Poland (Auschwitz and the Warsaw Ghetto foremost among them), concluding in Israel with observations of Israeli Memorial Day and Independence Day. The official March of the Living website may be found at <www.marchoftheliving.org/>. For background and perspectives on the March, see: Ruth Ellen Gruber, "This Year's March of the Living Raises Some Troubling Questions," *JTA–Jewish Telegraphic Agency*, April 28, 1994: 11; William B. Helmreich, "Visits to Europe, Zionist Education, and Jewish Identity: The Case of the March of the Living," in *Journal of Jewish Education* 61 (1995): 16-20; Allan Nadler, "Bibi's Misstep on the Grounds of Auschwitz," *Forward*, 22 May, 1998: 7; Peter Novick, *The Holocaust in American Life* (Boston: Houghton Mifflin, 1999): 160; "Tourist Attraction?" *Forward*, 29 April, 1994: 1.

19. Ruth Ellen Gruber is a freelance journalist who has written extensively on Jewish tourism to Eastern Europe. See her books: *Upon the Doorposts of Thy House: Jewish Life in East-Central Europe, Yesterday and Today* (New York: John Wiley, 1994); *Jewish Heritage Travel: A Guide to East-Central Europe*, rev. ed. (Northvale, NJ: Jason Aronson, 1999); and *Virtually Jewish: Reinventing Jewish Culture in Europe* (Berkeley: University of California Press, 2002). For the ethnographic perspective, see Jack Kugelmass, "The Rites of the Tribe: The Meaning of Poland for American Jewish Tourists," in *YIVO Annual* 21 (1993): 395-453 (previously published in *Museums and*

Communities, 1992), and his article "Missions to the Past: Poland in Contemporary Jewish Thought and Deed," in *Tense Past: Cultural Essays in Trauma and Memory* (New York: Routledge, 1996): 199-214.

20. When I was a child I asked my mother where her parents were born. "A part of Austria called Galicia," she replied. "Now it's in Poland."

21. "Routes to Roots Publications" <www.routestoroots.com/public.html>.

22. The Miriam Weiner Routes to Roots Foundation, Inc., "Introduction to Eastern European Archival Database" <www.rtrfoundation.org/archdta1b.html>. This introduction is revised and adapted from an article that appeared in *Avotaynu* 17, no. 3 (Fall 2001): 3-5.

23. The Miriam Weiner Routes to Roots Foundation, Inc., "Related Websites" <www.routestoroots.com/webs.html#anchor>. Links to many of the same websites are also found on JewishGen.

24. Some years ago I wrote about the mutually beneficial interactions of librarians and genealogists. See Zachary M. Baker, "What We Owe the Genealogists: Genealogy and the Judaica Reference Librarian," in *Judaica Librarianship* 6, no. 1-2 (Spring 1991-Winter 1992): 43-46, 48.

Index

Academic institutionalization, 152-153
Acquisitions-related issues
   future perspectives of, 92-93
   individuals associated with, 90-118
      Frenkel, A., 92,118
      Rosenberg, A., 90
      Tcherikower, E., 90
   institutions and organizations
      associated with, 89-91
      IDC Publishers, 90
      Institute Judaica, 91
   introduction to, 89-90
   reference literature about, 118
   at the YIVO Institute for Jewish
      Research, 89-118
   bibliographic data, 92-93
   book collections, 91-92
   conference, congress, and
      symposia literature, 115-118
   culture- and art-related
      literature, 108-115
   histories and biographies,
      96-103
   Holocaust literature, 103-107
   introduction to, 89-90
   periodical literature, 93
   reference sources and
      bibliographies, 94-96
Alliance Israélite Universelle, 35
Allony, N., 61-62,67
Archival-related issues
   archival surveys, 5-15. *See also*
      Surveys, archival
   documentary collections, 17-36. *See
      also* Documentary collections,
      Russian Jewry history
Art- and culture-related literature,
   108-115
Asiatic Museum of St. Petersburg,
   37-57
Association of Jewish Libraries, 151-152

Assouline, H., 36
Azerbaijan, current book publishing
   in, 82-83

Bacon, G. C., 155,166
Baker, Z. M., 1-4,37,68,151-152,156,
   166
Balaban, M., 155,166
Baltic States, documentary collections
   in, 17-36
Bampi, I., 41
Beider, A., 175
Beizer, M., 128
Belarus
   current book publishing in, 79-80
   documentary collections in, 17-36
Berlin Hochschule of Jewish Studies, 20
Bershadskii, S., 20-23
Bertel, D., 50
Bibliographical projects
   future perspectives of, 165-166
   individuals associated with, 151-166
      Bacon, G. C., 155,166
      Baker, Z. M., 151-152,156,166
      Balaban, M., 155,166
      Boyarin, J., 166
      Czajka, M., 167
      Engel, D., 154
      Gąsiorowski, S., 156,167
      Gierowski, J., 156
      Grygier, U., 156
      Hundert, G. D., 155,166
      Kugelmass, J., 166
      Lerski, H. T., 155-156,166
      Lerski, J. J., 155-156,166
      Mendelsohn, E., 155,166
      Muszyńska, K., 156-157
      Pilarczyk, K., 156-157,166
      Singer, I. B., 162-163

institutions and organizations
  associated with, 151-166
  Association of Jewish Libraries,
    151-152
  Brandeis University, 154
  Columbia University, 154
  Diaspora Research Institute, 154
  Hebrew University, 155
  Jagiellonian University, 156-157
  Jewish Historical Institute, 153-154
  Library of Congress, 159-163,166
  New York University, 154
  OCLC, 159-163
  Oxford University, 154
  Polish Society for Jewish
    Studies, 154
  YIVO Institute for Jewish
    Research, 152
introduction to, 151-152
on Polish-Jewish studies, 151-166
  academic institutionalization
    of, 152-153
  Bibliographies of Polish Judaica:
    International Symposium,
    159-160
  "Bibliography of Eastern European
    Memorial (Yizkor) Books," 156
  "Bibliography of Polish
    Judaica," 158
  Biuletyn Żydowskiego Instytutu
    Historycznego, 159
  development of, 154-166
  Gal-Ed: On the History of the
    Jews in Poland, 151,158-165
  Guide to Bibliographies of
    Polish Judaica, 159
  historical perspectives of,
    151-155
  introduction to, 151
  Kwartalnik Historii Żydów, 159
  online and electronic sources
    of, 164-165
  overview of, 155-158
  Polish Judaica of the Sixteenth
    and Seventeenth Centuries:
    Materials for Bibliography, 159
  poverty of, 152-153

Studia Judaica Cracoviensia:
  Series Bibliographica, 158-159
Studia Polono-Judaica: Series
  Bibliographica, 158-159
reference literature about, 166-167
at YIVO Institute for Jewish
  Research, 92-93
Bibliographies of Polish Judaica:
  International Symposium,
  159-160
"Bibliography of Eastern European
  Memorial (Yizkor) Books," 156
"Bibliography of Polish Judaica," 158
Biographies and histories, 96-103
Bislisches, E., 42
Biuletyn Żydowskiego Instytutu
  Historycznego, 159
Blank, M., 27
Book publishing
  current, 69-88. *See also* Current
    book publishing
  YIVO Institute for Jewish Research
    collections and, 91-92
Borodulin, N., 89-118
Boyarin, J., 166,172-173,180,183
Brandeis University, 154

CAHJP (Central Archives for the
  History of the Jewish People)
  archival surveys of, 9
  creation of, 19-20
  development of, 20-22
  document copies of, 26-32
  documentary collections of, 17-36
  in former Soviet archives, 22-32
  microfilm-related issues of, 60-61
  Russian collections of, 26-32
Censorship policies, 29
Center for the Preservation of Historical
  Documentary Collections, 10
Center of Academicians and Teachers
  of Judaica in Institutions of
  Higher Education "Sefer," 75

Central Archives for the History of the Jewish People (CAHJP), 9, 17-36, 60-61
Central Government Historical Archive, St. Petersburg (TsGIA SPb), 23, 34
Central Historical Archive of Kiev, 35
Central Management of Jewish Communities in Russia (TsEVAAD), 23
Central State Historical Archive of Ukraine (TsGIAU), 23-25
Central Zionist Archives, 9
Chwolson, D., 37, 43-45, 50-51
Classification systems, 13-14
Cohen, C., 20, 171
Cohen, D. J., 34
Cohen, Y. Y., 126-127
Columbia University, 154
Communities, documentary collections about, 29-32
Congress, conference, and symposia literature, 115-118
Consortial agreements, 10
Corrsin, S. D., 151-184
Culture- and art-related literature, 108-115
Current book publishing
　in Azerbaijan, 82-83
　in Belarus, 79-80
　development of, 71-73
　in Estonia, 82
　future perspectives of, 87-88
　in Georgia, 82
　historical perspectives of, 70-71
　of Holocaust literature, 85-86
　introduction to, 69-70
　in Kazakhstan, 83
　in Kyrgyzstan, 83
　in Latvia, 82
　in Lithuania, 80-81
　　introduction to, 80-81
　　Publishing House of the Vilna Gaon Jewish Museum, 81
　of local history literature, 83-86
　in Moldova, 80
　perestroika and, 71
　periodicals and, 86-88
　reference literature about, 88
　in Russia, 73-77, 84
　　Center of Academicians and Teachers of Judaica in Institutions of Higher Education "Sefer," 75
　　introduction to, 73-74
　　Izdatel'stvo "DAAT/Znanie," 74
　　Izdatel'stvo "Evreiskii mir," 76
　　Izdatel'stvo "Gesharim/Mosty kul'tury," 74
　　Izdatel'stvo "Lekhaim," 75-76
　　Jewish Community Center of St. Petersburg, 77
　　Project Judaica, 74-75
　　Research Center "Petersburg Judaica," 76
　　Russian Jewish Encyclopedia, 75
　　St. Petersburg Institute of Judaica, 76
　　Tsentr "ORT-Ginstburg," 77
　survey of, 73-83
　in Ukraine, 77-79
　　Institute of Judaica, 78
　　introduction to, 77, 84
　　Ministry of Culture and Arts of Ukraine, 78-79
　in Uzbekistan, 83
Czajka, M., 167

"DAAT/Znanie," 74
Daitch, R., 172
Davies, R. A., 62, 68
de Rossi, G. B., 38-39, 49
Deinard, E., 42
Diaspora Museum, 173
Diaspora Research Institute, 154
Dinur, B.-Z., 19-20, 34-35
Documentary collections, Russian Jewry history
　in Baltic states, 17-36
　in Belarus, 17-36

CAHJP (Central Archives for the
  History of the Jewish People)
  project for, 17-36
  creation of, 19-20
  development of, 20-22
  document copies of, 26-32
  in former Soviet archives, 22-32
  Russian collections of, 26-32
future perspectives of, 32-33
individuals associated with, 19-36
  Assouline, H., 36
  Bershadskii, S., 20-23
  Blank, M., 27
  Cohen, C., 20
  Cohen, D. J., 34
  Dinur, B.-Z., 19-20,34-35
  Dubnov, S. M., 35
  Eliashevich, D. A., 33
  Fodello, K., 27
  Friedman, I., 36
  Gessen, I., 20-23,34
  Ginsburg, S., 21-22,35
  Gofman, M., 27
  Greig, A., 28
  Katzenellenbogen (Rabbi), 27
  Krasnyi-Admoni, G. I., 34-35
  Kuperbant, M. M. A., 27
  Lenin, V., 27
  Lozinskii, S. M., 35
  Lukin, B., 33-34
  Meisel, J., 19-20,34
  Melamed, E. I., 33
  Men'shikov, A., 28
  Mikhoels, S., 35
  Motzkin, L., 35
  Mowshovitch, D., 35
  Nicholas I, 27
  Peri, A., 33
  Prombaum, E. M., 35
  Rein, A., 34-35
  Rosenthal, N., 27
  Sallis, D., 33
  Segall, A., 22-23
  Steinberg, A., 35
  Täubler, E., 19-20,34
  Tugenhold, V., 27
  Web, M., 33
  Zel'tser, L., 27
institutions and organizations
  associated with, 17-35
  Alliance Israélite Universelle, 35
  Berlin Hochschule of Jewish
    Studies, 20
  Central Historical Archive of
    Kiev, 35
  GARF (State Archive of the
    Russian Federation), 23
  GAZhO (State Archive of
    Zhitomir District), 24
  he-Haluts, 23
  Jewish Colonization
    Association, 35
  Jewish Committees (Fourth and
    Fifth), 28
  Jewish Historical Archeographic
    Commission, 22
  Jewish Historical General
    Archives, 19,33-34
  Jewish Historical-Ethnographical
    Commission, 20-21
  Jewish Historical-Ethnographical
    Society, 23,35
  JTSA (Jewish Theological
    Seminary of America), 33
  Kiev Central Archive, 22
  Moscow Archives on the History
    and Culture of the Jews, 33
  NARB (National Archive of the
    Republic of Belarus), 25-26
  National Library of Israel, 35
  NIARB (National Historical
    Archive of the Republic of
    Belarus), 23-25
  OPE (Society for the Promotion
    of Enlightenment Among
    Jews in Russia), 23
  Project Judaica, 33
  RGADA (Russian State Archive
    of Ancient Documents),
    23-24,30

RGAVMF (Russian State Archive of the Naval Fleet), 24
RGGU (Russian State University of the Humanities), 33
RGIA (Russia State Historical Archive), 23
RGVIA (Russian State Military Historical Archive), 24
Russian Jewish Historical Society, 34
Society for the Attainment of Equal Rights for Russian Jews, 23
TsEVAAD (Central Management of Jewish Communities in Russia), 23
TsGIA SPb (Central Government Historical Archive, St. Petersburg), 23,34
TsGIAU (Central State Historical Archive of Ukraine), 23-25
Tul'chin Jewish Pedagogical Technical School, 32
World Congress of Jewish Studies, 20
YIVO Institute for Jewish Research, 33
Zhitomir Jewish Academic Institute, 24
Zhitomir Rabbinical Seminary, 24
Zitomir Rabbi School Archive, 28
introduction to, 17-19
Istoriia everisjogo naroda v Rossii (The History of the Jewish People of Russia) and, 21
in Moldova, 17-36
perestroika and, 18
reference literature about, 33-36
in Russia, 17-36
subjects of, 28-32
   communities, 29-32
   economics, 29
   educational policies, 29
   forced exile and oppression, 29
   Karaite exemptions, 29
   military service, 28
   publication and censorship policies, 29
   religious life regulations, 29
   resettlements, 29
in Ukraine, 17-36
in Uzbekistan, 17-36
Dubnov, S. M., 14,35

Eastern European resources
   genealogical, 169-184. *See also* Genealogical resources
   manuscripts, microfilming of, 59-67. *See also* Microfilming-related issues
Economic-related literature, 29
Educational policies, documentary collections about, 29
Eisenstadt, M. E., 51
Electronic and online resources, 164-165,176-181
Eliashevich, D. A., 8,11,14,33,127-128
Engel, D., 154
Estonia, current book publishing in, 82
"Evreiskii mir," 76

Feldman, D. Z., 174
Firkovich, A., 65
Fodello, K., 27
Forced exile and oppression, documentary collections about, 29
Fragility, original documents, 65
Frenkel, A., 69-88,92,128
Friedland, L. F., 40-43,50
Friedland, M., 66-67
Friedlander, A. E., 175,183
Friedman, I., 36
Friedman, L., 37

Gal-Ed: On the History of the Jews in Poland, 151,158-165
GARF (State Archive of the Russian Federation), 14,23
Gąsiorowski, S., 156,167

GAZhO (State Archive of Zhitomir District), 24
Genealogical resources
  of Eastern European Jews, 169-184
    historical perspectives of, 171-176
    introduction to, 169-170
    JewishGen website, 176-179
    online and electronic resources, 176-181
    print resources, 179-180
  individuals associated with, 171-183
    Beider, A., 175
    Boyarin, J., 172-173,180,183
    Cohen, C., 171
    Daitch, R., 172
    Feldman, D. Z., 174
    Friedlander, A. E., 175,183
    Gruber, R. E., 183
    Hanover, N. N., 182
    Hoffman, D. B., 174
    Krasner, B. R., 174
    Kugelmass, J., 172-173,180,183
    Kurzweil, A., 174,180-181
    Luft, E. D., 174
    Mermelstein, M., 183
    Milamed, S., 180
    Mokotoff, G., 172,174-175,180
    Rhode, H., 175,180
    Rottenberg, D., 181
    Sack, S. A., 175,180,183
    Schwartz, R., 180
    Seigel, S. W., 174
    Sobel, N., 183
    Stankiewicz, E., 181
    Steinroe, M., 183
    Vashem, Y., 171
    Weiner, M., 177-180,184
    Weinreich, U., 181
    Wynne, S. F., 174-175,180,183
  institutions and organizations
    associated with, 170-184
    Diaspora Museum, 173
    Holocaust Memorial Museum, 173
    International Seminar on Jewish Genealogy, 174
    LDS (Latter Day Saints), 172-173,182
    Library of Congress, 170
    New York Public Library, 173
    RTR (Routes to Roots)
      Foundation, 178-179,184
    YIVO Institute for Jewish
      Research, 173,177-178
  introduction to, 169
  March of the Living and, 183
  reference literature about, 179-184
  Where Once We Walked: A Guide to the Jewish Communities Destroyed in the Holocaust, 171-172,182
Geographic-related issues of, 121-122
Georgia, current book publishing, 82
"Gesharim/Mosty kul'tury," 74
Gessen, I., 20-23,34
Gierowski, J., 156
Ginsberg, C., 49
Ginsburg, S., 21-22,35
Gofman, M., 27
Greenbaum, A. A., 127
Greig, A., 28
Gruber, R. E., 183
Grygier, U., 156
Guenzburg, D. and Guenzburg collection, 62-68

Hanover, N. N., 182
Harkavy, A. A., 66
Hebrew University, 155
he-Haluts, 23
Historical perspectives
  of archival surveys, 6-8
  of bibliographical projects, 151-155
  of current book publishing, 70-71
  of genealogical resources, 171-176
  of incunabula, 38-40
  of microfilming-related issues, 60-64
  of periodical literature, 120-125
Histories and biographies, 96-103
Hoffman, D. B., 174

Index

Holocaust literature
  current book publishing and, 85-86
  at the YIVO Institute for Jewish
    Research, 103-107
Holocaust Memorial Museum, 9,173
Hundert, G. D., 155,166
Hungarian Academy of Sciences, 61

Iakerson, S. M., 37-57
Iashunskiim I. V., 126
IDC Publishers, 90
IMHM (Institute of Microfilmed
    Hebrew Manuscripts), 59-68
Incunabula
  of the Asiatic Museum of St.
    Petersburg, 37-57
  description of, 37-45
  listing of, 51-57
  bibliographies of, 45-48
  future perspectives of, 45
  historical perspectives of, 38-40
  individuals associated with, 37-51
    Baker, Z. M., 37
    Bampi, I., 41
    Bertel, D., 50
    Bislisches, E., 42
    Chwolson, D., 37,43-45,50-51
    de Rossi, G. B., 38-39,49
    Deinard, E., 42
    Eisenstadt, M. E., 51
    Friedland, L. F., 40-43,50
    Friedman, L., 37
    Ginsberg, C., 49
    Kimhi, M., 43
    Landsberg, M., 42
    Marx, A., 49
    Mazel, J., 41
    Offenberg, A. K., 48,50
    Rabbinovicz, N. N., 42
    Rabinovich, L., 41
    Rondestvedt, K., 37
    Tishby, P., 49
    Tsukerman, S., 41
    Uvarov, S. S., 39
    Weiner, S., 40-45
  institutions and organizations
    associated with, 39,50
    RNL (Russian National
      Library), 39,50
    RSL (Russian State Library),
      39,50
  introduction to, 37-38
  inventory and description of, 39-45
  ownership markings, lack of, 42
  printed catalogs, lack of, 42
  reference literature about, 45-51
  typography and, 38
Institute Judaica, 91
Institute of Judaica, 78
Institute of Microfilmed Hebrew
    Manuscripts (IMHM), 59-68
Institutionalization, academic, 152-153
International Seminar on Jewish
    Genealogy, 174
Internationalization issues, 9
*Istoriia everisjogo naroda v Rossii
    (The History of the Jewish
    People of Russia)*, 21
Ivask, U. G., 126
Izdatel'stvo "DAAT/Znanie," 74
Izdatel'stvo "Evreiskii mir," 76
Izdatel'stvo "Gesharim/Mosty
    kul'tury," 74
Izdatel'stvo "Lekhaim," 75-76

Jagiellonian University, 156
JAS (Jewish Archival Society), 5-14
Jewish Archival Society (JAS), 5-14
Jewish Colonization Association, 35
Jewish Committees (Fourth and Fifth),
    28
Jewish Community Center of St.
    Petersburg, 77
*Jewish Documentary Sources in the
    Moscow Archives*, 11
Jewish Historical General Archives,
    33-34
Jewish Historical Institute, 62,153-154

Jewish Historical-Ethnographical Commission, 20-21
Jewish Historical-Ethnographical Society, 23,35
Jewish National and University Library (JNUL), 9,59-67
Jewish Theological Seminary of America (JTSA), 5-14,33
JewishGen website, 176-179
Jews in Russia conference, 7
JNUL (Jewish National and University Library), 9,59-67
JTSA (Jewish Theological Seminary of America), 5-14,33

Karaite exemptions, documentary collections about, 29
Karasik, V., 119-150
Katsch, A., 62,68
Katzenellenbogen (Rabbi), 27
Kaufmann, D., 61
Kazakhstan, current book publishing in, 83
Kazovskii, G., 14
Kel'ner, V. E., 127-128
Kiev Central Archive, 22
Kimhi, M., 43
Klimenko, I., 128
Krasner, B. R., 174
Kugelmass, J., 166,172-173,180,183
Kuperbant, M. M. A., 27
Kupfer, E., 62,68
Kupovetski, M., 15
Kurzweil, A., 174,180-181
Kwartalnik Historii Żydów, 159
Kyrgyzstan, current book publishing in, 83

Landsberg, M., 42
Language-related issues, 123-124
Latter Day Saints (LDS), 172-173,182
Latvia, current book publishing, 82

LDS (Latter Day Saints), 172-173,182
"Lekhaim," 75-76
Lenin, V., 27
Lerski, H. T., 155-156,166
Lerski, J. J., 155-156,166
Library of Congress, 159-163,166,170
Lithuania, current book publishing in, 80-81
Local history literature, 83-86
Lozinskii, S. M., 35
Luft, E. D., 174
Lukin, B., 14,17-36

Manuscript migration, 8
MARC/AMC format, 10-11
March of the Living, 183
Marx, A., 49
Mazel, J., 41
Meisel, J., 19-20,34
Mekor Haim Yeshiva, 63-64
Melamed, E. I., 33
Men'shikov, A., 28
Mermelstein, M., 183
MGAIA (Moscow State Historical Archive), 14
Microfilming-related issues
  of Eastern European manuscripts, 59-67
  fragility, original documents, 65
  future perspectives of, 66-67
  historical perspectives of, 60-64
  individuals associated with, 61-68
    Allony, N., 61-62,67
    Baker, Z. M., 68
    Davies, R. A., 62,68
    Firkovich, A., 65
    Friedland, M., 66-67
    Guenzburg, D. and Guenzburg collection, 62-68
    Harkavy, A. A., 66
    Katsch, A., 62,68
    Kaufmann, D., 61
    Kupfer, E., 62,68
    Richler, B., 67-68

Sever, S., 63
Shatzman, I., 63
Sirat, C., 67
Steinsaltz, A., 63-64
Strelcyn, S., 62
Weiser, I., 63-66
institutions and organizations
   associated with, 59-68
   CAHJP (Central Archives for
     the History of the Jewish
     People), 60-61
   Haifa University, 63
   Hungarian Academy of
     Sciences, 61
   IMHM (Institute of Microfilmed
     Hebrew Manuscripts), 59-68
   Jewish Historical Institute, 62
   JNUL (Jewish National and
     University Library), 59-67
   Mekor Haim Yeshiva, 63-64
   RNL (Russian National
     Library), 64-67
   RSL (Russian State Library),
     59-67
   Russian Academy of Sciences,
     Oriental Institute, 59-67
   Russian State Military Archive,
     66-67
   Universitätsbibliothek, 62
   introduction to, 59
   objectives, 66-67
   reference literature about, 67-68
   texts, types of, 60
Mikhoels, S., 35
Milamed, S., 180
Military service, documentary
   collections about, 28
Ministry of Culture and Arts of
   Ukraine, 78-79
Mokotoff, G., 172,174-175,180
Moldova, documentary collections in,
   17-36
Moscow Archives on the History and
   Culture of the Jews, 33
Moscow State Historical Archive
   (MGAIA), 14

Motzkin, L., 35
Mowshovitch, D., 35
Muszyńska, K., 156-157

NARB (National Archive of the
   Republic of Belarus), 25-26
National Archive of the Republic of
   Belarus (NARB), 25-26
National Historical Archive of the
   Republic of Belarus
   (NIARB), 23-25
National Library of Israel, 35
New York Public Library, 173
New York University, 154
NIARB (National Historical Archive
   of the Republic of Belarus),
   23-25
Nicholas I, 27

OCLC, 159-163
Offenberg, A. K., 48,50
Online and electronic resources,
   164-165,176-181
OPE (Society for the Promotion of
   Enlightenment Among Jews
   in Russia), 6,23
Oppression and forced exile, documentary
   collections about, 29
Ownership markings, lack of, 42
Oxford University, 154

Perestroika
   current book publishing and, 71
   documentary collections and, 18
Peri, A., 33
Periodical literature
   current book publishing and, 86-88
   future perspectives of, 124-125
   individuals associated with, 126-128
     Beizer, M., 128
     Cohen, Y. Y., 126-127

Eliashevich, D., 127-128
Frenkel, A., 128
Greenbaum, A. A., 127
Iashunskiim I. V., 126
Ivask, U. G., 126
Karasik, V., 127
Kel'ner, V. E., 127-128
Klimenko, I., 128
Pinkus, B., 127
Shkoliarenko, O., 126
Suetnov, A., 127
Valk, E., 128
Zeltser, A., 128
introduction to, 119-120
reference literature about, 123-129
in Ukraine, 119-150
    bibliographies of, 125-129
    geographic-related issues of, 121-122
    historical perspectives of, 120-125
    ideals of, 122-123
    introduction to, 119-120
    languages of, 123-124
    periods, listing of, 121
    titles, listing of, 130-150
    at YIVO Institute for Jewish Research, 93
Pilarczyk, K., 156-157,166
Pinkus, B., 127
Polish Judaica of the Sixteenth and Seventeenth Centuries: Materials for Bibliography, 159
Polish Society for Jewish Studies, 154
Polish-Jewish studies, 151-166
Project Judaica, 9-11,14,33,74-75
Prombaum, E. M., 35
Publishing House of the Vilna Gaon Jewish Museum, 81

Rabbinovicz, N. N., 42
Rabinovich, L., 41
Reference sources and bibliographies, 94-96
Rein, A., 34-35

Religious life regulations, documentary collections about, 29
Research Center "Petersburg Judaica," 76
Resettlement, documentary collections about, 29
RGADA (Russian State Archive of Ancient Documents), 12-13,23-24,30
RGAVMF (Russian State Archive of the Naval Fleet), 24
RGGU (Russian State University of the Humanities), 5-14,33
RGIA (Russia State Historical Archive), 23
RGVIA (Russian State Military Historical Archive), 24
Rhode, H., 175,180
Richler, B., 59-68
RNL (Russian National Library), 39,50,64-67
Rondestvedt, K., 37
Rosenberg, A., 90
Rosenthal, N., 27
Rottenberg, D., 181
Routes to Roots (RTR) Foundation, 178-179,184
RSL (Russian State Library), 39,50,59-67
RTR (Routes to Roots) Foundation, 178-179,184
Russia
    current book publishing in, 73-77,84
    documentary collections in, 17-36. *See also* Documentary collections, Russian Jewry history
Russia State Historical Archive (RGIA), 23
Russian Academy of Sciences, Oriental Institute, 59-67
Russian Jewish Encyclopedia, 75
Russian National Library (RNL), 39, 50,64-67

Russian State Archive of Ancient
   Documents (RGADA),
   12-13,23-24,30
Russian State Archive of the Naval
   Fleet (RGAVMF), 24
Russian State Library (RSL), 39,50,
   59-67
Russian State Military Archive, 66-67
Russian State Military Historical
   Archive (RGVIA), 24
Russian State University of the
   Humanities (RGGU), 5-14,33

Sack, S. A., 175,180,183
Sallis, D., 15,33
Savitskii, E., 10,15
Schwartz, R., 180
Segall, A., 22-23
Seigel, S. W., 174
Sever, S., 63
Shatzman, I., 63
Shkoliarenko, O., 126
Singer, I. B., 162-163
Sirat, C., 67
Slavic Judaica
   acquisitions-related issues, 89-118.
      See also Acquisitions-related
      issues
   archival-related issues, 5-15,17-36
      archival surveys, 5-15. See also
      Surveys, archival
   documentary collections, 17-36.
      See also Documentary
      collections, Russian Jewry
      history
   bibliographical projects, 151-167.
      See also Bibliographical
      projects
   current book publishing, 69-88. See
      also Current book publishing
   genealogical resources, 169-184.
      See also Genealogical
      resources

incunabula, 37-57. See also
   Incunabula
introduction to, 1-4
microfilming-related issues, 59-68.
   See also Microfilming-related
   issues
periodical literature, 119-150. See
   also Periodical literature
Sobel, N., 183
Society for the Promotion of
   Enlightenment Among Jews
   in Russia (OPE), 6,23
St. Petersburg Institute of Judaica, 76
St. Petersburg Jewish Historical and
   Ethnographic Society, 6
St. Petersburg Jewish University,
   6,11,14
Stankiewicz, E., 181
State Archive of the Russian
   Federation (GARF), 14,23
State Archive of Zhitomir District
   (GAZhO), 24
Steinberg, A., 35
Steinroe, M., 183
Steinsaltz, A., 63-64
Strelcyn, S., 62
*Studia Judaica Cracoviensia: Series
   Bibliographica,* 158-159
*Studia Polono-Judaica: Series
   Bibliographica,* 158-159
Suetnov, A., 127
Surveys, archival
   of former Soviet archives, 5-14
      classification systems and, 13-14
      consortial agreements and, 10
      current perspectives of, 8-14
      document searches and, 13-14
      historical perspectives of, 6-8
      internationalization of, 9
      introduction to, 5-6
      Jews in Russia conference and, 7
      manuscript migration and, 8
      promotion of Jewish learning
         and, 6
   future perspectives of, 13-14

individuals associated with, 8-15
  Dubnov, S. M., 14
  Eliashevich, D., 8,11,14
  Kazovskii, G., 14
  Kupovetski, M., 15
  Lukin, B., 14
  Sallis, D., 15
  Savitskii, E. M., 10,15
  Veidlinger, J., 15
  Veisberg, A., 14
  Web, M., 15
  Zeltser, A., 14
institutions and organizations
  associated with, 9-14
  CAHJP (Central Archives for
    the History of the Jewish
    People), 9
  Center for the Preservation of
    Historical Documentary
    Collections, 10
  Central Zionist Archives, 9
  GARF (State Archive of the
    Russian Federation), 14
  JAS (Jewish Archival Society),
    5-14
  JNUL (Jewish National and
    University Library), 9
  JTSA (Jewish Theological
    Seminary of America), 5-14
  MGAIA (Moscow State
    Historical Archive), 14
  OPE Historical Commission, 6
  Project Judaica, 9-11,14
  RGADA (Russian State Archive
    of Ancient Documents), 12-13
  RGGU (Russian State University
    of the Humanities), 5-14
  St. Petersburg Jewish Historical
    and Ethnographic Society, 6
  St. Petersburg Jewish
    University, 6,11,14
  U.S. Holocaust Memorial
    Museum, 9
  Yad Vashem Archives, 9

  YIVO Institute for Jewish
    Research, 5-14
  introduction to, 5-6
  *Jewish Documentary Sources in the
    Moscow Archives*, 11
  MARC/AMC format and, 10-11
  reference literature about, 14-15
  Symposia, congress, and conference
    literature, 115-118

Täubler, E., 19-20,34
Tcherikower, E., 90
Texts, types of, 60
Tishby, P., 49
Tsentr "ORT-Ginstburg," 77
TsEVAAD (Central Management of
  Jewish Communities in
  Russia), 23
TsGIA SPb (Central Government
  Historical Archive, St.
  Petersburg), 23,34
TsGIAU (Central State Historical
  Archive of Ukraine), 23-25
Tsukerman, S., 41
Tugenhold, V., 27
Tul'chin Jewish Pedagogical Technical
  School, 32
Typography, incunabula and, 38

Ukraine
  current book publishing in, 77-79
  documentary collections in, 17-36
  periodical literature of, 119-150
Universitätsbibliothek, 62
Uvarov, S. S., 39
Uzbekistan
  current book publishing in, 83
  documentary collections in, 17-36

Valk, E., 128
Vashem, Y., 171

Veidlinger, J., 15
Veisberg, A., 14
Vilna Gaon Jewish Museum, 81

Web, M., 5-15,33
Weiner, M., 177-180,184
Weiner, S., 40-45
Weinreich, U., 181
Weiser, I., 63-66
Where Once We Walked: A Guide to the Jewish Communities Destroyed in the Holocaust, 171-172,182
World Congress of Jewish Studies, 20

Yad Vashem Archives, 9
YIVO Institute for Jewish Research, 173,177-178
   acquisitions-related issues of, 89-118
      bibliographic data, 92-93
      book collections, 91-92
      conference, congress, and symposia literature, 115-118
      culture- and art-related literature, 108-115
      histories and biographies, 96-103
      Holocaust literature, 103-107
      introduction to, 89-90
      periodical literature, 93
      reference sources and bibliographies, 94-96
   archival surveys of, 5-14
   bibliographical projects of, 152
   documentary collections of, 33
   genealogical resources of, 173,177-178
   periodical literature of, 93

Zeltser, A., 14,128
Zel'tser, L., 27
Zhitomir Jewish Academic Institute, 24
Zhitomir Rabbinical Seminary, 24
Zitomir Rabbi School Archive, 28

SPECIAL 25%-OFF DISCOUNT!

Order a copy of this book with this form or online at:
http://www.haworthpress.com/store/product.asp?sku=5046
Use Sale Code BOF25 in the online bookshop to receive 25% off!

Judaica in the Slavic Realm, Slavica in the Judaic Realm
Repositories, Collections, Projects, Publication

___ in softbound at $22.46 (regularly $29.95) (ISBN: 0-7890-2280-X)
___ in hardbound at $29.96 (regularly $39.95) (ISBN: 0-7890-2279-6)

COST OF BOOKS _____	❏ BILL ME LATER: ($5 service charge will be added)
Outside USA/ Canada/ Mexico: Add 20% _____	(Bill-me option is good on US/Canada/ Mexico orders only; not good to jobbers, wholesalers, or subscription agencies.)
POSTAGE & HANDLING _____	
(US: $4.00 for first book & $1.50 for each additional book)	❏ Signature _____
Outside US: $5.00 for first book & $2.00 for each additional book)	❏ Payment Enclosed: $ _____
SUBTOTAL _____	❏ PLEASE CHARGE TO MY CREDIT CARD:
in Canada: add 7% GST _____	❏ Visa ❏ MasterCard ❏ AmEx ❏ Discover
	❏ Diner's Club ❏ Eurocard ❏ JCB
STATE TAX _____	Account # _____
(NY, OH, & MN residents please add appropriate local sales tax	Exp Date _____
FINAL TOTAL _____	Signature _____
(if paying in Canadian funds, convert using the current exchange rate, UNESCO coupons welcome)	*(Prices in US dollars and subject to change without notice.)*

PLEASE PRINT ALL INFORMATION OR ATTACH YOUR BUSINESS CARD

Name
Address

City	State/Province	Zip/Postal Code
Country		
Tel	Fax	
E-Mail		

May we use your e-mail address for confirmations and other types of information? ❏Yes ❏ No
We appreciate receiving your e-mail address. Haworth would like to e-mail special discount offers to you, as a preferred customer. **We will never share, rent, or exchange your e-mail address.** We regard such actions as an invasion of your privacy.

Order From Your Local Bookstore or Directly From
The Haworth Press, Inc.
10 Alice Street, Binghamton, New York 13904-1580 • USA
Call Our toll-free number (1-800-429-6784) / Outside US/Canada: (607) 722-5857
Fax: 1-800-895-0582 / Outside US/Canada: (607) 771-0012
E-Mail your order to us: Orders@haworthpress.com

Please Photocopy this form for your personal use.
www.HaworthPress.com